Telephone S

FOR

DUMMIES®

by Dirk Zeller

CEO, Sales Champions and Real Estate Champions

Telephone Sales For Dummies®

Published by
Wiley Publishing, Inc.
111 River St.
Hoboken, NJ 07030-5774
www.wiley.com

WILEY

Telephone Sales For Dummies®

Cheat Sheet

Three Clicks to Insider Info on Your Prospect

Before you can make any sales presentation, you first need to know as much as you can about your prospects. No matter who the prospect is, remember the following to get a leg up. (Chapter 4 offers more advice for preparing for a sales call and putting together a phone script.)

- **Visit the corporate Web site.** Familiarize yourself with the company products and services, senior management, mission statements, upcoming projects, recent news — and even contact phone numbers.

- **Google the company.** Using Google or another search engine can bring up sometimes *thousands* of mentions of the company on sites that may give you a *different* perspective from that of the corporate site. You can also use Zoominfo or Linked In to get the information on companies. Don't overlook the lowdown from the competitors!

- **Google your contact.** The Internet holds valuable information about the individual you plan to contact at the company. You can gather both professional *and* personal details — both help you sell.

Making a Powerful Seven-Second Opening

First impressions are everything. When you have the prospect on the phone, the first seven seconds can make or break you. Keep these pointers close by to help your opening zing. (Chapter 9 presents even more ways to open calls with a successful close in mind.)

- **Greet the prospect by name.** Grab the contact's attention immediately — and hold it — by using his name.

- **State your full name.** Don't be a stranger! Identify yourself clearly and completely.

- **Identify your company.** Don't assume you're a household word — say the name and add a brief description of your firm's specialty.

- **Explain the purpose of your call.** Get to the point. "The reason I'm calling is. . . ."

- **Link in a benefit statement.** Make your "purpose" something relevant to the contact: "I'm calling to help you save money/increase revenues/do your job better."

- **Add a close or bridge.** Wrap up the opener with a concise question or statement that leads into further discussion.

For Dummies: Bestselling Book Series for Beginners

Telephone Sales For Dummies®

Take Back Your Time

Time management is one of the most important skills a telephone sales professional can have. (To sharpen yours further, read Chapter 7.) Here are a few tips:

- **Manage distractions.** When you're on task, turn off your cell phone, hold your calls, switch off the you've-got-mail notice, sign out of instant messaging, and hang up a do-not-disturb sign.

- **Keep phone calls short.** Schedule phone calls for no longer than 15 minutes.

- **Take advantage of voice mail.** When simply delivering information, time the calls for early morning or evening. You're more likely to get voice mail and avoid a lengthier conversation.

- **Maximize drive time.** Keep a collection of self-help, professional-improvement, and motivational CDs in the car, and pop them in when driving to work or to an appointment.

Staying Motivated

Sometimes you're going to feel like you've hit a brick wall because you're not getting the sales numbers you envision. Don't despair. Allow these six methods to be your motivational mantra to help you keep charged. (Chapter 18 is packed with suggestions for maintaining motivation and positive attitude.)

- **Stay disciplined.** Sticking to "the plan" keeps the positive energy flowing.

- **Be your own cheerleader.** Daily affirmations help boost your out-look to the positive mark: Even if you don't believe it, say it anyway: "I'm a successful salesperson"; "I'm good at what I do"; or "I'm skilled at helping people." It's one of life's miracles: Tell yourself you're motivated and — *voila!* — you're motivated.

- **Take care of yourself.** Staying upbeat is nearly impossible if you run yourself to exhaustion, eat poorly, and forgo your health.

- **Protect against negative forces.** Whether they're doom-and-gloom friends, nay-saying coworkers, or doubting spouses, keep the bad attitudes of others from sinking your motivation.

- **Follow a warm-up routine.** Before you begin a sales call — or any activity calling for positive energy — warm up with a mood-lifting ritual: Review or practice your script or simply relax to music.

- **Continue learning.** The process of increasing your knowledge and skills gives you further security in your abilities and potential, which feeds your motivation.

For Dummies: Bestselling Book Series for Beginners

About the Author

Dirk Zeller started his sales career almost 40 years ago through lemonade stands and selling newspaper subscriptions door-to-door. Dirk has been recognized as a top sales performer in every sales field he's entered from business-to-business sales of advertising, marketing, and event sponsorship to consumer-direct sales fields like real estate.

Dirk proceeded to turn his sales success into creating significant business income and life-change when he founded Sales Champions in 1998. Sales Champions provides premier coaching and training to the sales industry with clients worldwide. Dirk has created revolutionary programs like Stewardship Selling™, Selling the Way the Prospect Wants to Buy™, and The Champion Salesperson™. These programs and others like them have transformed the lives of hundreds of thousands of salespeople worldwide.

Dirk is one of the most published authors of success, life balance, sales training, sales force development, and business development in the sales field. He has over 300 published articles to his credit, and his weekly sales newsletter is read by over 350,000 salespeople and sales managers.

Dirk is one of the most sought after speakers in the sales arena. He has spoken to hundreds of thousands of salespeople and sales managers at the regional, national, and international level. He has also authored five top selling books in the field of sales, and he wrote *Success as a Real Estate Agent For Dummies,* also published by Wiley.

With all of the blessings and success Dirk has attained, his faith and his family are still the primary focus of his life. He and his wife of 18 years, Joan, are active with their children, five-year-old son, Wesley, and two-year-old daughter, Annabelle. He and his family reside in Bend, Oregon. You can reach Dirk at: Sales Champions, 5 NW Hawthorne Ave., Suite 100, Bend, OR 97701; phone 541-383-0505; e-mail Info@SalesChampions.com.

Dedication

To salespeople — the backbone of any successful company. You possess the power to make your companies grow and prosper. Nothing is accomplished without someone making a sale somewhere at sometime. Be proud you are a salesperson. Your profession is noble and essential to the world.

Author's Acknowledgments

I thank the team at Sales Champions and Real Estate Champions, my two sales training companies. Without your dedication to helping salespeople reach their full potential in selling, this book wouldn't be possible.

Special thanks must be expressed to my senior management team Don Cunningham, Director of Coaching; Dan Matejsek, VP of Marketing; Roger Marti, Sales Manager; and Julie Porfirio, VP of Operations. You all take on extra duties while I am focused on writing. Also, to Rachelle Cotton who typed and proofed the manuscript . . . thanks.

Thanks to Tracy Boggier, Acquisitions Editor, Chad Sievers and Georgette Beatty, Project Editors, and Sarah Westfall and Carrie Burchfield, Copy Editors, for taking on this project and keeping us all on schedule. Thank you to Betsy Sheldon who did a masterful job of taking my writing, thoughts, and ideas and converting them into the *For Dummies* format that you can learn from and enjoy.

To the home team — my wife, Joan, my son, Wesley, and my daughter, Annabelle, you make the challenges of a sales career all worth the effort. Without you all, the rewards of sales and success would have diminished value.

Publisher's Acknowledgments

We're proud of this book; please send us your comments through our Dummies online registration form located at www.dummies.com/register/.

Some of the people who helped bring this book to market include the following:

Acquisitions, Editorial, and Media Development

Project Editors: Chad R. Sievers, Georgette Beatty

Acquisitions Editor: Tracy Boggier

Copy Editors: Sarah Westfall, Carrie A. Burchfield

Editorial Program Coordinator: Erin Calligan Mooney

Technical Editor: Mark Swanson

Contributor: Betsy Sheldon

Editorial Manager: Michelle Hacker

Editorial Assistants: Joe Niesen, Leeann Harney

Cover Photos: © George Dryle/Getty Images

Cartoons: Rich Tennant (www.the5thwave.com)

Composition Services

Project Coordinator: Erin Smith

Layout and Graphics: Reuben W. Davis, Melissa K. Jester, Barbara Moore, Christine Williams, Erin Zeltner

Anniversary Logo Design: Richard Pacifico

Proofreaders: Laura Bowman, Jessica Kramer

Indexer: Potomac Indexing, LLC

Publishing and Editorial for Consumer Dummies

    Diane Graves Steele, Vice President and Publisher, Consumer Dummies

    Joyce Pepple, Acquisitions Director, Consumer Dummies

    Kristin A. Cocks, Product Development Director, Consumer Dummies

    Michael Spring, Vice President and Publisher, Travel

    Kelly Regan, Editorial Director, Travel

Publishing for Technology Dummies

    Andy Cummings, Vice President and Publisher, Dummies Technology/General User

Composition Services

    Gerry Fahey, Vice President of Production Services

    Debbie Stailey, Director of Composition Services

Contents at a Glance

Table of Contents

Introduction

"*A* born salesman." You know the expression. People love to slap that label on those who seem to come naturally to selling. Maybe *you've* been told you were born to sell at some point in your life:

- ↙ When you were 6 years old and persuaded the guy in the ice-cream truck to buy your lemonade, your Mom said it.

- ↙ When you got the prize for selling the most candy for the school fundraiser, the other kids said it.

- ↙ When you talked your way from a C to a B, your English lit teacher said it.

- ↙ When you turn your trash into treasure by selling it on eBay, your spouse says it.

But whether you call it the power of persuasion, the capacity to convince, or the wit to win over — I'm here to tell you this: Dynamite salespeople aren't born. They're the result of commitment, discipline, and the drive to learn the best and *smartest* ways to earn the business of their prospects.

Take it from me: I'm the penultimate salesperson. Sure, sales is my passion, my path to career success. Sales has helped me attain and even exceed my financial goals and has allowed me to realize my most-valued life dreams. But I didn't start out that way.

When I started out in the field, I was the youngest, greenest sales agent in my office. Some tried to convince me I'd fail, that I didn't have what it took. However, I put forth a lot of effort in those first few months. During the day, I'd work through breakfast, lunch, and dinner to make as many calls as possible. And after hours, I'd review my performance and numbers and devise the most effective methods for selling over the phone.

Within months, I earned the title of top salesman for the entire division. My progress continued, and I earned my first million at the ripe old age of 32. In 1998, I launched my coaching company, Sales Champions, to help others become top-notch salespeople and reach their career goals and life dreams.

I wrote *Telephone Sales For Dummies* for the same reasons I started my company — to guide others to develop their full potential as a sales professional and achieve their highest aspirations.

About This Book

This book is a how-to guide for gaining the skills and knowledge you need to become a champion telephone salesperson. You can also use it to acquire the organizational habits, time-management techniques, personal motivational strategies, and positive attitudes you need to rise to the top.

Telephone Sales For Dummies isn't a book of theory but of "real stuff" that works. I've packed it with proven programs and processes, tested techniques, and tried-and-true skills, strategies, and scripts.

In classic *For Dummies* fashion, the book is designed to give you easy access to the precise information you're looking for. You can read the book from cover to cover or zigzag your way through, flipping to the content you need *when* you need it. You can keep the book close at hand and turn to it for a fast reference — whether by combing the Table of Contents or Index or zeroing in on a particular chapter section, sidebar (those gray shaded boxes), or list.

Conventions Used in This Book

To make this book as easy to use as possible, the following conventions are followed throughout:

- All Web addresses appear in monofont.

    Note: Some Web addresses break across two lines of text. In such cases, no hyphens were inserted to indicate a break. So if you type exactly what you see — pretending the line break doesn't exist — you can get to your Web destination.

- New terms appear in *italics* and are closely followed by an easy-to-understand definition. I also use italics for emphasis once in a while.

- **Bold** font highlights keywords in bulleted lists or identifies the action parts of numbered lists.

- I indent and *italicize* all scripts used throughout the book. You can use them verbatim or with minor tweaks to increase your sales success.

What You're Not to Read

I understand your life is busy, and you want to read only the need-to-know information. If you're on a fast-track learning mission, you can safely skip the sidebars. Shaded gray boxes, *sidebars* serve as examples or support material. They're meant to reinforce and illustrate a concept (giving you a little extra oomph), but aren't critical to your understanding of the concept.

Foolish Assumptions

When I wrote this book, I assumed a few things about you, my dear reader. I assumed that you picked up this book because you want to improve your phone-sales skills. I didn't assume, however, that you're a working person with the title of *telephone salesperson.* You may be

- ✔ A real estate agent
- ✔ A financial consultant
- ✔ An insurance agent
- ✔ An account executive for a business-to-business product
- ✔ A volunteer for a phone fundraising campaign
- ✔ A telemarketer
- ✔ A customer service professional
- ✔ A savvy businessperson who understands that telephone-sales skills are valuable to success in any job

No matter your title or your job, you want to elevate your game and improve your sales numbers.

How This Book Is Organized

I divide *Telephone Sales For Dummies* into six major parts to help you find just what you need as quick as possible. The content is organized so that you can choose to read only the topics that interest you — or the entire part. Check out the Table of Contents or the Index to find your area of interest, and then go to the chapter that addresses the topic. At a glance, here's what you can find:

Part I: Picking Up on Telephone Sales

Part I presents an overview of the most important matters to master in order to achieve telephone-sales success. I begin with a walk-through of the phone-sales process in Chapter 1, and then follow with ways to increase your sales and income in Chapter 2. In Chapter 3, I untangle Do-Not-Call regulations for easy understanding.

Part II: Laying the Groundwork for Telephone-Sales Success

Phone-sales success requires plenty of groundwork *before* you place a finger on the first touchtone. And a game plan is the best foundation for a champion sales effort. Chapter 4 takes you step by step through the process.

Ready to get in touch with future clients? Chapter 5 covers the what, who, when, why, and how of prospecting for business. And in Chapter 6, I show you how to overcome that common malaise: call hesitance. I identify this malady and reveal my sure cure. And because time is your most valuable asset, Chapter 7 addresses another challenge to your sales endeavors: time management.

Part III: You Make the Call!

The call is the *core* of telephone sales. And (no surprise) making a call that closes is a complex process — complex but easily mastered if you have a handle on the process and the players. Part III contains the how-to instructions for executing a winning call, starting in Chapter 8 with tips to get past the gatekeepers that guard your prospect's phone access. In Chapters 9, 10, and 11, you discover how to craft an attention-getting opening, how to *ask* and *listen* before you *tell* and *sell,* and how to ask the questions that garner the best answers. Finally, Chapter 12 shows you how to smoothly shift into the delivery of your sales presentation.

Part IV: Going for the Close

So close to the *close!* This stage is one of the most critical parts of the sales process — the spot that can make or break the sale. This part contains the secrets to overcoming close barriers: Chapter 13 covers the most frequently cited objections and presents my six-step process for defusing them. In Chapter 14, I show you how to lock in your prospect's commitment and close the order *now*. And Chapter 15 shows how you can turn a failed close into a future sale.

Part V: Increasing Your Sales

This part contains tips to help you read your clients and adapt your behavior to increase your odds of closing, no matter the prospect's behavioral style. In Chapter 16, I cover different selling styles and show you how to make the most of yours. Recognizing your prospect's communication style over the phone can be a challenge, but Chapter 17 gives you the tools to meet that challenge head on. And finally, I give you some tricks of the trade for staying motivated through discipline, attitude, and ongoing training and professional development in Chapter 18.

Part VI: The Part of Tens

Every *For Dummies* book ends with the famous Part of Tens (drum roll, please). In mine, you get three tip-packed chapters to help you polish your delivery when talking on the phone, steer clear of do-not-use phrases, and abide by the ten commandments for phone-sales success.

Icons Used in This Book

To help you navigate this book a bit better, you can rely on icons in the book's margins. The icons are similar to little signposts pointing out the important info.

This bull's-eye icon points out little-advertised nuggets of knowledge that are certain to give you an edge in increasing your telephone sales.

This icon denotes critical information that you really need to take away with you. Remember these points if nothing else. They address the issues that you come across repeatedly in your phone-sales efforts.

Consider this icon the flashing red light on the road to making a sale. When you see a Warning icon, you know to steer clear of whatever practice, behavior, or response I indicate.

"Did you hear the one about the salesman and the . . .?" Not to worry. When you see the anecdote icon, expect to find a G-rated, short personal story from my own archives of experience — one that is meant to drive home the point I'm making in the text.

Where to Go from Here

To get the lay of the land of telephone sales, Part I is a good place to start. This part introduces you to the big picture and the big benefits of acquiring and honing your telephone-sales skills.

From there, you can use the Table of Contents or the Index to pick out the topics that most interest you. If you're new to sales, you can feel comfortable jumping to and fro in any order that suits you — without feeling that you've missed something.

If you've got some years of professional experience under your belt, you may want to jump to Part V. Here, I address how to get yourself to the next level through an understanding of sales psychology and continuing development through ongoing education. No matter where you start, you can find tons of valuable info that you can use to elevate your sales performance.

Part I

Picking Up on Telephone Sales

The 5th Wave   By Rich Tennant

"He's a weasel in real life, but smooth and likable on the phone."

In this part . . .

Telephone sales may focus on the sense of hearing, but you have to be able to *see* the big picture. The chapters in this first part offer a wide-angle view of what it takes to make it to the top — valuable information whether you're brand-new to the business or a veteran who's won your share of sales awards.

From the best ways to set up for sales calls to surefire strategies to "work" those calls to following up to secure the sale, I outline the crucial steps to making sales calls in Chapter 1. Chapter 2 reveals the four ways guaranteed to increase sales and income and other tried-and-true tactics for achieving the success you desire. Lest I leave you with the idea that the route to phone sales success is a walk in the park, I lead you into the land of "Do Not Call" in Chapter 3. The regulations that affect telemarketing are full of twists and turns, but trust me, they're not as impenetrable as you may think. Be sure to read Chapter 3 if you have any questions about these latest regulations. (And who doesn't?)

Chapter 1

Calling All Sales Professionals!

*T*he surge in telecommunications technology has changed the very nature of — well — communication. From anywhere in the world, you can reach out and touch someone. Or text-message them. Or at least leave a voice mail. You can even arrange a conference call so that several parties meet remotely, or set up a videoconference and put faces to voices. There's no doubt about it — you're in the era of the telephone. (And if you *have* any doubt, just listen to the orchestra of cellphone rings in the middle of a shopping mall, or count the drivers who whiz by with a phone attached to their ears.) So it's natural that the telephone is the most important tool at the disposal of any salesperson.

If you're a sales professional, you may not consider yourself to be in *telephone* sales — maybe because your job title isn't "telemarketer" or because you don't work in a call center. But in today's world, *all* salespeople rely on the telephone to be successful in their work.

In any sales scenario, the first contact with a potential customer is likely to be via the phone, even if follow-up is face to face. Although more and more commerce is carried out on the Internet, few business-client relationships are forged without regular phone contact. The days of the door-to-door encyclopedia peddler are long past. In fact, it's not unusual for, say, a printer in the Midwest to serve a magazine publisher on the West Coast, executing business entirely over the phone.

Now is the time for all sales pros to step up to the phone and master this amazing sales tool. This chapter gives you a quick rundown on telephone sales and serves as a jumping-off point to this book and to the world of telephone sales.

Plugging In to Telephone Sales

Telephone sales is much more than simply picking up the phone and asking someone to buy something. Telephone sales is the primary sales communication system for any salesperson on the planet. The formula for telephone-sales success is complex if not complicated. It's more involved than just picking up the receiver and punching in a phone number. Just as any sales effort requires planning, preparation, and practice, telephone sales demands much effort before you can count on closing sales at regular intervals.

Are you telephone-sales material?

Do you have to be a certain "type" to succeed at phone sales? Nope. In order to be a good telephone-sales pro, you must be organized, detailed, persistent, and able to read people and situations in a single call. Although individuals with certain qualities may be faster to adapt, I believe that anyone with the drive and desire to succeed can do so.

Sure, those outgoing types who are fearless about meeting new people, who love a challenge, and who thrive on competition may dive right into the sales pool and find the temperature just right. But phone-sales success demands more than personality. Whether you're the classic "sales type" or you have other qualities valuable to effective selling, all salespeople benefit from honing their knowledge and sales skills, as well as maintaining a positive attitude. (Check out Chapter 2 for more on what a thriving telephone-sales pro needs.)

Obeying the Do Not Call laws

Critical to any salesperson who uses the phone to sell is a clear and thorough understanding of national and state Do Not Call laws. More than 150 million people have registered to have their names and phone listings added to these Do Not Call lists, which blocks them from most telemarketing calls.

Salespeople who sell products or services direct to consumers — life, auto, and health insurance; long-distance or cable services; real estate; replacement windows; and myriad others — must be aware of the Do Not Call registries and adhere to their restrictions.

 If you sell business to business, you don't have to worry about the no-call issues, because businesses can't register with national or state Do Not Call lists.

 If you're caught breaking the Do Not Call law, the federal fine is $11,000 per offense — not an inconsequential amount of money. For more information about the Do Not Call Registry and state laws involving telemarketing restrictions, read Chapter 3.

Gearing Up for Winning Calls

Great telephone-sales calls don't just happen, whether you're a veteran or a newbie. A lot goes into a sales call before your fingers ever hit that first touch button. You master all the details about the service or product you sell, and you research everything possible about the person or company you're calling. You practice your delivery, prepare for questions or challenges, and — last but not the least — you prepare yourself! This section gives a quick 4-1-1 on preparing to make your calls. (You can also check out Part II for more in-depth info.)

Studying up for call success

When it comes to making the most out of your telephone-sales career, the same advice that applied to your classes in high school or college still applies in the workplace: Keep up with the daily assignments, and the big tests seem to take care of themselves.

 Each day, when you arrive at the office, set aside some time for reviewing your schedule. Then study up for each and every phone call. Review your notes to refresh your knowledge, and if you discover some gaps, do what you must to fill them, whether digging deeper into your files or researching on the Internet. (Refer to Chapter 4 for more advice.)

Prospecting smarter, not harder

Telephone sales demands work, but you can manage your prospecting work in an efficient way. *Prospecting,* the heart and soul of telephone sales, simply means you invest effort consistently seeking new customers.

The following tips can help you work smarter and increase your effectiveness and productivity when prospecting. You can also check out Chapter 5 for more info.

✔ **Batch like calls together.** By addressing similar questions, challenges, objections, and related issues, you gain a smoother flow and greater efficiency. For example, call all small, independent tire dealers in one batch, and then call the attorneys in the next batch, then the dentists, and so forth.

You also can batch by sales stage — make all your presentation appointments at the same time, all your lead follow-up calls together, and all client-referral calls in a group.

✔ **Recognize your limits.** No one can stay on the phone for eight hours straight. To maximize your production and maintain a high energy level, plan a 10- or 15-minute break after each hour of calling. Stretch, grab a snack, and get back for another hour of calls. An hour to 75 minutes is really the maximum time to be calling back-to-back.

Overcoming sales aversion

No matter how experienced or how successful, all sales pros are stricken with sales-call aversion from time to time. *Sales call aversion* is when you try to avoid, delay, or divert your prospecting and lead follow-up calls to later or never. A few examples may be boredom, stress, or fear of calling. The best cures, however, work for almost all forms of sales aversion.

 Sticking to routine is a healthy way to control the condition. If you're in the habit of setting aside every morning for calls, you likely have an easier time moving forward even if you're temporarily uninspired. For more prescriptions for sales aversion, check out Chapter 6.

Making the most of your time

Telephone salespeople are plagued by time burglars. Taking a bite out of time crime is critical — and it's not so hard after you identify what is preventing you from using your time wisely. The following two culprits can steal a lot of valuable time. If you can eye them and make them a priority, you may be able to increase your productivity.

✔ **Low-return activities:** Held captive by service calls and paperwork duties, the sales pro watches as valuable opportunities slip away. Zero in on the high-return activities and make them your number-one priority. In sales as in other disciplines, 20 percent of your efforts bring in 80 percent of your successes. So determine what comprises the 20 percent and make it a priority. This, combined with a zero tolerance for time stealers, is certain to control time loss.

✔ **In-between call breaks:** They may be a few seconds — but sometimes these breaks are three, four, or even five minutes. However, these seemingly small breaks can add up. For example, say you spend five hours making 100 calls a day, with three minutes between each call. If you reduced your in-between call breaks from three minutes to one minute, you could make an additional 200 calls per day.

Instead of allowing these thieves to steal from your telephone-sales success, zero in on the high-return activities and make them your number-one priority. (Read Chapter 7 for more ways to free yourself up to become a more productive member of your sales force.)

Making the Call

The time has come — you're ready to pick up the phone and sell! What to expect? Well, at the most fundamental level, you may antici- pate a yes, a no, or a maybe. That outcome depends largely on what you do from the moment you connect with the prospect until you ask for the business. This section looks at the possibilities.

Reaching the right person

The *gatekeeper* is the person who guards the decision maker — the person you want to talk to. You must be able to get past the gatekeeper to make the sale. If you're stopped at the administra- tive assistant's extension, a few tricks are at your disposal:

✔ If you know the decision maker's extension, call before or after the close of business and hope the assistant isn't at work — and the boss is.

✔ Call someone else within the company, apologize, and say you were transferred to the wrong extension. This individual may transfer you to the exec's direct line.

✔ Based on the assistant's extension, try keying in a number higher or lower. For example, if the assistant's extension is 234, it's highly probable that the decision maker's extension is 233 or 235. (If you don't reach the executive, then try one of the other two ploys.)

For more hints and tips for reaching the decision maker, read Chapter 8.

Opening moves

The *opening* is the most critical step in charting your sales call. Your first seven seconds determine whether you get the sale. You *don't* want to leave it to chance. Put in time to craft a powerful, stop-in-your-tracks opening, and then practice it until it's perfect.

Every successful opening is built on certain key components. You must also avoid certain words or phrases like the plague (see Chapter 20). Chapter 9 is a great source of statement templates, as well as other ideas for winning greetings.

Asking the questions first

The best way to sell is through questioning. A masterful telephone salesperson focuses on the questions because well-crafted questions elicit answers that can be used to guide the successful sale.

Without an effective questioning process, you can't determine desire, motivation, needs, wants, expectations, ability, authority, time frame, competition, priority of needs and wants, and a host of other factors that influence the buying decision.

After you get the answers to these questions, *then* it's your turn to talk. You have a lot to consider in crafting and preparing your questions. Chapter 10 provides more on questioning.

Hear this!

Salespeople are cast as talkers, not *listeners.* But all good sales pros — and especially *telephone-sales* pros — are successful because they listen, not because they talk. The better you are at listening, the more you learn about the prospect and the better equipped you are to sell to the prospect when it comes your turn to talk.

But listening is more than shutting your mouth. In order to pick up and process valuable information that helps you to shape your sales presentation, you have to be proactive — even if you feel like listening is a passive exercise.

Learning to love the pause and making peace with the awkward silence are two important skills that make you a master listener. Chapter 11 shows you the way to these and other valuable tricks.

Delivering dynamite presentations

The sales presentation is where *you* do the talking. And if you've followed all the other guidelines to phone-sales success, a powerful presentation is likely to follow.

Presentations that turn a prospect into a client don't happen by accident. Ever watch those courtroom dramas on TV? You know, the ones where the lawyers chase down every last detail and anticipate every move from objections to surprise witnesses? That's the kind of work that results in a winning sales presentation. And if you prepare your presentation as if it were your closing statement to the jury, you're well on your way to success. For more advice, turn to Chapter 12.

Closing the Deal

If you do an effective job throughout the sales process, the *close* is merely the natural — and successful — ending to your effort. Closing does require careful attention, as much preparation as any other step of the process, and an artful reaction to any last-minute objections. This section shows what you need to do for a successful close.

Dealing with objections

You know you've reached savvy-sales status when you come to welcome objections from sales prospects! Because, indeed, objections are a positive sign — and they signal promising potential for a sale.

Objections, you see, are evidence of *interest*. Instead of reading an objection as a don't-waste-my-time message, look at it as a please-*please*-convince-me-to-buy plea. Chapter 13 spells out, step by step, how to prepare and respond to objections in a way that transforms that reluctant prospect into a satisfied customer.

Getting to yes

If you've ever read advice about job hunting, you no doubt discovered that you must always ask for the job — even if you're not certain you want it. The same holds true for making a sale . . . except for the part about not wanting it.

Oh sure, you can find all kinds of closing techniques and strategies that you may want to try — and I spell them all out in Chapter 14. But whatever technique reels in the prospect, you still want to ask for the sale. Always.

Looking on the no-sale bright side

By handling that rejection in the right way, you may earn yourself a client down the road, a glowing referral, or even a sale a lot sooner than you may expect. Although losing a sale can be a downer, you can tap into ways to turn this failure into a future success. Read Chapter 15 for some ways to use this rejection in a positive way.

Keeping Motivated

No matter where your sales career path takes you, staying motivated is critical to your success and growth. Motivation comes from within, but it must be nourished from the outside. Begin with an understanding of your values and your goals and maintain them through discipline, attitude, routine, habit, and further self-development.

Staying motivated is the picture of the Porsche (or resort in Tahiti, or mansion in Montana) tacked on your bulletin board. But it's also the checkmarks in your day planner, the commitment to your daily call schedule, and the hours of practice and rehearsing. In short, your ongoing motivation calls on efforts both grand and humble. (Check out Chapter 18 for how you can stay motivated.)

Chapter 2

Thriving as a Telephone-Sales Pro

. . . .

In This Chapter

▶ Discovering the required traits and skills for phone-sales success

▶ Applying the Four Probabilities of Success for greater results

▶ Counting out the four ways to increase your sales

. . . .

A little more than a year ago, I was interviewed in a monthly trade magazine for an international sales association with 1.4 million-plus members. The interviewer asked me this question: "What is the very best sales tool currently available to our sales association members?" When I gave her my answer, she was so surprised she dropped the phone. I got in a good chuckle, while she fumbled around for the receiver.

The greatest sales tool for the last 30 years, I told her, remains the *telephone*. I knew she expected me to say, "the Internet," "the Blackberry," or some other 21st-century high-tech device. They're dandy gadgets and certainly aid in organization and lead generation — but none of them directly helps make a sale. The telephone is still the best tool with which to convey your sales message in a personal way — the only tool that allows you to inject emotion, urgency, passion, and conviction and enables you to immediately address questions and objections and guide your prospect to action.

However, thriving as a telephone-sales professional takes more than a phone. The winning salesperson must have the skills, knowledge, attitude, and habits that make the best use of that tool. In this chapter, I identify what it takes to succeed — the personality traits and skills that shape a successful phone pro — and how to acquire them. I reveal the four components that lead to top sales achievements, and offer four proven ways to raise your sales productivity.

Understanding What You Need to Succeed in Phone Sales

The toolkit for success in the world of telephone sales contains a variety of instruments. To maximize your potential, you need to gain command of all of them. The good news? You don't have to be a "born" salesperson in order to shine in your career. Unlike sports celebrities, blessed with physical build and innate skills, telephone-sales professionals can achieve stardom in their jobs through diligence, commitment, and development of positive behaviors. This section explains the most important tool you need and lists helpful personality traits and skills for telephone-sales pros.

Mastering the primary tool: Words

Every profession has its primary tool and its secondary tools. Although all tools are important, without that primary tool, the secondary tools are of little value. Mastering that number-one tool separates the successful professionals from the rest of the pack, distinguishing them from the competition and positioning them as world-class in earnings, prestige, and recognition.

Words are your primary tool when it comes to achieving success in telephone sales. I know, I know . . . at the beginning of this chapter, I say that the *telephone* is the most important tool. In the case of the telephone-sales professional, however, the telephone is the means for conveying your words. The two are inextricably entwined.

For example, my father was a dentist for more than 30 years. He was, by most people's definition, extremely successful. He relied on countless tools: drills, explorers, probes, amalgam fillings, gold and porcelain fillings, sealants, adhesives, and Novocain. But one tool was absolutely essential — his skillful hands. Without them, my father's efforts would have resulted in a different outcome.

The quality of your words conveyed via the phone is what enables you to rise to the top of the field in any sales profession. Whether you're selling rain gutters, windshield repair, real-estate services, insurance, or financial services, your ability to thrive — not just survive — is linked to the mastery of that tool. In Parts III and IV, I provide tips for mastering the words of your sales calls, from start to finish.

Becoming a sales star with a few essential personality traits

Most folks have a pretty clear definition of a "sales type." You know, a real people person who's not shy about meeting strangers. An upbeat sort — always seeing the glass as half-full. A tireless go-getter. Doesn't take rejection personally. Lots of tenacity.

I've met countless successful salespeople who fit that description. Indeed, a positive attitude, a social orientation, and a high tolerance to rejection are personality traits that definitely serve the sales professional well. And strong commitment and passion increase the odds of success. These champions win through desire and willpower because of their willingness to pay the price. If I'm describing you, then the odds of your success are very high!

I understand this type well because my personality is the same. When I began my sales career more than 20 years ago, I made calls for hours to get sales or secure appointments. I was willing to walk through a wall of fire to earn an income for my family.

But even if you have less natural drive and a lower tolerance for rejection, you can still succeed at telephone sales by tapping into other strengths critical for sales, training yourself to take on certain personality traits, and avoiding other personality traits. Although turning into a telephone-sales superstar may be more of a challenge, you can consistently produce month after month and serve as a valuable team player. You can create revenue, sales, and measurable returns on investments for the company and for yourself.

What are some of these traits that serve the telephone-sales professional well? They include the following:

- ✔ Consistent
- ✔ Disciplined
- ✔ Enthusiastic
- ✔ Optimistic
- ✔ Patient
- ✔ Persistent
- ✔ Stable
- ✔ Strong belief in the product or service

Chapter 18 discusses many of these traits and how you can use them to stay motivated.

Surveying skills that suit a sales pro

Although you can strengthen positive personality traits and break the negative ones, *skills* are practices that are learned. The successful salesperson must master a number of disciplines, including those in the following list. (Some are so critical, I've devoted an entire chapter to them.) Check the list to assess your skills in the following areas. And if you find yourself lacking, get the training you need (check out Chapter 18 for more on training).

- ✔ Closing techniques (see Chapter 14)
- ✔ Communication
- ✔ Follow-up
- ✔ Handling objections (see Chapter 13)
- ✔ Listening effectively (see Chapter 11)
- ✔ Organization
- ✔ Phone skills
- ✔ Prospecting (see Chapter 5)
- ✔ Script-writing (see Chapter 4)
- ✔ Time management (see Chapter 7)

One skill deserves special attention: discipline. Now I'm not talking about having you sit on the time-out chair. *Discipline* is the ability to do what you know needs to be done even when you don't feel like doing it. This ability helps you acquire the other necessary skills, and can significantly improve your career and earnings. As a speaker and coach of peak sales performers, I consistently observe that the top salespeople have more discipline, whether conquering a new skill, overcoming a challenge, or just attending to the paperwork and administrative details of their jobs. Discipline isn't a mystery; it's an act of will.

Achieving Your Goals with the Four Probabilities of Success

In the world of sales — especially telephone sales — you must be on a constant quest to understand the odds for success and focus on the improvement of those odds. With an increase of the odds comes improvement of income, reduction in work time, higher conversion ratios, greater career satisfaction, and a better home life.

One of the secrets to achieving your sales and life goals is conquering the Four Probabilities of Success. When you can grasp their direct connection to achieving your dreams and desires, you're better able to formulate a plan for your growth. You're also able to put the plan into action and attain the success you desire.

I call these important areas the Four Probabilities of Success, because when applied, they raise the probability of your increasing your sales, income, quality of life, and quality of relationships. These Four Probabilities of Success carry with them the power to transform your bank account, status at work, and personal life. The following section leads you through the four.

Identifying the Four Probabilities

What you accomplish is the net result of the proper application of the Four Probabilities of Success: knowledge, skill, attitude, and activities. If you raise any one of these, you increase the chances of achieving your personal or business goals. You virtually guarantee your success if you improve all of them.

Knowledge

If you increase your knowledge of the products or services you sell, you enhance your income and success. If you gain more knowledge of your competitors' offerings, you increase sales by selling more effectively against the competition. If you learn more about your customers before they buy, you increase the likelihood of making more sales for higher dollar amounts. (Chapter 4 has the basics on doing your homework for winning calls and increasing your knowledge.)

Skill

Do you have the skills you need to have telephone-sales success? If you can focus on just two skills, I recommend the following:

✔ **Sales skills** arm you with the ability to convince customers to take an action (buy your product, for example) or to persuade them to do it faster. Sales skills include your prospecting, lead follow-up, qualifying, presentation, objection handling, and closing abilities.

✔ **Time-management skills** increase the time you invest in direct income–producing activities over production-supporting activities. Time management is one of the largest challenges for most salespeople. (Check out Chapter 7 for more info.)

Both of these critical skills require ongoing attention if you want to increase performance, but each salesperson must work to perfect many other skills (see the list in the earlier section "Surveying skills that suit a sales pro"). As you improve your skills, you'll see the odds swing more and more in your favor.

Attitude

Most salespeople report that attitude influences their results. The ability to control and improve your attitude leads to increased sales, because as a human being, you're inevitably influenced by outside forces, which is especially true for salespeople. You're on the front line of rejection and a "no" is always a nearby threat. A positive attitude is a choice you make each day. The easiest way to improve your attitude is to choose it yourself, rather than let other people dictate it. In other words, be proactive, rather than reactive, with your daily attitude.

 In telephone sales, you run the risk of letting someone on the other end of the line influence your attitude. Don't allow a faceless, unknown person control the rest of your day because you caught them at a bad time or they didn't want what you were selling. Make a decision today — right now — to improve your attitude. Also, commit to being the only person you allow to control your attitude. If you stand around waiting for someone else to improve your attitude, what happens if they don't show up? (For more about improving your attitude, head to Chapter 18.)

 During my formative years, I watched a mother who chose, each day, to have a positive attitude when a negative one would have been easier. My mom was diagnosed with multiple sclerosis when I was 3. By the time I entered second grade, she had taken her last step and was confined to a wheelchair. Over the next 35 years, as I watched MS ravage her body to the point of total incapacitation, I saw that her power was in her attitude. I, like most people who knew her, didn't notice the wheelchair to which she was confined. Her attitude lifted her out of it. Her attitude also raised the probability of success for her children.

Activities

When a salesperson focuses on the activities necessary to increase her sales success, positive things come quickly. Top sales performers perform activities that bottom sales performers can't or won't do. Top salespeople do more prospecting, lead generation, lead follow-up, and appointment booking — and end up with more sales. If you want to increase your probability of success, increase the success-producing sales activities. (I go into more detail on direct income–producing activities in Chapter 7.)

Prioritizing the Four Probabilities to maximize success

When considering the Four Probabilities of Success, you must prioritize. Two of the probabilities have a larger influence on your sales growth than the others. You may even call one of them the "choke point" for most salespeople. Take a moment without reading further (no peeking!) and rank the following probabilities from 1 to 4, with 1 being what you think is the most important and 4 being the least important.

_____ Knowledge

_____ Skill

_____ Attitude

_____ Activities

Before I reveal the correct order, I want to share with you what I've discovered after speaking to hundreds of thousands of salespeople about the Four Probabilities of Success. Universally, I've found that 85 percent rank attitude as number one. Each of the other probabilities (knowledge, skills, and activities) earn top billing from only about 5 percent of the voters.

A very compelling case can be made for attitude as the top priority. You can say that without a proper attitude, nothing positive will happen. My years of coaching and training have led me to another conclusion, however: I find that most salespeople have a good enough attitude to dramatically increase their sales. The true number-one priority is activities, because most salespeople aren't doing the success-producing activities of prospecting, lead follow-up, and booking enough presentation appointments to drive the sales they desire.

But you may find yourself faced with the age-old question: Does your attitude influence your activities more than your activities influence your attitude? Which way is it for you? For most salespeople, even top performers, attitude has a greater affect on their activities than their activities have on their attitude. For the top salesperson, though, I find that the influence is reversed. To reach the highest levels in telephone sales, your activities must have greater influence on your attitude than your attitude has on your activities. (Chapter 7 has ways to help you use your time well.)

I hear the following from salespeople all the time: "I didn't feel like prospecting." Since when does *feeling* like it have anything to do with what you must do? I can tell you I rarely felt like changing my children's diapers, but I did it anyway. I rarely feel like skipping dessert, but it needs to be done if I want to maintain my weight.

If you're waiting to *feel* like doing challenging sales activities such as prospecting, you may be waiting a long time. You may as well say to a wood stove, "Give me some heat, and then I will put the wood in." You must be willing to move activities to the top of the Four Probabilities of Success and to the top of your daily personal to-do list.

From activities as number one, attitude is the second most important. Knowledge or skills can be next depending on where you are in longevity and success in your sales career.

Tackling one probability at a time

Although each of the Four Probabilities holds the potential to create explosive growth in your sales career, focusing on all of them at once is impossible. Instead, target one or two to work on *right now* by answering the following questions:

- ✔ Which of these probabilities is the choke point or limiting step for you?
- ✔ Which one would have the greatest positive influence on your sales career if you mastered it in the next year?

After you've determined the answers, then you know which probability you must tackle first. You can have positive results in a short period of time, as little as a few weeks. But to achieve *mastery* over each one of the Four Probabilities of Success, you'll need as much as a year. The sooner you make a commitment to start, the sooner you can conquer that one probability — and begin your next 12-month journey to master another.

Charting the Four Pathways to Increased Sales

When you tally what contributes to increased sales, the number of choices are fewer than you may think. Sure, you've seen ads for courses and books that claim to reveal *hundreds* of ways to multiply your sales. The truth is that all these options for increasing sales are mere footpaths that fall under four major avenues to increased sales. Each category carries tremendous power to help you increase your sales, as you can see in the following sections. Apply them effectively, and the road to success becomes much smoother.

Chart it — and achieve it

I have a wish for every salesperson I have the privilege of serving, a desire born out of the best day I've ever had in sales in my more-than-20 years in the business. I woke up early on January 12, 1993. I had just finished my best sales year. I was in the shower at 6:15 a.m., using that time to review my business plan and sales ratios in my head. All of a sudden, like a lightning bolt, the realization that I could make any amount of money I wanted struck me. I knew my sales ratios so thoroughly that I could calculate exactly how to achieve any financial goal I set for myself. It was one of the most empowering feelings I've ever experienced: to know with certainty, less than two weeks into the new year, that I would achieve my income goals for that year.

My objective that year was to make $250,000 — a quarter million dollars — *more* than I made the previous year. And on December 27, 1993, I cashed a $4,700 commission check that put my annual income in 1993 at $252,000, more than in 1992. The best part wasn't the extra income; it was knowing that I had the power to chart my course to success — and that I would do it again.

My wish is that every sales professional could realize that this power is within reach. That sales success — whether measured by income, position, or fulfillment — is attainable. That by increasing contacts and using other strategies that are part of the Four Pathways, individuals can truly chart their course.

Growing your number of contacts

A reliable predictor of performance is the number of contacts you make on a daily, weekly, monthly, and yearly basis. A salesperson who consistently achieves his daily contact goal — no matter the distractions — goes a long way in locking in a successful sales future.

In the world of sales, numbers do matter. Making a personal commitment to meet predetermined performance standards on a daily basis separates you from the pack. Your grasp of and attention to sales ratios is critical to meeting your sales goals — and the first component of that ratio is *contacts to leads.* How many contacts do you need to engage in order to generate one lead? Top salespeople know the connection between not only their contacts to leads, but also their leads to appointments and appointments to sales.

I adhere to a narrow definition of *contact:* a phone-to-phone or face-to-face meeting with a prospect who could either purchase your products or services or refer someone who could. Others may include hits on a Web site or recipients of a marketing piece as a contact. Any other definition allows you to delude yourself. Tracking the results from Web hits and direct-mail lead generation is harder than tracking the cause-effect relationship between your telephone contacts, leads, presentations, and sales. When you're making direct contact via the phone or in person, you're also using your personal sales skills to create urgency, motivation, emotion, and desire for your products or services on the prospect's part. You can't do that as easily or effectively through your Web site or direct mail.

Using the telephone effectively as your method of contact

Most salespeople are more effective selling face to face than over the phone. At minimum you have to use the phone to book those face-to-face presentations, so any salesperson must be a master of the telephone. Some salespeople can conduct the complete sales process over the phone.

If you're selling high-ticket, personal, or professional services, as do financial planners, mortgage originators, real-estate agents, and insurance agents, the best strategy is to use the phone to book personal, face-to-face presentations for your services. However, if you're selling cable television, magazine subscriptions, long-distance service, or many other products or services that may be considered more of a commodity, booking face-to-face presentations is probably an unnecessary step. You'll be able to complete the whole sale over the phone, maybe even in just one call.

As a method of contact, the telephone is highly effective. You can control who you contact and your message. You have the opportunity to convey your message with power, passion, and persuasion. And I show you how to do so throughout this book!

Upping your revenue through the quality of your prospects

A salesperson who makes consistent contacts in a personal manner and uses strong presentation skills can still suffer from low sales if the prospect is a poor match for your product. In the following list, I give you some guidelines on determining the quality of your prospects.

- ✔ **The 80/20 Rule:** To increase the odds for success, you can apply the 80/20 Rule — that 80 percent of your effort creates 20 percent of your results — to your prospecting strategy. The rule also dictates that 20 percent of your prospects create 80 percent of your sales. (For more about the 80/20 Rule, see Chapter 7.) A dynamite salesperson focuses time, effort, and emotion on the 20 percent that yields the 80 percent.

✓ **The 20/50/30 Rule:** Prospects can be further broken down (from the 80/20 Rule in the previous bullet) with the use of a rule I call the *20/50/30 Rule*. Around 20 percent of potential prospects will do business with you easily. They trust and connect with you quickly, and their barriers come down easily. You have to convince about 50 percent of prospects that they should do business with you. The remaining 30 percent is toxic. This segment can't be satisfied. As a group, these prospects can ruin your sales, motivation, and attitude.

If your compensation is essentially 100-percent commission or a small-base fee with a large commission incentive, your prospect's commitment becomes an even more critical consideration. Why? If you expend a lot of time and energy on a person with a low commitment level, that's time and energy you're *not* spending on prospects who are more likely to buy.

With each prospect, you need to ask yourself: Is this person a possible sale or a *probable* sale? Do you have a greater than 50-percent chance of making a sale, or are the odds much lower than that? In order to gauge a prospect's commitment level, you need to ask qualifying questions (see Chapter 10 for more info).

My experience is that the larger the order, the lower the odds or probability of a sale that most salespeople are willing to accept. You wouldn't go to Las Vegas and bet more money with longer odds and expect to win more frequently. The size of the sale shouldn't influence the quality of the prospect you're willing to work with. Your evaluation of the odds and quality of the prospect can't be influenced by your earnings, or you will get burned.

Improving the quality of your message: Two theories

Too many telephone salespeople operate on the edge of insanity — doing the same things over and over but expecting different results. If you have quality leads, and you're making the number of contacts you need daily with the appropriate method of contact (see previous sections on these topics), the problem is clearly the quality of your message. It can't be anything else!

What you say and how you deliver that message matters — a lot. The careful preparation, practice, and role playing of your presentation skills can yield amazing results. I believe that for every 15 hours you spend on the phone, one hour must be invested in practicing what you're going to say and role playing.

To improve the quality of your message, you can rely on the two following theories:

- ✔ **The X Theory of Success:** Becoming proficient at anything always takes people a certain amount of time, which I call X. X is different for each person based on your innate talents and previous experiences and skills. The more innate talent and previous experience you have, the less practice you need.

  For example, perfecting your presentation may take you 100 practice sessions, in order to deliver it with power and conviction, handle objections, and persuade the prospect to sign the contract. I may have a tougher time perfecting my message. I may need to practice 200 times before I get it down pat. However, the issue isn't that I take twice as long as you to achieve success, but that I have an idea of where X is, and I'm working toward it regularly.

- ✔ **The Y Theory of Choice:** I now have a decision to make: Because I know I must practice my presentation 200 times, I have a choice of how long I will take, which is the Y Theory of Choice in action. I can take ten years, five years, two years, one year, or perhaps even just six months. If I only conduct my presentation *live*, in front of prospects, and don't practice, it'll take me a long time to reach my 200. For example, say I'm in front of prospects three or four times a month, I may need more than five years to complete my 200 presentations. This is where too many salespeople miss a critical opportunity to make a positive choice: They don't factor in greater frequency of practice in their equation.

  Your success in improving the quality of your message is determined by crossing the finish line (X) and using the shortest amount of time (Y) to get there. A top salesperson uses a combination of presentations to prospects and a larger number of practice or role-play sessions to advance farther faster when striving to improve her message quality.

Chapter 3

Brave New World: The Laws of Telesales Land

In This Chapter
▶ Understanding the basics of Do Not Call
▶ Keeping your sales methods legal under Do Not Call
▶ Finding opportunity in the challenges of Do Not Call

*T*he rules of telephone sales changed forever on October 1, 2003. That was the day the National Do Not Call (DNC) Registry went into effect. The Federal Trade Commission (FTC) amended the previously standing Telemarketing Sales Rules (TSR) to prohibit telemarketers from calling individuals who place their home phone numbers on the DNC list. The list has more than 150 million phone numbers from consumers who have indicated that they want to limit the telemarketing calls they receive. Registration is voluntary and must be initiated by the consumer.

For the world of telemarketing, the change was met with concern and trepidation. Many swore the list would bring about the end of companies that relied on telephone sales and lead to an economic collapse. Others were hopeful that the restrictions would signal doom only for dishonest telemarketers. Consumers who signed up on the registry were thrilled that the telephone would never again interrupt a family dinner.

The conscientious phone-sales pro must be aware and adhere to the newest addition to the Telemarketing Sales Rules. Abiding by the law takes some attention and extra work. But on the other hand, the new legislation has also presented some positive opportunities for telephone salespeople. In this chapter, I help clear up exactly what the Do Not Call Registry restricts and permits, and I point out how the limitations may even improve the salesperson's success and quality of leads.

The registry is managed by the FTC and enforced by the Federal Communications Commission (FCC), as well as state consumer protection agencies; more than 30 states have Do Not Call registries, as well. To access further information or to receive a copy of the Do Not Call list, go to www.telemarketing.donotcall.gov.

Coming to Grips with the Rules

The impact of the Do Not Call Registry is neither black nor white. Although it hasn't brought down the U.S. economy, the DNC Registry has certainly thrown some challenges at companies that count on telephone sales to meet their financial goals. Plenty of scam artists still manage to stay in business even with the DNC list. And consumers still have to put their fork down to take calls in the evening. As a salesperson, you need to understand how this law affects you. This section helps you get a firmer grasp.

Defining telemarketing

The establishment of the Do Not Call list gives households the chance to opt out of receiving telemarketing calls. But how that list and the term *telemarketing* are defined is often misinterpreted by both telephone-sales companies and consumers.

This is how the FTC defines telemarketing calls:

> "The do not call provisions of the TSR cover any plan, program, or campaign to sell goods or services through interstate/intrastate phone calls. This includes calls by telemarketers who solicit consumers, often on behalf of third-party sellers. It also includes sellers who are paid to provide, offer to provide or arrange to provide goods and services to consumers."

In short, *telemarketing calls* are those that solicit the sales of goods and services to consumers — even if the business or individual isn't identified as a "telemarketer." Anyone who generates sales leads and sells to consumers over the phone is covered by the rule.

Examining exceptions

You can find a number of exceptions to the Do Not Call Registry on the books. Exempted are charitable organizations and telephone surveyors. And the politicians who passed the law also excluded themselves and political organizations — imagine that! The following situations also are exempted from the Do Not Call prohibitions.

Business-to-business sales

For salespeople who sell to other businesses, Do Not Call has had zero effect, because the DNC law only encompasses home telephone numbers. However, many businesses are home based. If a business is home based, then the number is exempt from DNC coverage. Savvy phone-sales pros make every effort to get a work phone number for every prospect and client they meet. They're steering clear of the Do Not Call restrictions by calling prospects at their offices.

Established business relationships

Sales calls are permitted — even if the consumer's number is on the Do Not Call list — if the salesperson or company has established a business relationship with the consumer within the previous 18 months of the call. Markers of this relationship may be a final payment, previous purchase, or recent delivery.

This relationship extends to all company employees and divisions — meaning you may call a prospect even if the established business relationship was with another department. For example, if you're selling life insurance, and your company also has a mortgage division, you can call all the people who originated mortgages from your company in the last 18 months.

This provision has proven a valuable exemption, allowing salespeople to call indefinitely without repercussions. When was the last time you paid your credit card bill? Last month? Technically, even if you stopped paying your bill for the next 17 months, the card company can call to sell you other products without violating the Do Not Call rule.

Inquiries

If an individual calls about your company, product, or services — or even to ask for directions — that's considered an *inquiry*. Because the consumer initiated the contact, he's just created a 90-day window that allows you to call back for the purpose of selling to him. If a prospect hits your Web site and leaves contact information, that is also considered an inquiry.

Make your contacts within that 90-day period. After that time passes, you can't contact people who had inquiries unless they make another inquiry or give you written permission to call them.

Written permission

You can continue to contact anyone beyond the 90 days after an inquiry or 18 months after an established business relationship (see previous sections on these topics) provided that the person gives you written permission to do so. I recommend, for example, that real estate agents include a phrase at the bottom of every open house sign-in sheet: "By providing us with your name and telephone number, you grant us permission to contact you via the telephone." This allows an agent to contact the people who attend the open house long after the 90-day inquiry period has ended.

Any other salesperson can use the same language and technique. You must acquire the prospect's signature on some document with the language printed on the bottom. You can also put it at the bottom of your Web page where the prospect fills out an inquiry for more info. You can also e-mail brochures and place it on the bottom.

Forming your own list

Most companies that a telephone salesperson would work for would handle the task of forming a list of individuals. The company would require each salesperson to daily hand in the names of people that have requested to be taken off their call list. If you're an independent contractor or own your own business, you have to keep track of this information. I suggest establishing a spreadsheet of the names and phone numbers of people who have requested to be removed from your calling list.

You're required to update your list every 90 days if you're going to call consumers directly.

What to do when customers are upset with legal calls

If someone has placed herself on the Do Not Call Registry and then receives a call from you, the individual may react with anger. She may not be aware of the key exemptions that allow you to call — and may not *care* that the call is legal. You may receive a tongue-lashing, a hang-up, or even a demand to be taken off your call list forever. If that happens, your best option is to use the best four-letter word in sales . . . *next!*

If anyone asks you to not call again or tells you to put them on your in-house no-call list, you have to comply with their wishes — even if you have an established business relationship or if they provided written permission for you to call. If you don't comply, you may be hit with the $11,000 fine from the FCC.

Adhering to the Registry's Rules

Following the rules of the DNC Registry usually isn't high on the list for most salespeople. Some salespeople want to bend the rules in order to get the sale. Be warned though! The DNC Rules are rigid and the fines are steep (usually $11,000 a fine). This section explains what you can and can't do to make sure that your sales calls fully comply with the rules of the DNC.

Making the most of what you can do

Despite its restrictions, I believe that the Do Not Call list has provided a real opportunity for success-minded salespeople. Norman Vincent Peale, the famous author and speaker, described *problems* as the outside wrapping for opportunities. The exterior looks daunting and impenetrable, but after you break through the tough exterior, the inside is easy-going.

Although some of the most attractive prospects have opted themselves onto the Do Not Call Registry, exemptions such as businesses, consumers who've established a business relationship, and people who've made inquiries to your company pump plenty of prospects into the sales pipeline. (I cover exceptions to the no-call rule in more detail earlier in this chapter.) And in many ways, the rule works to filter out many of the leads that would most likely fail to produce sales anyway.

Instead of viewing DNC as an expensive, inconvenient barrier that hampers your ability to make sales contacts, shift your perspective and treat it as motivation to focus your efforts on the most qualified leads. Such a philosophy can result in higher close ratios.

Documenting call activity

The new Do Not Call restrictions make it more critical than ever to document your sales activities: each call, all correspondence, topics discussed, and outcome of contact. If you intend to use the established business relationship and inquiry exemptions to contact names on the list, you must record a history of delivery of service to back up your action. *Delivery of service* is a very broad provision, and is open to interpretation. If you can make a case that your service to the client hasn't ended, then you may be able to fall under this provision. The more diligently you document your prospect and client contact, the longer you can extend the established business relationship provision.

The best way to document your activity is through the use of your customer relationship management (CRM) software. Whether you use ACT, Goldmine, or salesforcc.com, document every phone, mail, or e-mail contact into the software log. You should also get into the habit of recording the detail immediately after the contact — leave it until later and you run the risk of forgetting important details.

Using telephone surveys as a contact method

Telephone surveys are also exempt from the Do Not Call restrictions. By conducting a survey, you can approach individuals who may be good prospects — even if they're on the list.

This method works *only* if you refrain from promoting your product or service, attempt to make a sale, or process an order as part of that survey phone call. If you don't refrain from such actions, you'd be breaking the law.

But the primary reason you'd be conducting that survey is to identify potential leads, not to make the sale right away. And that's legit — nothing wrong with having an ulterior motive! In the following examples, both salespeople can use the info they've gathered to determine which respondents qualify as good prospects:

- ✔ A real estate agent may conduct a phone survey among area home owners, asking questions about buying and selling trends, neighborhood activity, age of homes, and services consumers want from a real estate agent.

- ✔ An insurance agent can survey folks about their most important insurance needs, quality of their current service, and types of insurance they currently carry.

But that's where the phone contact must end! The only way you can market to people you've surveyed is through going to their front door or direct mail or e-mail. Then (and only then) if they respond expressing interest in further information (called an *inquiry*), you're allowed 90 days to follow up with them on the phone. To get their home and e-mail address, you must ask carefully. One way is to offer to send them the results of the survey and then ask them for their address or e-mail address.

You can also pay a personal visit. Yes, instead of sending a direct-mail piece, you can drop off information and ask for permission to follow up with a prospect. I have coached numerous salespeople in the last few years who have employed the survey method and techniques with tremendous sales results, so don't be afraid to get out there yourself. With this technique, you don't have to wait on an e-mail inquiry or a response to a direct mail request. You get the answer from the horse's mouth right now!

Tapping into technology to create inquiries

The explosive expansion of the Web as a marketing vehicle presents another way to skirt the limitations of DNC. Free online reports, streaming audio files, complimentary newsletters, podcasts, and blogs are all proving to be effective in generating inquiries and harvesting leads that can be pursued via the phone within 90 days.

Another breakthrough for the world of telephone sales is the *call-capture system,* a service that provides a toll-free access point to consumers who want to hear about your company and its products or services. Through marketing efforts, you can persuade the prospects to dial the call-capture system, and in turn, they listen to a recorded message and learn about specific products or services by entering codes. Because you can record all activity, you have a great way to measure the effectiveness of your marketing efforts.

So what are the advantages of a call-capture system to the telephone salesperson? Oh, let me count the ways:

- ✔ After consumers dial into the call-capture system, their phone numbers are available for you to use for follow-up solicitations — even if their names are on the registry. Because they're initiating calls into this system, they fall under the inquiry provision of the Do Not Call law (which I discuss earlier in this chapter). And because your company is paying for the call-capture system, you're entitled to call them. You have 90 days after the call is captured to follow up to make a sale.

- ✔ Many call-capture services offer instant notification for the salesperson. Within minutes, you receive a phone call, text message, or e-mail notifying you of the contact and providing the phone number and information about the caller. This means you can call the prospect *immediately,* when she's most likely still at the number she called from minutes earlier.

- ✔ The call-capture system encourages a high inquiry rate. For one thing, people can use the service any time they wish — which means the system may be gathering leads while you're sleeping. Consumers are further motivated to call because they know they don't have to talk to a salesperson — no personal contact and no pressure. In fact, I've seen marketing response rates increase by 75 percent — or even double — when call-capture is used.

The birth of Do Not Call

Laws regulating telephone sales had been on the books for years. But in January 2003, the Federal Trade Commission (FTC) amended the Telemarketing Sales Rules to create the National Do Not Call Registry — a change that has had far-reaching consequences for the world of telephone sales.

Even today, years later, you can still find confusion and controversy over DNC. The initial rule was drafted to protect consumers from predatory telemarketing salespeople selling scam products and services. The original intent was to restrict interstate prospecting; for example, you live in California, and you get a phone solicitation call from someone in Arizona. A number of amendments were added to significantly expand the reach of the law to include intrastate calling, as well. These amendments caught up a number of service sectors — including real estate agents, insurance agents, financial planners, and many others — that were not part of the original version.

Knowing what you can't do

You *don't* want to disregard the Do Not Call regulations. If your product or service is sold directly to the consumer, you can't ignore the law. The penalty is too high for the company and for the errant salesperson. The fine is set at $11,000 per offense. It's easy to get nicked because any consumer can turn you in.

Calling from unscrubbed lists

If you cold call from a database of prospects, you must have the list *scrubbed* — or cleared of the names of people who have opted onto the Do Not Call Registry. By law, a call list must be scrubbed every 31 days. To scrub your list, just compare your list of prospects to the phone numbers on the DNC list and delete the prospects' numbers who appear on the list.

What are the odds that, in the last month, many of the folks on your list have added themselves to the registry? What would it hurt to go ahead and call a few numbers from the database? Don't even go there. The DNC list contains more than 150 million phone numbers — and the registry is growing all the time. Don't risk picking up that phone until you've updated your list.

Neglecting to establish a Safe Harbor compliance program

A burgeoning sector of the telephone-sales world is dedicated to assisting sales companies with managing their prospecting lists, DNC compliance procedures, sales staff training, and other related areas. When navigating the DNC waters, engaging such a service is a wise move for sales businesses, because it establishes what is known as a Safe Harbor compliance program and guides the sales-call practices with a specific set of predetermined standards of compliance, monitoring, and training.

The *Safe Harbor compliance provisions* offer some protection from violation simply through the protocols and oversight of an outside company. In most cases, if a company is working with a compliance program, the company is less likely to incur a fine if a few unintentional mistakes are made.

 A number of credible companies offer safe harbor compliance programs. Check out `www.export.gov/safeharbor/Sh_Checklist.asp` or `http://consulting.possiblenow.com/sub_audit_harbor.asp` for more information.

Facing the Future of Telephone Sales in Three Easy Steps

If you think that the Do Not Call list has made life more difficult for phone-sales pros, you're right. If you have the attitude that the DNC list has improved things for good salespeople, you're *also* right. With the right attitude and expectations, you can discover that the DNC registry has been a blessing to your job.

For example, fewer people are cold calling to generate prospects than ever before. In fact, the number of direct calls to people who aren't on the DNC list has reduced since the advent of the laws. Now, when you cold call from a scrubbed list (see the previous section for more on this topic), you're likely to experience a higher response rate. In the following sections, I share with you some steps to help start your journey into the future of telephone sales in the right direction.

Review your database

For most salespeople, their database is a black hole. Almost anything goes in — and never comes out. Many pour names into the database and never speak to the prospects again. Some salespeople may mail something on occasion, but for the most part, these potential clients are swallowed up and forgotten.

In order to avoid sending prospects into the black abyss, take the time to review every single name in your database, assessing each person's value as a viable prospect or referral source. You should separate the prospects in your database based on two key factors:

- ✔ **Timeframe:** How soon is the prospect going to take action? How long before he intends to purchase your product or service?

- ✔ **Odds of making a sale:** How committed is the prospect to you as a service provider? What are the odds that you can make the sale? Is the person a possible prospect or a probable prospect?

A *possibility* is something that happens less than 50 percent of the time — and that could be even 1 percent. A *probable* prospect would buy your product 50 percent of the time or more. Great salespeople always evaluate the odds of the game that they're playing.

Contact everyone regularly

After you've reviewed everyone in the database (check out the preceding section), you need to contact each one. I don't mean send another mailing. The time has come for personal contact. Talk to them over the phone or face to face, if possible.

This personal contact is an opportunity to discover how the individual felt about your service or whether she is satisfied with your product. Using direct contact is also a chance to call past and current clients and gain permission to continue to talk to them — which means if they're on DNC, you can move them out of the 18-month established-business-relationship category and put them under free-to-call-indefinitely portion of your list.

Ask for the business — always

Asking people for their business can be scary. You don't want to appear too pushy or "salesy." But, my friends, you are in sales! That is your job: to sell. Prospects are calling, surfing your Web site, asking for a brochure, or inquiring about your products and services because they have a need or a want. You're exactly the person to provide the solution for them to achieve a better life. You sell solutions.

Anything is possible for anyone who wants it badly enough. And you work in the greatest profession in the world — sales. More millionaires have been created in sales than in any other profession. But in order to reach that level of success, you must ask for the number, the appointment, the order, and the referral. Head to Parts III and IV for details on making the sale effectively.

Part II
Laying the Groundwork for Telephone-Sales Success

The 5th Wave   By Rich Tennant

SALES PICNIC

"Get names!"

In this part . . .

*J*ust as professional athletes win through preparation
and practice, telephone-sales success requires plenty
of hard work *before* you place a finger on the first touchtone. This part takes dead aim at the preparations required
for a championship sales season. In Chapter 4, I coach
you through creating your game plan and cover all the
steps critical to being the best-prepared telephone salesperson you can be. An outstanding telephone salesperson
knows that prospecting is the pathway to career success.
Chapter 5 covers the how, why, and when of contacting
prospects.

Even with plenty of preparation, salespeople are susceptible to a serious telephone sales condition: call aversion.
The prognosis is good for a quick recovery if you follow
my prescription. In Chapter 6, I identify call aversion and
offer a few cures. Finally, in Chapter 7, you can explore
a telephone salesperson's most valuable asset — time.
I pinpoint some of the most challenging time drains
and help you plug up the leaks with tested and proven
strategies.

Chapter 4

Doing Your Homework for A-Plus Calls

*Y*our days in the classroom may be over, but life learning never ends. Dynamite salespeople read books such as *Telephone Sales For Dummies* and enroll in seminars to sharpen their skills. They also know the value of routine preparation. The best way to stay at the top of the class is to complete those daily assignments — in the sales world, that translates to doing your prep work for sales calls on a regular basis.

Your sales-call homework involves many of the practices you probably recall from school: research, analysis, review, and rehearsal. It enables you to stay on course of your long-term goal — graduating to the top performance level — by successfully performing the day-to-day assignments.

Preparing diligently for your calls means that you not only do well on the day-to-day challenges — whether making a sale or building your appointment schedule — but you're better positioned to successfully handle the bigger tests that your career as a telephone salesperson inevitably brings. Before you pick up the phone (in terms of crafting high-quality results-oriented scripts, practicing those scripts to perfection, and investing the time to research the prospect), look over these actions. They can help swing the results in your favor. Not only does being prepared increase sales, but it also decreases the time you invest to make the sale along with shortening the sales cycle. This chapter shows you how to figure out what you want to achieve, who you want to reach, and how to get there with a well-constructed script.

Focusing on Your Objectives: What Do You Want to Achieve?

In order to be successful at telephone sales, or anything in life for that matter, you need to know what you want to accomplish. You simply can't pick up the phone and make that killer sale without having an idea of why you're doing it in the first place. Figuring out your goals and objectives is paramount before jumping into the call.

After you figure out your goals — short, medium, and long range — staying focused on them isn't easy. However, before you pick up the phone for the first time today, you need to pause and look at the larger picture for the day, week, and month. Doing so helps ignite the positive energy and keeps you on track. The greater the clarity of purpose, the easier it is to stay on the path toward your ultimate destination. This section helps you figure out what your own goals and objectives are. After you have a clearer picture of them, you increase your chances of success in telephone sales.

Identifying and assessing your achievement goals

When figuring out what you want to accomplish when you're working in telephone sales, you want to establish what your own specific achievement goals are. Your *achievement goals* are a blueprint for your actions; they can be broken down into short-, medium-, and long-range goals. After you establish your goals, you want to revisit them on a regular basis to assess how you're doing.

For example, your long-term goal may be to retire comfortably at the age of 50. In the meantime, short-term goals help you get there. And your daily preparation helps you achieve these short- and medium-range objectives. (Continue reading this chapter for more info on how to study your prospects and prepare your script.)

Consider what you must accomplish to stay on course to achieve your goals. Look at the next month:

- ✔ How much money in commission do you need this month to fund your lifestyle?
- ✔ How much money in commission is your goal for the month?
- ✔ How many sales do you need to achieve the commission goal?

✔ How many appointments or sales presentations do you need to achieve the number of sales to reach the goal?

✔ How many contacts must you secure to meet the required number of appointments?

✔ How many dials will it take to reach the contact goal?

✔ What must you do this week to achieve at least one-fourth of your monthly goal?

✔ Who are your most probable targets for achieving sales this week?

✔ Do you have enough good targets to reach your weekly goal?

✔ If the number of probable targets is low, what action must you take to change the outcome?

Telephone-sales success relies on a consistent formula: Identify your goals, determine what course can get you there, act upon that course, and refine your action plan as required as you progress.

Reviewing your sales cycle

Knowing your field's or company's *sales cycle* — the process from first contact to final sale — is invaluable, especially when focusing on your objectives. This information can allow you to manage your time and get the necessary preparation done for each sale. The more familiar you are with your sales cycle, the easier it is to prepare for and keep on top of the process and determine whether you're meeting your goals and objectives or falling short.

A sales cycle for a product or service is the order of action taken to achieve the sale. For example, if you're selling long-distance telephone service to individuals, your sales cycle may look like this:

✔ Secure a targeted list that your company will probably provide for you.

✔ Make initial calls to the people on the list using approved scripts and dialogues for opening statements.

✔ Find out their current provider with in the first three minutes of the call.

✔ Bridge to your pre-scripted comparison evaluation between their current service and yours.

✔ Confirm that they see the clear advantages they would enjoy by changing services.

✔ Close for the order and confirm a good decision was made.

This example is obviously a smaller sales cycle because of the one-call close objective of selling long distance. If you were selling business long distance rather than individual long distance, the sales cycle may be longer, with a few more calls and more comparison and evaluation between services.

Chances are slim that you can speed up the timeframe or streamline the process. The average sales cycle reflects a successful sales history in your company or field. Depending upon the product or service you sell and the type of client you sell to, your sales cycle may be as short as ten minutes or as long as six months.

Be sure you know the answers to these questions regarding the sales cycle:

- ✔ What is the length of the sales cycle for your product, company, or industry?

- ✔ What are the phases of the typical sales cycle (phone calls, presentations, follow-up calls, information packets, and so on)?

- ✔ What actions must you perform in order to complete the sales cycle?

These questions can help you have the right timing for the sale. Some of selling is being there at the right time. If you're too early or too late with a wonderful offer or opportunity, you won't acquire the sale.

Preparing for daily assignments

High scores in telephone sales require daily preparation. The successful telephone salesperson has a game plan for the day — every day. If you want to meet your goals and objectives, you need to do more than just walk in the door, put your stuff away, grab a cup of coffee, switch on your computer, put your headset on, and make the first dial. The following sections help you prepare your own game plan.

Planning for every call

Begin by preparing for each and every call . . . no exceptions. Before you pick up the phone, have the answers to the following questions:

- ✔ Why are you calling this person? To book an appointment? To confirm receipt of information? Are you making a presentation?

✔ If you're making a presentation, do you have your questions prepared? Your script? Have you personalized your presentation for this particular call?

✔ What is the desirable outcome for this call?

Anything can derail a sale. You want to avoid derailment through knowing clearly the goals and objectives of each call that you invest your time, effort, and energy into.

Setting the call objective

No matter how inconsequential you think a call may be, setting a goal for every call is important. Make your primary objective a *tangible* one; instead of "Convince the prospect to consider my product further," be sure an action is attached to it: "Take an order." "Book an appointment." "Gather full profile from lead." "Ask all qualifying questions." When you hang up the phone, you then have a material reflection of the results.

Be prepared with a back-up objective, too. If your primary objective is to make an order and that doesn't happen, what's the secondary outcome you'd like to have? Getting the prospect to agree to a face-to-face meeting? Procuring a referral from the prospect? Getting permission to call the prospect in a few months to see whether circumstances have changed?

When establishing objectives, be sure that you balance your optimism with reality. Be forward-thinking, but not delusional. Expecting the prospect to switch to your services and commit to a five-year contract for $100,000 a year with the first call is just this side of deranged. A primary objective of a single, smaller sale is optimistic — and a back-up objective of booking an appointment is realistic. All in all, try to strike a good balance.

Rehearsing your words

In order to meet your overall objectives, you want to take a few minutes before making a call to practice and know what you're going to say. What you say to the prospect is guided by your objective: If you're trying to determine whether the company is a good fit for your product, you prepare your list of qualifying questions. (See Chapter 10 for more about qualifying prospects.)

If you're planning to sell, you pull out your sales script. (More about script-preparation later in this chapter in the "Delivering a Straight-A Script" section.) And if you're anticipating specific objections, you plan for some compelling responses. (Turn to Chapter 13.) If you don't take a few moments to rehearse, you won't be prepared, and you risk blowing the call and blowing the lead, sometimes for good.

Establishing call length

To keep control of your schedule, establish your call length in advance. This doesn't mean you have to abruptly cut the call short if you're still tying things up or if an enthusiastic prospect is asking more questions. And, of course, you need to invest the time in building a personal connection. But giving yourself an average timeframe helps keep you on track.

In most cases, longer calls don't bring better results. In your business, a time standard has most likely been set for the typical follow-up, presentation, booking, or service call. When you exceed the planned call length, then you have to evaluate why. If, for example, you're investing too much time on meeting your primary objective, it may be necessary to switch to your back-up goal.

Studying Your Prospects

Knowledge is the key to the door of opportunity. When you study up on your prospects before your calls, you gather information that is bound to unlock sales success. As a side benefit, prospects are impressed and flattered when you show you're acquainted with their business. And your pre-call research also helps you avoid being sideswiped by sensitive situations you may not have been aware of.

Before the Internet, doing such research was much more difficult. Today you can find a ton of reliable and valuable info online. This section shows you what to look for and where to turn when studying your prospects. (For more on prospecting, turn to Chapter 5.)

Boning up on the company

Remember your job-hunting days? You were advised to walk into every interview with a solid background on the company. Your pre-call research should uncover similar information. You want to make sure you're familiar with a prospect's company, including:

- Core business
- Key management, including president, CEO, COO, and CFO
- Company history
- Size: number of employees, divisions, and locations
- Financial information, including recent annual report
- Market share

✔ Stock-market history

✔ Major competitors

✔ Management in the division your contact works in

✔ Sales figures for that division

Gathering any other information that gives you a glimpse of the company's character — press releases, news articles, corporate mission statement, core values, and even employee policies and benefits — is a good idea.

Taking the three-click crash course

By investing even five minutes before an important sales call to dig up a little dirt on your prospect, you can dramatically increase your knowledge, improve your call performance, and increase the odds of success. And it's as easy as three clicks on your computer.

Click one: Visit the corporate Web site

On the company's Web site, you can find plenty about its services and products. Check for information about the senior managers. Often, their e-mail addresses are listed — and you may need those in the future. Review the mission statement or core values. Quickly read any recent press releases (ideally published in the last three to six months).

Don't put too much value on company-issued press releases. Press releases, in most cases, skew positive — announcing achievements and successes or launches of cutting-edge products or strategic projects. Most are written to position the company as a leader in their field. You may want to check an independent source to verify some of that info.

Click two: Search online

Checking up on a company via an Internet search engine brings up references on other Web sites, from news and trade e-zines to personal blogs. Read a few articles about the company in third-party publications (although you're likely to see a regurgitation of the same press releases you discovered on the company's Web site). Find out whether others are critical or whether the company has some public relations issues. Be sure to check the date — an article that's three years old may not depict the present state of the company.

You may also come across the sites of competitors in your Internet search. Frequently, other companies buy ads around their competition's search-engine traffic. So find out what's up with the competition — you may even identify some future prospects!

Click three: Research your contact

Finally, research your company contact by typing the name into an Internet search engine. Of course, you may find information about her on the corporate Web site, but unless she's senior management, there's a good chance she's not included.

When you type the name into a search engine, you bring up references both professional and personal. You're as likely to learn that your prospect leads seminars in your industry as you are that she's president of the PTA. You could discover that she has won top professional awards — and that she won a blue ribbon in the state fair quilting exhibit. Personal information about a prospect comes in handy when trying to build rapport.

With this information you can guide the conversation to areas that you know will peak their interest. You know in advance that if they are president of the PTA that they are very active in school functions and issues.

Posing as a Customer

Gathering info the company freely gives out to the general public is completely above board — and *smart*. The best way to access this info oftentimes is to act like you're a prospective client. In fact, to fully understand the company and best serve the client, you certainly want to experience its services from the consumer's viewpoint. This section gives you a couple ways to find out more about your prospect by acting like one of its customers.

"Send me a brochure"

If you want to find out more about a company, just ask for a brochure. Granted, some of this info may be repetitive to info on the company's Web site (check out the earlier section, "Click one: Visit the corporate Web site"), but you also may uncover a tidbit you didn't know. Most companies are prepared to provide consumers with a brochure or information packet that explains and promotes their business, product, or service. And in most cases, getting your hands on this material is as easy as clicking a link on the company Web site.

If you want to dig further, you may find that a phone call will produce more results. The source for this information is likely to be someone in administration — or possibly sales — but not typically the contact you're trying to win as a client. You may ask, for example, whether the company offers more detailed information about specific services — or the activities of a particular division (the one you're trying to secure as a client, of course).

This type of research means advance preparation, though. Rather than starting your research gathering the day before your sales call, you need to work a week to ten days ahead in order to receive and digest the company materials. If you want to speed up the process and reduce the company's costs, ask it to e-mail the info to you.

"In the market for some stock"

Another great way to find out information is to buy some stock. Call the company for some information or contact your broker. Stockholders of publicly traded companies receive insider information, including copies of annual reports. These year-end summaries typically include financial information and a description of short-term and long-term projects.

When you read the annual report, you're getting the straight story —but told in as positive a light as possible. This report is an opportunity for the company to share its success stories with investors in order to encourage them to invest even more.

So become a shareholder and get in on the news. Owning even one share can give you an advantage in a couple ways:

- ✔ It puts you on the mailing list for corporate communication and keeps you abreast about your investment — your investment in this company as a client, that is.

- ✔ You can also share with the prospect that you own stock in the company. He'll be impressed that he's dealing with not *just* a salesperson, but a stockholder, as well.

Delivering a Straight-A Script

Ever take part in a school play? I'm willing to bet you followed a script, which led you word by word through the performance. You probably rehearsed for weeks, until you could read the lines in your dreams. But could you imagine accepting the role of, say, Juliet, and simply showing up for the performance without ever having looked at a script, *only* knowing that you were playing a star-crossed teenage lover destined to die?

Plays, oral reports, bar mitzvah speeches, class lectures — they all require a script. And the most effective deliveries are from those individuals who prepare and follow that script. The same goes for telephone salespeople. Using a script ensures the quality of the call, increases impact, guides your prospects and clients more effectively, shortens your call time, and increases sales and customer satisfaction. The net result is that you make more calls in the day for more sales. Who wouldn't want that?

Are you not sure where to start with your script? Not to worry. This section explains what to include in a script, how to rehearse, and what you can add to it to personalize it.

Following the company line

Businesses often insist that their phone-sales staff follow an approved script, which is a wise practice. Good companies have distilled their years of sales experience into presentations that have historically delivered results. Scripts are designed to help you and the company achieve sales, so don't be too quick to change them — that only moves you from the proven to the unproven.

If you're new to sales or new to selling this product or service, my best guidance is to follow the company scripts, at least until you've established yourself in the upper-middle tier of the sales force. If the company doesn't provide scripts for telephone-sales efforts, bring up the situation with your sales manager. In a positive way, explain that a company-endorsed script could help you — and the others on the sales force — to improve your calls and results and ensure a consistent message and image to prospective customers. In this section, I include all you need to know about constructing, rehearsing, and even personalizing your sales script.

The ABCs of a well-constructed script

The best rule anyone can give you in sales is to use scripts. A good script should be structured with three elements in mind:

> ✔ **The purpose:** The script for completing a sale isn't the same as the one for booking an appointment. Qualifying a prospect requires a different approach than delivering a presentation.

The purpose of your call dictates the content of your script. Determine this before you finalize your script.

✔ **The recipient:** Who are you intending to reach? A consumer? A business person? The receptionist? The CEO? A purchasing agent? The script varies, depending upon the answer to this question.

✔ **The offer:** If you sell a line of products or services, your script may be targeted to a single item or a family of items. In order to select the proper script, you want to know this first.

A good script also follows the sales cycle for your product or service, moving you up one rung at a time (refer to the "Reviewing your sales cycle" earlier in this chapter for more info). If your typical sales cycle takes the form of three initial calls to introduce yourself, send information, and qualify the prospect, your scripts must be designed in that manner. A four-step process and a two-script sales arsenal just don't add up.

Just as an A-plus class paper has an accepted structure with consistent components, so does a telephone-sales script. If you're following the company script, try to identify its key parts. If you find yourself in a situation in which you must write your own script, this information is critical. A good call script includes

✔ **An opening statement:** This opening launches the call with ease, quickly introduces you and your product, and piques interest in a few seconds. (Turn to Chapter 9.)

✔ **A request for an appointment (phone or face to face):** If the appointment is part of the sales cycle, you want to ask for an appointment. If you're selling a product in which the sales cycle is a one-call close, then you omit this step.

✔ **Questions to qualify the prospect:** Ask questions in order to ensure that your time on the appointment is well spent. You want to find out about the prospect's typical purchasing process, and specific needs, wants, problems, and desires.

✔ **The core presentation:** Show how your product or service fits the prospect's needs. (Chapter 12 includes the scoop on designing and scripting presentations.)

✔ **The initial close:** This is the first asking for the order of your presentation, which will usually be followed with objections by the prospect. (See Chapter 14 for more on the types of closes you can use.)

✔ **Objection handling:** Although you don't include all possible objections, you definitely need to have them at hand and ready. (See Chapter 13.)

✔ **The final close:** After you get the objections out of the way, your job is to go back and gain the final commitment for the sale and confirm that the prospect made a good decision.

Rehearsing for a winning delivery

Scripted calls seem to have a bad rap among salespeople. I often hear complaints that scripts sound unprofessional. I laugh at that because, in my view, stuttering and struggling for the words to say are much more unprofessional than following a script. I suspect that what sounds unpolished about script reading to these folks is salespeople who haven't *rehearsed* or prepared enough. The script is rarely at fault.

Before you actually pick up the phone and make the call, you want to take a few minutes to rehearse the call and make your call seem fresh and not canned. However, rehearsing is more than simply parroting the words to get successful results from a good script. You can make it or break it with nuances in pauses, tonality, feedback-response techniques, pace, voice inflection, and conviction. Incorporating, tweaking, and testing these components with a few practice sessions is bound to make for a smoother, more-natural reading.

Translating written script to speech

When you rehearse, you can work out any awkward spots where written dialogue doesn't translate naturally in verbal mode.

For example, while writing *Success as a Real Estate Agent For Dummies* (Wiley), I came to loggerheads with the editorial staff. They wanted to make some changes to the sample scripts in the book in order to correct grammar. They were clearly right . . . about the grammar. But all our scripts have been tested and proven by hundreds of thousands of real estate agents over more than 15 years.

Those grammar glitches were designed into the scripts to make them more conversational — a critical component of a winning sales script. A couple of phone calls cleared things up between us, and my scripts appeared in the book untouched. My advice is to not get hung up on grammar . . . get hung up on the results. Does the script work? Then it's correct!

Planning pauses and indicating voice inflections

You may be thinking, "What? Planning pauses and marking voice inflection?" Yes; you want to note on your script where to pause and where to change the tone of your voice. These techniques may seem too rehearsed, but, paradoxically, they help create a more natural, conversational tone. And they yield fabulous results for the salespeople who plan, prepare, and use them on calls.

When rehearsing a winning script, make notes on the script about pauses and changes in voice inflections:

✔ **Pauses:** Pauses are important because they give the prospect time to think and consider your points. After you're on the call, you may rush right through your lines — whether out of nervousness or a desire not to take up too much of the prospect's time. However, pauses allow you to keep an effective pace. Highlight pause points or insert an ellipsis to indicate a pause.

✔ **Tone or voice inflection:** Do you want to deliver with a downswing in your voice at the end of a sentence? The downswing conveys power, authority, and conviction of your statement or question.

By properly employing pauses, inflections, and other techniques, you can avoid sounding like a prerecorded automated customer-service line.

Testing, testing . . . one, two, three

During your rehearsal, you can't just sit down for a few minutes, read through the script, and then pick up the phone. Make sure you follow these three steps of the rehearsal process:

1. **Read through the script aloud, getting a feel for the delivery speed, pauses, downswings, and convictions.**

   You may have your sales manager review the script, too. If you feel it has some weakness, the two of you may agree on some minor changes for improvement.

2. **Role-play with your sales manager or another salesperson, and be sure to have the other person read the script, too.**

   Put yourself in your prospect's shoes to gauge reaction. Listen to the pause points when your role-play partner delivers the script. Did you get them in the right spot to increase the power?

3. **Test your script with the prospect.**

   At least one individual has to serve as a guinea pig. Listen for the reaction on the phone. Does the prospect seem confused? Are there gaps of silence because she can't answer your questions? Your attention to the response helps you fine-tune your delivery for greater effectiveness.

Taking time to revise

Your script doesn't end when you hang up the phone. After you hang up, take a moment to debrief:

- ✔ What did you do well?
- ✔ What area needs improvement in your delivery?
- ✔ Were there parts that went over like a lead balloon?
- ✔ Was undue resistance created at any part?
- ✔ Did the script lead to a discussion by the prospect?
- ✔ Were the pauses right?
- ✔ Do you need to change the pace of delivery or tonality?
- ✔ Did it work better than the script you were using before?
- ✔ What do you need to change?

After you answer some of these questions, revisit the script, make notes, and determine whether you need to make changes to improve the script.

Don't change the script because your first delivery is less than stellar. Testing is essential to define a script as a success or a flop. Test it — as is — at least 25 to 30 times by tracking such factors as contacts to leads, leads to appointments, and appointments to sales. If your numbers aren't where you want them at that point, go ahead and tweak the script. By the time you cross the 50 to 75 threshold, you should know whether you need to start over. Don't undertest scripts!

Personalizing the script

For people who are new to sales or who may have been struggling with their sales numbers, I encourage you to stick with tried-and-true company scripts. But don't misunderstand — I'm not endorsing *generic* scripting! A good script, whether for lead generation or closing, is formatted to allow for personalization. This section points out a few easy ways that you can personalize your script without straying off the path.

What's in a name?

No sound is sweeter than the sound of your own name. So when speaking to a prospect, inserting his name into the script is bound to get a positive reaction.

Before you can effectively use the name, however, you have to be able to say it. And how is it that your call list is exploding with 20-letter last names containing two vowels and unfamiliar accents? What to do — risk butchering the name? Stick to the first name? Or in the case that the first name is the challenge, refer to them as Mr. or Ms. Whomever? I recommend three options:

- ✔ **Plan ahead.** Call the assistant or receptionist and ask for help with the pronunciation before calling the prospect.

- ✔ **Call the prospect well before the opening of the business day.** You want to reach her voice mail greeting — not her. Listen carefully as she says her name — and write it out phonetically.

- ✔ **Confess at the get-go that you're clueless.** Trust me, this won't be the first time the prospect has heard this. Expressing some interest into the name's origin may help distract from any awkwardness. As the prospect pronounces the name, write it down phonetically, then repeat it back, asking if you've said it correctly. Your care, diligence, and desire to get it right may just launch your relationship in a successful direction.

Once upon a time . . .

You can also personalize scripts through short stories and anecdotes about your product or service and its effectiveness for others. This works well, no matter what you're selling. By sharing success stories, you increase the credibility of your product and your company. The stories can't be novels, however. You want your anecdotes to be easy to grasp, illustrative, and compelling, such as the following:

> *"Fred, my client, Bob Smith, at XYZ Company had the same challenges you are describing. When he started using our machine, he reduced his costs by 35 percent in less than a month."*

> *"Stan, my client Susan Jones, of ABC Company, had a similar problem. When we placed our machine in her company, she saw an immediate return of $5,000 in additional sales in just two weeks. So, our machine paid for itself in that short amount of time."*

Earning trust

You're only as good as your word, as they say, and when dialoguing with prospects, one of the strongest tools you have is your personal guarantee. Whether it's for on-time delivery, lowest price, or lifetime service, when you give your word that you and your company will come through, you make big points with the customer.

Make sure your script has room for personal guarantees. *But,* be absolutely positive that you can stand by your commitment, whatever it is. For example, if you know you have absolutely no control over escalating costs, don't promise a locked-in price. Instead, you may be able to commit to alerting the prospect about upcoming price increases.

Chapter 5

Prospecting Your Way to Success

*P*rospecting: Brings to mind images of the Old West, doesn't it? History has made the determined prospector who spent every backbreaking day panning for gold in a churning river or swinging a pickaxe into hard rock mythological. However, lots of miners returned to their homes with nothing. Some were seduced by get-rich-quick schemes — card playing, stagecoach robbing, and so on. And plenty, after a brief taste of the demands of the work, realized that an easier way to make a living had to be out there somewhere. But a handful of dedicated and persistent 49ers withstood the harsh conditions and, day in and day out, continued the grueling task. To these folks came the fortunes of the Gold Rush.

Prospecting really isn't so different for the telephone-sales professional. They just mine for a different kind of reward: sales! And success is still the result of hard work, determination, and fortitude. It requires rolling up your proverbial shirtsleeves and digging in — committing to the day-to-day chore of making telephone calls. Any shortcut to bypass this effort leads only to fool's gold.

I have yet to meet a salesperson who is dying to prospect. *No one* gets up in the morning, leaps out of bed, and says, "I'm excited today — I get to make 200 cold calls!" But face it: Prospecting is the bedrock of sales success. And it can even be fun if you approach it with a can-do attitude and the right tools. Honest. In this chapter, I outfit you for your search for gold — I mean, sales — and help guide you along the surest path to the mother lode of leads. Eureka!

Plenty of sales trainers may try to convince you otherwise; they may swear they've discovered a miraculous prospecting-free route to riches. But, believe me, anyone who tells you that you can become a champion sales leader without prospecting is nothing more than a snake-oil salesman. So the next time you're offered a ticket to the "greatest show on earth," pass it up and get back on the phone.

Understanding What Prospecting Is — and Isn't

Webster defines prospecting as "seeking a potential customer, seeking with a vision of success." You can find two key concepts worth considering here:

- ✔ **Seeking:** Notice that Webster's definition doesn't say *waiting, hoping,* or *praying.* Action is implied here. You require effort to go find these potential customers.

- ✔ **Vision of success:** Effective prospecting requires an optimistic approach, a belief in a positive outcome. It forbids the influence of other salespeople who may have bought into other definitions of prospecting.

You may find various other definitions for prospecting in *your* dictionary. But in the language of the telephone-sales world, the word may have a narrower meaning than in other translations. Prospecting is limited to a very specific action: *talking.* Not mailing, not blogging, not advertising. If you're not on the phone or face to face with a person, you're not prospecting.

Table 5-1 shows the differences between prospecting activities and other tasks.

Too often salespeople only work the leads that they have currently. A salesperson always needs new leads to work, and that is what prospecting creates — new leads. Like I always say: "The pathway to riches in sales is the prospecting pathway."

The power of prospecting: A first-hand account

In 1991, I joined a new sales firm. The sales office was populated with experienced and high-producing professionals. To succeed, I knew that I needed to prospect more than the other salespeople. My prior experience prepared me to do what was necessary — to make a certain number of dials and contacts each day.

I arrived at the office at 7 a.m. every day. I was on the phone by 8 a.m. — list calling and cold calling. Heck, as long as those prospects had phone numbers, I'd call them as long as they had a pulse. The other salespeople laughed about the "new kid's" zeal. The laughing died down in less than six months when I moved into the top production category. The laughter stopped when I made more than six figures in earnings my first year. And my grin started when I held the number-one sales position in less than three years. If you make this same commitment to prospecting, you too can see this kind of sales success.

Table 5-1   Prospecting versus Other Activities

What Prospecting Is	What Prospecting Isn't
Calling past clients	Mailing magnets, calendars, marketing pieces, anything
Calling sphere of influence (people you know)	Setting up a Web site
Cold calling	Putting magnetic signs on your car
Calling targeted lists of prospects	Sponsoring a community sports team
Calling and asking for referrals	Answering e-mails
Add-on selling to previous orders	Pinning your business card up on a bulletin board
Personally meeting with your past clients and sphere of influence face to face to solicit referrals or more business.	Running advertisements in any publication

Prospecting: The Cornerstone of Your Business

Prospecting must be the foundation of your business. E-mail correspondence, support marketing pieces and brochures, or any other tool is the icing on the cake. Prospecting *is* the cake. Without a solid foundation, a house won't be safe, secure, or stand for decades into the future. Without the foundation of prospecting, a sales career won't hold up, either.

In the following sections, I explain how to make prospecting the cornerstone of your sales career with a strong support system. I also show you how to aim for the best prospects and work toward specific prospecting goals.

Setting and achieving goals

When you're first starting out in sales — or in a new sales job — start with easily attainable goals as you build healthy prospecting habits. You don't run a marathon without having trained for weeks or months to increase your endurance. Nor would you set the goal of 100 contacts in a day of sales prospecting — that's marathon-level prospecting!

In setting daily and weekly prospecting goals, concentrate on following these three steps, which all flow into each other and help you establish your goals:

1. **Establish a number of contacts.**

   The number of qualified prospects — decision makers who are able to purchase your product or service or can refer you to someone who could — that you decide to call must be based on your goals, sales cycle, and sales ratios.

   When I coach a new sales client, I like to start him at realistic goals for daily contacts. Of course, sales numbers of any kind vary greatly, based on product or service, cost, sales cycle, presentation length, and any number of factors. But as a general rule, a safe minimum is 15 to 25 contacts a day. Seem low? Remember, a contact is two-way conversation with a potential prospect. It's not a voice mail message, a discussion with a gatekeeper, or a call to gather background information.

It may take several weeks for you to build up to this number. After you find yourself comfortably achieving 15 to 25 contacts a day for three weeks straight without missing a single day, you're ready to ratchet up: 30, 35, 40 a day.

2. **Calculate the number of leads.**

   After you review the list of all those people you *contacted,* this list is the total number of contacts who demonstrated a motivation and desire to make an investment in your product or service. They said something that led you to believe that your product or service is a viable solution to their problem — and that they have the financial capacity to make the investment.

3. **Project a number of appointments.**

   From that list of leads, you must establish a list of follow-up face-to-face or phone meetings that you must schedule. During this appointment, you discuss in more detail their needs and wants, share more information about your service or product and how your company works, and build the foundation for a relationship. The more you can secure an exclusive relationship, the more control you can have in the sales process.

Building the four pillars of prospecting

You need a system of support for your foundation of prospecting. You can't just go at it without a little forethought and elbow grease. You need some specific guidelines for carrying out your plan in order to accomplish your sales goals. My four pillars of prospecting are just the thing to stabilize your sales efforts and build long-range success.

Pillar #1: Find a set time and place for daily prospecting

Many salespeople make the commitment to prospect every day — but their mistake is trying to work it in around their day. That approach doesn't work long term. Instead of working your prospecting around your day, work your day around your prospecting. Schedule a segment of your day — same time every day — to prospect, and have a set place for it.

If you're unable to reach whom you're calling, you need to vary your approach. You may want to periodically add additional prospecting sessions on differing days and at different times. You may be trying to catch someone who will never be available in your primary prospecting block.

In a previous sales position, I had set up a prospecting space in my private office. It was a standup area with a computer and a telephone with a headset. My prospecting scripts were tacked on the wall where I could see them. On the other wall were my objection-handling scripts. Having all my tools within reach or in sight allowed me to not fumble for a moment with a prospect — I was ready for anything.

Here are two helpful tips that I gathered from setting up this space:

✔ A good-quality headset is one of the best investments a telephone-sales professional will find. Check for features such as sound quality, comfort, fit, and range. You may have to spend a few hundred dollars, but the expense is worth it.

✔ Standing up while prospecting is an amazing technique to pump up your passion and energy. Your body language accounts for 55 percent of your communication — even when you are on the phone. A headset frees up your hands so that you can use them to engage in the sales process more effectively. The combination of standing and freeing up your hands is guaranteed to raise the level of passion, conviction, and enthusiasm your prospect hears when talking to you.

Pillar #2: Fight off distractions

First of all, distractions are a fact of sales life. And truth be told, most people are *looking* for them: the inbound phone call, a difficult client, an e-mail, another salesperson who wants to talk, a problem sale, a broken fingernail. Any excuse will do — you can call it creative avoidance.

And don't think you're off the hook after you achieve telephone-sales success — top salespeople have more potential for distraction because they have a greater volume of business. The sooner you accept the fact that distractions are a constant threat, the better prepared you'll be to fight them off.

So what do you do when distractions hit? The best way to fend off distractions while you're prospecting is to not let them happen in the first place! Hold all calls and messages. Put up a do-not-disturb sign on your office door. Take whatever steps are necessary to divert distractions. (See more tips on eliminating distractions in Chapter 7 on time management.)

Ironically, your own effective prospecting efforts may be the biggest distraction-making culprit. Prospecting calls always generate production-supporting activities. Many prospects want further information, future contact, comparison data, and outside input. And, of course, each call may require a follow-up thank-you note or recap of your discussion.

Don't break your stride now. Take a moment to jot down a few notes about the tasks you need to do, so you can remember them later and get back on the phone now. Be in the moment. Stay on your prospecting path — the quickest route to sales success.

Pillar #3: Follow the plan

Prospecting is only effective if it generates a truly qualified lead — someone who is interested in what you offer, needs the service you provide, and has the ability and authority to become a client of your business — or refers you to someone who could. A contact isn't a secretary, voice mail, an assistant, the babysitter, a 10-year-old, or a teenager. Those salespeople who strike it rich at prospecting set their sights on the best opportunity for making sales. They don't waste their time calling *iffy* contacts that may not even be in the market for their product or service.

Success boils down to some very simple formulas. Following the right steps in the proper order is one of those formulas. In short, you need a plan. For best results, set up your daily prospecting plan at the end of the prior workday. Before you leave your office *today,* lay out your call schedule for *tomorrow.* Set everything you need on your desk so you're ready the minute you walk in the door in the morning.

Establishing a daily routine reinforces your commitment to the process and helps build good habits. It can be as simple as the following steps:

1. **Research prospects and set up your call list the day before.**

   Invest the time in determining who you're going to call tomorrow before you leave today. If you can invest time in researching before you leave you'll be better prepared for tomorrow's calls. Turn to Chapter 4 for how to research your prospects.

2. **Set aside time to practice your script and rehearse responses just before you begin your calls.**

   You want to spend about 20 minutes practicing your scripts and dialogues before your pick up the phone for the day. See Chapter 9 to know what scripts to practice.

3. **Do a quick review of your list and daily goals.**

4. **Repeat (out loud) your favorite affirmation statements.**

Using affirmations is a great way to get your mind in a positive state before you make your prospecting calls. You can say your own, or try out some of the following:

- "I am a great prospector."
- "I will generate _____ leads today."
- "I am going to make _____ sales today."

By following a similar routine, you can be warmed up and ready to give your task your best effort — just like any professional. The minute you pick up the phone, practice is over — the limelight's on you.

One note of caution: Adequate preparation and warm-up is important, but too much can be a sign of creative avoidance (see Pillar #2)! If you spend more than 30 minutes to get ready to call, you're spending too much time.

You can target qualified leads by purchasing better lists that target income, geography, demographics, or job titles. You may need to target a CEO, a CFO, purchasing agents, or sales managers depending on what you're selling. You can also target by company size in sales, employee numbers, and number of offices or branches. You can target past clients for additional sales or referrals. I would suggest that you talk with your sales manager to understand what groups of prospects offer the highest probability of success.

Pillar #4: Finish what you start

In order to win, you have to finish the race. The *whole* race. That means fulfilling your daily goals every day, down to the very last contact on your list. Don't accept anything less!

If it's been a particularly grueling day, throwing in the towel and cutting your calling short is easy: "What's the point? One more call won't pull up my stats." If you've hit record numbers, justifying quitting before you're done is also easy. "Hey, I've exceeded my goal — I don't need to make any more calls today." Again, resist the tendency to seek any excuse to avoid fulfilling your prospecting goals. Don't settle; finish what you start.

Finishing what you start is more than just making it through your list. You must also follow through with the contacts you made. A great way to wrap things up most effectively with a contact is to compose a handwritten thank-you note and mail it in a small (*not* a standard business size) envelope. Unlike an e-mail or even a generic, preplanned regurgitated form letter, your personal note will get noticed. The typical consumer receives dozens of e-mails a day, selling everything from no-interest loans to Viagra. And the post office delivers stacks of junk mail. Although most of this ends up in the "circular" file, a handwritten letter breaks through the clutter to land in the A pile, which means it gets read — and keeps your relationship alive until you talk again.

Connecting the Dots between Numbers and Income

You've probably heard of cause and effect — a basic law of physics. But you don't have to be a rocket scientist to understand that your prospecting efforts today can influence the results you receive tomorrow. And as a telephone-sales professional, the more you understand this connection, the better you can identify the actions that will bring you the outcome you desire. And after you've mastered this principle, you may see quantum leaps in your sales activity.

In order to get you there, you need an understanding of the cause-and-effect relationship between numbers and income as well as a record of your past performance, so you can chart your future success. This section helps.

Harnessing the power of sales ratios

Sales ratios explain the relationship between various factors involved in the selling process in a form that you can use to measure performance and establish goals. For example, take the daily prospect list and number of contacts made for Salesman A:

- ✔ If Salesman A calls 80 prospects a day and has a voice-to-voice conversation with 40 of them, he achieves a 2 to 1 (or 2:1) call-to-contact ratio. (Not too shabby.)

- ✔ If he then succeeds in persuading 20 of these contacts that they are candidates for his service, his contact-to-lead ratio is 2 to 1. (Pretty good work.)

- ✔ Say he's able to secure ten appointments from these leads. Again, that's a 2 to 1 ratio of leads to appointments. (This guy's on fire!)

- ✔ After completing those appointments, Salesman A has closed five sales — at a ratio of, yes, 2 to 1.

You can also convey other relationships with ratios: prospects to appointments; prospects to sales; number of closes to sales dollars; and any other pairing.

 These ratios help take the guesswork out of success by helping you establish clearer expectations and goals. Measuring yourself against the averages for your office or industry can give you an indication of where you stand — and where you need to go. But in order to do this, you need to keep track of your ratios (which I tell you how to do in the following section).

Sales ratios also help you identify what areas you need to work on. If I see your sales ratios, I can tell you exactly what you need to do to dramatically increase your sales. For example:

- ✔ If your prospect-to-contact list is low, I may advise you to check the quality of your list to be sure it's up-to-date or suggest that you try calling at a different time of day.

- ✔ If your contact ratio is good, but your contact-to-lead ratio is poor, you'd want to see whether you have the right kind of customer for your service.

- ✔ If your lead-to-appointment ratio is below average, I'd say it's time to brush up on your phone presentation skills (which you can do in Part II).

But you don't need *me* to diagnose your strengths and weaknesses. By understanding sales ratios, you can figure out on your own what skills you need to attend to. That's the power of sales ratios.

Tracking and recording everything

In order to use sales ratios to assess the effectiveness of your prospecting efforts, you must capture the details of your sales activity. Consistent tracking of your numbers creates a record that can serve you well. You can break sales activity down to a series of repeatable numbers that, over time, produces a predetermined result. If you track your numbers over a few months, you can determine what you need to do to earn the income you desire.

 Sales averages aren't built in a day! Or even a week or month. Your ratios are most effective as measuring sticks when they reflect your consistently documented activity over a period of at least three months. I had days when I didn't set an appointment. I probably had weeks that I got skunked. Over a three-month period, however, I was always within a 5-percent margin of error on my numbers.

Keep a complete and accurate record of your sales numbers. Table
5-2 is a sample tracking sheet you can use. (Feel free to create your
own.) You want to use this tracking sheet daily so you establish your
sales ratios. It will take three months worth of daily use to achieve
accuracy in your sales ratios.

Table 5-2	Daily Goals and Results	
Activity	*Goals*	*Results*
Prospecting dials made		
Leads obtained		
Phone appointments scheduled		
Qualified phone presentations made		
Face-to-face appointments scheduled		
Qualified face-to-face presentations made		
Orders written		
Orders closed		
Activity	*Total "Real Working Hours" Invested*	
Prospecting hours		
Lead follow-up hours		
Presentation hours		
Contract hours		
Rate Your Day (1–10)		

Obeying the law of accumulation

The *law of accumulation* states that everything in life accumulates
either positively or negatively in disproportionate amounts. For
example, if you were to save $2.74 a day from the time you were 20
and you received an average rate of return of 9 percent over those
years, you would be a millionaire at 65. You would have saved only
about $45,000 over that time, but the law of accumulation did the
rest of the work. If you asked most people if they would trade
$45,000 for $1 million, they would say yes, but few people do.

The law of accumulation rules the world of prospecting, as well. The daily amount of time and effort you invest in prospecting is a manageable amount, but the return is greater than the sum of its parts. And as with saving money, the payoff doesn't come right away. It may be 60 days later — or months and months, depending on your particular sales situation. You have to make deposits in daily prospecting over a period of time before you receive withdrawals of commission income. The only way to ensure sales success is the daily deposit approach.

Success without Prospecting? Shattering the Myth

I hear a lot of myths in my work as a sales coach: "*My* market is different." "*My* product is not like others." "You don't understand how we do things here in Mayberry." And some salespeople think they can get by or even make it big with little to no prospecting. But these ways of thinking are myths through and through.

The prospecting guidelines I give you work in any market, with any product or service, at any place in the world at any time. The reason I'm so confident is because I have taught and coached this strategy to salespeople all over the world in numerous industries with different products and services. And the fundamentals I share with all of them are the same fundamentals you can read in this chapter. The results for these companies and individual salespeople have been outstanding; many of these salespeople rise to the top level in their company in a short period of time.

In the following sections, I break down the myth that you don't need prospecting for telephone-sales success, and help you know how to deal with people who promote prospecting-free sales schemes. Believe me — everyone needs to prospect!

Realizing that prospecting won't disappear

Sorry to be the one to disappoint you, but you can't find a miracle pill or magic solution that makes the prospecting part of sales vanish. Championship sales results are built upon solid practices and supportive actions, and you can't take prospecting out of that ratio!

Plenty of folks may try to convince you that the fundamentals in this chapter don't apply to the salespeople who follow their short-cut to success. Look out for promotions to buy their book, e-mails to subscribe to their Web sites or e-newsletters, or — and this is the jab that stings me the most — a phone invitation to their semi-nars. Just imagine: A roomful of telephone salespeople making calls to convince you that phone prospecting is obsolete!

These sales-meisters may allude to a secret selling method that only they have discovered, promise a scientifically calculated for-mula to quick success, or hint at a strategy so effective that you'll have prospects calling *you,* begging for your services. And that's about as likely as going fishing and watching the fish jump into your boat. And it bears repeating one more time: Prospecting is the foundation for sales success. You can't leave it out any more than you can skip laying the cornerstones for a 30-story building.

Determining fraud from sales god

Enthusiastic peddlers of quick-fix tactics do a great job of selling their schemes. Getting drawn in by tales of effortless sales pickings and fantasizing yourself on that sales-associate-of-the-year grand-prize trip to Tahiti are easy. Indeed, some self-proclaimed sales gurus paint a golden picture of possibility. But, there's more (or less, actually) to the picture than these wizards of prospect-free wealth like to reveal.

Before believing any get-rich-quick sales schemes, pull back the curtain and discover the truth. Demand hard evidence for their method's success: the connection between actions and results and quantifiable measures of effectiveness. In at least 95 percent of the cases, you'll most likely find nothing there. So next time you're approached about such as scheme, ask these questions — and if the great and powerful wizard of sales can't answer them, you'll know it's time to head back to Kansas:

✔ How many sales does this technique generate for you annually?

✔ How much time do you need to invest personally to set this up and maintain it?

✔ What does it cost you to use this marketing service to generate your leads?

✔ What conversion ratio does this technique generate?

✔ What percentage of your business comes from using this method?

✔ How many clients did you get?

> ✔ What was the average sale made to those clients?
>
> ✔ What was your average commission earned from those clients?
>
> ✔ What is your net profit from this after all your costs?
>
> ✔ Have you included the value of your time in that equation?

Committing to the never-ending task of prospecting

The best nugget of advice I can give any salesperson is to start prospecting today — and never, ever, *ever* stop prospecting. I commend the dedicated telephone professionals who've discovered that consistent and regular prospecting is the bedrock of sales success. The wisest also know that even after you strike it rich, daily prospecting is still the best tool for mining an untapped wealth of sales opportunity.

You may have been hoping that after you made it big in sales you could say adios to the daily chore of generating new leads? No such luck. When you commit to an effective and disciplined prospecting process, you're virtually guaranteed to create sales — which in addition to income *also* creates more work: order-taking, paper-signing, follow-up, problem-solving, customer service, and so on. But growing income and increasing workload aren't reasons to stop prospecting. Does a concert pianist stop practicing after she plays Carnegie Hall? Would a tennis pro quit working out just because he won at Wimbledon? No — and neither should you (never ever!).

Doing the math: Putting a prospect-free scheme to the test

I recently received a marketing piece from a salesperson touting his prospect-less lead-generation strategy. In his third year of business, he made 60 sales — a very enviable number for the high-ticket, personal service he sold. His brochure also noted that he generated 1,200 leads per month. I immediately grabbed my calculator (that's just what the sales coach in me does) and computed his leads per year as 14,400. So his 60 sales against 14,400 results in a conversion ratio turned out to be less than half of 1 percent (0.004167, to be exact). That means he converted only one person out of the 240 leads he generated through his so-called "no-fail" prospect technique. Either his leads are marginal at best, or he is extremely ineffective at converting them. I'll leave you to draw your own conclusion.

Chapter 6

Conquering Sales Call Aversion

. . . .

In This Chapter

▶ Diagnosing sales call aversion

▶ Enlisting strategies to fight sales call aversion

▶ Eliminating sales call aversion for good

. . . .

*O*ne of the most sinister threats to the aspiring telephone-sales professional is sales call aversion. This condition is particularly insidious because it starts out so mild that you may not even notice you have it. And by the time you recognize the problem, you may have already suffered the damage — low sales results.

Sales call aversion is one of the most common afflictions to salespeople everywhere. This condition eats away at the productivity, calls, and results of any salesperson. It can affect even salespeople who are skilled and successful. Sales call aversion costs companies worldwide billions of dollars a year in sales.

For salespeople, the most reliable measure of their future success is the number of consistent contacts they make to prospects. In short, salespeople have to rely on their ability to pick up the phone each day and make large volumes of calls. This fact is especially true with new salespeople who are untested, unproven, and don't have extensive product or service knowledge yet.

All salespeople face the dreaded sales call aversion at one time or another in their sales careers. But this chapter helps you identify the symptoms of sales call aversion, determines which forms of the conditions are more common and which you're more susceptible to, and offers strategies to build up your sales call aversion immunity.

Recognizing Sales Call Aversion

To fully understand sales call aversion, you need to be able to identify the signs. Some salespeople have difficulty recognizing when they're suffering from sales call aversion — but here's an easy way to test: Use your sales ratios and goals to take your temperature. If you're not making the required number of calls per day to achieve your sales goals, that's all the evidence you need to know . . . you have sales call aversion!

So what exactly causes this condition? Although varied theories exist, the following are some of the more popular:

✔ **Your environment:** Both your upbringing and work can lead to periodic bouts with sales call aversion.

- **Your upbringing:** Maybe you were raised in a household (as was mine when I was growing up) where sales wasn't a highly regarded career choice. My parents wanted us to be professionals like doctors, dentists, accountants, attorneys, and so on. Being a salesperson wasn't viewed as a pathway to success.

- **Your work environment:** Some people, maybe even your manager, will raise your level of sales call aversion and stunt your performance. For example, some low-performing salespeople will want you to join their coffee and donuts bunch. They'll try to get you to join the complainer convention of "how poor the leads are that the company provides." Don't do it!

✔ **Your sales field or company you work for:** How do the salespeople view themselves at your job? Do they view themselves as salespeople, account managers, coordinators, customer service representatives, account representatives, sales consultants? People affix this never-ending list of job titles to themselves either personally or corporately to avoid being a salesperson. But face it, you're all salespeople. Don't let a job title make you think you're not at risk; you're all susceptible to call aversion.

✔ **Your DISC behavioral style:** This style can influence your frequency and intensity of sales call aversion. Your DISC behavioral style influences how you do everything in life, so it can influence how you make calls and how many calls you will make. (For more on your behavioral style, turn to Chapter 16.)

If you're the reserved, introspective, introverted, noncompetitive type, your likelihood of coming down with sales call aversion is higher. If you score higher on the Steady or Compliant scale of a DISC assessment, you'll have more difficulty initiating new sales calls to people you don't know. Your dial numbers will usually be lower than someone whose high scores are in the Dominant or Influencer scale.

If you can see marketing opportunities for what you're selling and don't seize the opportunities, you may be letting sales call aversion suppress your decision to act. Logically, most people with sales call aversion admit that they need to take action. The problem is if they're experiencing sales call aversion, few of them do take action.

Good Medicine: Treating Call Aversion

What do most telephone salespeople do when call aversion hits? They avoid making calls — the very worst action they can take. That makes about as much sense as deciding not to breathe when you have a stuffy nose.

Avoiding the task only aggravates and increases the severity of sales call aversion. The more you succumb to its symptoms, the more difficult it is to overcome. Before it gets any worse, commit to the following.

Reducing aversion in your life

Sales call aversion is the psoriasis of phone-sales disorders. You can treat it, you can reduce its damage, and it's not likely to kill you, but it's hard to get rid of it for good. In this section, I recommend two paths to reducing the threat of sales call aversion and its damaging impact on your productivity and your sales career.

Clarifying the "why"

Making calls is a day-to-day commitment. Its importance can often be overlooked when your sights aren't set on your values and goals. In short, you have to know why you make the calls. After you have clarity of the *why*, the *how* becomes easy.

My father, a dentist, only worked Monday through Thursday. He was always around on Fridays when I came home from school. In the summer, we spent three days a week on a lake near the Oregon Coast. My father worked harder in four days than most people work in five in order to meet the financial goals he set for himself. His *why* was borne out of his love for my mother. When I was 3, my mother was diagnosed with multiple sclerosis. By the time I was in the second grade, she'd lost her ability to walk. She spent the last years of her life without the use of her arms or legs. My father was determined to provide her with the most extraordinary life possible. Through his clarity of purpose, he managed to travel with my wheelchair-bound mother and three sons to Mexico, Asia, Hawaii (annually), and many other places. And he cared for her as her condition worsened in the home they raised their children in.

As soon you achieve clarification of purpose — the *why* — the *how* makes itself known and you have an easier time staying on the right path. For salespeople, goals are typically wrapped up in their success in selling. And the most direct *how* is making a consistent number of yearly, monthly, weekly, and daily telephone calls.

Admitting you have a problem and then getting help

Sales call aversion isn't a theoretical condition. It's a real problem with real costs attached to it. According to numerous studies, the reluctant salesperson defaults on an average of four pieces of new business a month. To bring that home to your own backyard, take the average commission you earn for an average sale and multiply that number by four. That's what's lost each month by a salesperson with sales call aversion.

The first step to conquering a condition is to recognize that you have it. If, after reading this chapter, you feel you suffer from call aversion, respond to it quickly by taking action. If you're still not quite sure, then here is one final option. I have an assessment at Sales Champions that can measure and benchmark your sales call aversion. It can help you identify the barriers and benchmark your levels against top sales performers in a wide range of sales industries. For more information about this assessment, visit my Web site at www.SalesChampions.com/CallAversion.

You can also take the following actions to help you treat this condition:

- ✔ **Chart your progress daily.** Doing so leads to results. For example, set a written goal of making 100 calls a day, and then track your progress. Writing down the goal and then monitoring your results helps keep you on track and doesn't let you off the hook.

- ✔ **Establish benchmark goals for dials and contacts for each day.** Set them at a level that will make you stretch, but also keep them attainable. Being able to consistently meet your goals for dials and contacts on a daily basis contributes to the reduction in sales call aversion.

What can lead to greater sales call aversion is the up and down numbers of calls that most salespeople make each day. For example, Monday may be a high call day for you, but Tuesday and Wednesday are slow. Thursday can be good, but then you leave Friday afternoon for a round of golf. With this typical week, far too many salespeople lack the consistency; they never establish clear benchmarks, so sales call aversion can take root.

All salespeople grapple with sales call aversion to some degree. Even the best salespeople exhibit tendencies toward call aversion. The question is whether it affects your sales performance? If you believe it's affecting your performance to the point where you're losing sales, take action *sooner* rather than later.

The taking-stock strategy

Chronic call aversion can stem from low self-esteem, lack of comfort-level with the product or service, or even uncertainty about personal values and goals. The process of *taking stock* — of self, sales products, and values — addresses all these root causes, and helps boost confidence and clarity.

Stick to the following when taking stock to help you maximize your efforts:

1. **Take inventory of your personal skills and attributes.**

   Those qualities make you a good salesperson and a valued employee. What are your problem-solving abilities, years of experience in fundraising, and your attention to detail?

2. **If you get stuck, call past satisfied clients.**

   Such an exchange can remind you of your winning qualities. This boost can counter those feelings of self-doubt that may be keeping you off the phone!

3. **Then, before you hang up, ask if the client needs anything, ask for a referral, or share information about new products.**

   This step primes the pump, so to speak, adding another success to your score and leading you to a potentially lucrative follow-up call.

4. **After your personal inventory, tally up the features and benefits of your company's offerings.**

   When taking stock of what you and your company bring to the table, ask these questions:

- What do we do for the prospects?
- What makes us different from our competition?
- What qualities make me the person they should work with?
- What are the specific benefits of our services?
- If I had to select one reason above all others why someone should do business with me, what would it be?

5. **Keep your completed inventory report close at hand as a quick attitude picker-upper and a helpful reference of product/service highlights.**

   If you're struggling with sales call aversion over an extended period of time, review the list every day. Keep it handy to raise your confidence and the conviction of your message.

The setting-daily-goals strategy

Unrealistic goals can aggravate sales call aversion. If you hang a "must-increase-productivity-by-500-percent" directive above your head, you may be so overwhelmed by the big picture that you can't take the first step.

Don't get ahead of yourself — sure, you may want to hit $1 million in sales by the end of the year. But instead of gazing out at that lofty goal, break it down into smaller pieces: $1 million in sales a year is $20,000 a week. Is it possible in your wildest imagination? If not, adjust your goal and make it more attainable.

If the goal is realistic, break down your week into days and determine what steps to take each day to achieve it. At your close ratios, how many calls per day must you make? For more about managing your time for maximum productivity, turn to Chapter 7.

The ban-negative-self-talk strategy

Sometimes, the salesperson's inner voice is his biggest fan and encourager. However, at other times, that little voice chains the sales pro to a cement block and pushes him into a deep river. Have you heard comments in your head like "They're going to reject you" or "Why would they use me?" If you suffer from sales call aversion, you want to get rid of any negative self-talk.

Negative thoughts and talk generate stress and anxiety, which are certain to influence the course of the call. To utilize the ban-negative-self-talk strategy, confront and put the handcuffs on this criminal influence. For example, you can do this by repeating daily affirmations out loud, while driving in the car to work or right before you make the call. This negative self-talk still may pop up again from time to time, but with repeated daily affirmations, the voice gets quieter, and after a few calls, it goes away completely. (Check out Chapter 18 for how to use daily affirmations.)

If your inner voice is a particularly fierce critic, try writing down the negative self-talk messages. Capturing them on paper helps you refute the statements. Write down your positive self-talk responses, too, and you can feel the shift, giving the supportive self-talk a greater voice.

The visualize-the-perfect-call strategy

Human nature often drives the salesperson to imagine the *worst* possible outcome of a sales call. However, if you're going to fanta-size, make it a story with a happy ending. Before starting a call, picture it playing out the best way possible.

Just before your scheduled call, follow these steps:

1. **Visualize yourself on the phone, speaking with confidence.**

   Visualizing good thoughts serves as a rehearsal for the real call. The more you run your story line through the mental projector, the more likely it is to become reality.

2. **Imagine a receptive prospect, asking questions.**

3. **Picture your exchange, building toward the climactic moment when the prospect says, "I'll take it!"**

The ten-minute strategy

Anticipating hours on the phone may not be the most motivating thought — even for the most positive and successful of salespeople. But for the reluctant caller, that anticipation can delay or preempt the activity entirely.

If you find yourself in this situation, try the ten-minute strategy: Give yourself permission to blow off the phone calls for the morning, afternoon, or day. *But* before you're permitted to walk away from the telephone, resolve to make ten minutes' worth of calls. Promise yourself that when the ten minutes is up, you can quit.

The benefit of the ten-minute strategy is that you break the negative pattern. Sure, you only stayed on the phone for ten minutes — made a few or even just one call — before you quit for the day. But you took the first step — it's still progress! When you perceive this as positive, a good attitude helps reinforce good habits. Maybe tomorrow you'll do it again, possibly even for longer.

After you take the hardest step of picking up the phone, the rest isn't so difficult. In fact, you may find that your 10 minutes turned into 30. Or more. All without you suffering a bit.

Chapter 7

Investing Your Time Wisely

● ●

In This Chapter

▶ Accomplishing more in less time with the 80/20 Rule

▶ Putting direct-income-producing activities first

▶ Using time blocking and to-do lists as tools for sales success

▶ Keeping your time management on track

● ●

*T*he effective use of time is a critical skill for anyone in sales —
particularly phone sales. And *particularly* phone sales in which
you're responsible for your own schedule. Peter Drucker, the famous
management expert, said, "We can't manage our time; we can only
manage ourselves." Time management is *self-management*. The ability to control the distractions, procrastination, interruptions, and
low-priority activities in order to increase effectiveness separates
the top producers from the rest of the sales force.

A casual approach toward time may result in low production, incon-
sistent sales numbers, income fluctuation, and frustration — which
can lead to discouragement, or even termination. But if you recognize time for what it is — a precious resource — you can use it to
your advantage to maximize your sales power. I call time a resource
because it's something you invest in for an expected return. And
because you only have a limited supply of it — a nonrenewable
resource, if you will — the first step to better time management is
to recognize the scarcity of time.

Making the most of your time requires urgency, focus, and intensity:

- ✔ **Urgency** attends to deadlines and goads you to accomplish a given task within a given time frame.

- ✔ **Focus** empowers you to think single-mindedly and drown out distractions — whether the chatter of other telephone salespeople, e-mails, inbound problem calls, or mindless administrative tasks.

- ✔ **Intensity** helps you overcome the inclination to procrastinate.

By exercising these three traits and enhancing them with some time-tested self-management tools, you can find yourself accomplishing dramatically more in less time — which translates to more sales success and increased revenue. This chapter tells you how.

Acquainting Yourself with the 80/20 Rule

In 1895, Vilfredo Pareto articulated what he observed as a universal phenomenon. In his home country of Italy, he saw that a small contingency of citizens — 20 percent — held most of the power, influence, and money — about 80 percent of the power, he figured. He described these people as the *vital few*. That, of course, meant that the other 80 percent of the population held only 20 percent of the financial and political power in the country.

This principal became known as the *80/20 Rule* (also known as the *Pareto Principle*), and can be applied to almost any situation. I've heard it used in nonprofit groups ("20 percent of our volunteers do 80 percent of the work"), the workplace ("20 percent of my staff make 80 percent of the revenue"), and even by investors ("20 percent of my stocks generate 80 percent of my income").

The 80/20 Rule works when we're talking about time, as well: 20 percent of the activities you invest your time in generate 80 percent of your achievement. In the world of telephone sales, those who consistently earn the high incomes know how to work the 80/20 Rule to perfection. They have monitored, watched, evaluated, and determined what 20 percent of their time and efforts bring in 80 percent of their income.

The better you are at applying the 80/20 Rule to your own sales efforts — not to mention all areas of your life — the more successful you will be. The secret to this success, however, is finding out *on what* and *how* you should be investing your time in order to achieve the 80-percent return. I introduce the basics of the 80/20 Rule in the following sections.

Determining where your time currently goes

Anybody can make the 80/20 Rule work for them. But *not* before they understand exactly how they're currently spending their time. This understanding may require an upfront time investment — say, a week — to record and track where the time goes.

For at least five working days, keep a running tab of your daily activities. Track everything: the review of your date book, the water cooler chat with colleagues, your follow-up calls to resolve problems with an account, your prospecting efforts, and your sales calls. Chop up your day into 15-minute increments — no bigger — and account for each quarter-hour.

A handy schedule for this task has lines for each quarter hour so you can fill in the activity you performed. Each entry notes whether the activity falls under the category of *direct income–producing activities* (DIPA) or *production-supporting activities* (PSA), both of which I cover in more detail later in this chapter. The schedule concludes with spaces for total hours spent on DIPA and PSA. (You can create your own schedule; I've started one for you in Figure 7-1 to show you what it looks like.)

Condensing seven days into four

My focus and productivity intensified when I went from seven days of work to six days, and then to five days. I experienced the largest production increase, however, when I went to a four-day workweek. My wife, Joan, and I were constructing a vacation home some three hours away in Bend, Oregon. Because Joan was the general contractor, we had to be in Bend every Friday to check on the progress. We did that throughout the eight months of construction. After the home was done, I decided not to revert back to working five days a week. I didn't *need* to. Through intensity, urgency, and focus, I was able to accomplish as much in four days as I had previously in five. And we've continued with our lifestyle, driving to Bend every Thursday late afternoon and coming home Sunday.

Activity Tracking by the Quarter Hour

Name: _____ Date: _____

7:00 - 7:15 _____ DIPA PSA

7:15 - 7:30 _____ DIPA PSA

7:30 - 7:45 _____ DIPA PSA

7:45 - 8:00 _____ DIPA PSA

8:00 - 8:15 _____ DIPA PSA

8:15 - 8:30 _____ DIPA PSA

8:30 - 8:45 _____ DIPA PSA

8:45 - 9:00 _____ DIPA PSA

9:00 - 9:15 _____ DIPA PSA

9:15 - 9:30 _____ DIPA PSA

9:30 - 9:45 _____ DIPA PSA

9:45 - 10:00 _____ DIPA PSA

etc.

DIPA Payoff Hours _____

PSA Payoff Hours _____

Total Hours   _____

Figure 7-1: Keep track of your days in 15-minute blocks to see how you spend your time.

In tracking your time every 15 minutes, you want to be able to separate your direct income–producing activities like prospecting, lead follow-up, and presentation appointments from all the other things you do. You want to track your PSA compared to your DIPA. Ask yourself how much time is spent on DIPA versus PSA. Do PSA take over a time of your day? What are the changes you need to make to increase your DIPA time by at least 20 percent right now?

At the end of a week, you'll have a pretty accurate read on where you allot your efforts. This critical piece of evidence can then help you to take the next step: redirecting your time into revenue-producing activities.

Identifying the tasks that matter most

A salesperson's time is spent in two areas:

- ✔ Creating new customers
- ✔ Serving current customers

I often ask telephone salespeople, "If you had to select only one area to be exceptional at, which would you choose?" Well, you must be skilled at both. But of the two, *creating* customers is undeniably the more critical effort. Many salespeople are skilled at keeping their customers happy. These service-oriented folks hope that through their attentiveness, their customers will send more business their way, and that's good. But it's a risky basket to put all your eggs in — especially if it results in neglecting the development of *new* customers.

As a salesperson, you must invest time daily, regularly, in creating new customers through outbound prospecting. *This* is the 20 percent of your time that will bring you the 80 percent of your income. Nothing is more important than investing your time in creating new leads, pursuing prospects, and following up on potential opportunities — all efforts that result in more customers. The creation of new customers qualifies as a direct income–producing activity; I discuss the importance of such activities later in this chapter. (For more on prospecting, check out Chapter 5.)

Turning time from enemy to ally

Telephone sales is a demanding job. An eight-hour day of prospecting, following up on leads, delivering presentations, handling objections, and closing sales can wear you down faster than a 100-meter dash. Few people have the stamina to maintain a high level of focus and performance for eight hours or more every day. In the following sections, I explain how to figure out your peak performance period so you can accomplish more in less time and stick to the 80/20 Rule.

Discovering your peak performance period

Whether you're a night owl, early bird, or reach your peak at some point in between, identifying your highest-performance period and scheduling your most important tasks (in other words, those related to creating customers) at that time is a tried-and-true technique to rev up your productivity and boost your sales numbers.

Decide when you have the most energy during the day. When are you more focused, and when does your mind wander? Most people tend to have more energy, intensity, and focus during a certain time of day. Mine happens to be in the morning. The middle of the afternoon — when my energy level is lower — is my *down* time. I'm just not as effective at prospecting at that time. And I've met hundreds of telephone salespeople just like me.

The solution for us early birds is to concentrate our mornings on creating clients, and reserve the afternoons — when we have less energy — for client service. Those who spend all morning struggling to wake up, but then come alive in the afternoon, want to flip-flop this schedule.

Pre-empting the 11 a.m. Rule

It's uncanny, but no matter what time zone you live in, it seems the world starts delivering problems and challenges to your doorstep just before mid-day. This phenomenon is known as the *11 a.m. Rule*. So to pre-empt those troubles that could derail a productive day, get as much of your lead generation and prospecting done first thing. The more you can accomplish *before* 11 a.m., the higher your productivity rises.

And if 11 a.m. is the start of your peak period, you can protect your time with a couple of strategies:

✔ In some telephone-sales jobs, particularly in the insurance, finance, mortgage, and real estate sectors, salespeople must be available to clients to resolve problems and answer questions. To minimize distractions during high-production hours, it's okay not to answer the phone. Your voice mail message can assure callers that you will return calls after a certain time. By doing so, you've created a win-win solution: Your customers are comfortable that their needs will be met in a reasonable timeframe — and you haven't sacrificed your productivity.

✔ You can move your paperwork and servicing segments to later in the day. If you need to research information for a prospect or write a business letter, do it after 11 a.m. to increase your effectiveness.

Separating High-Return Activities from Other Tasks

Champion performers in any field quickly discover which actions account for the great majority — the 80 percent — of the results they achieve. They save their best time of day for the activities that result in the highest return on investment, while minimizing the time they spend on required activities that take up a lot of time.

Targeting direct income–producing activities

I describe high-return activities as *direct income–producing activities* (DIPA). In the world of sales, for example, DIPA might include:

- ✔ Prospecting (see Chapter 5)
- ✔ Lead follow-up
- ✔ Sales presentations (see Chapter 12)
- ✔ Practicing, role-playing, and rehearsing your sales skills
- ✔ Writing and negotiating contracts

As an example, in order to make it in an entrepreneurial sales field such as real estate, insurance, or financial services, you must spend a minimum of 15 hours a week on these activities. An outstanding salesperson goes beyond this — 30 percent, 40 percent, and more. I have watched countless entrepreneurial salespeople add $100, $200, even $300 to their per-hour value in less than six months, simply by concentrating on and devoting more hours per day on DIPA.

Checking out other necessary (but time-draining) activities

In addition to DIPA, telephone salespeople have two other job activity categories:

- ✔ **Indirect income– producing activities (IIPA):** These tasks help create income, but not in a direct way. Developing a sales brochure or a mailing for consumers and placing an advertisement in the local paper are examples. Although mailings, ads, and sales materials are certainly important to making sales, they can't be tied to revenue the way a one-on-one sales closure can.

- ✔ **Production-supporting activities (PSA):** These involve follow-up service to clients. After you make the sale, the faxing, copying, filing, and letter writing are required. This type of activity also includes all the phone calls taken from clients who have questions about their purchase.

Of course, IIPA and PSA are as much a fact of telephone-sales life as DIPA — although they're often the activities that cause the most stress, frustration, and challenges. But the more you can accomplish these tasks in a minimum amount of time, the more effort you can invest in those activities that directly bring in revenue (read more about these in the preceding section).

IIPA and PSA may be hazardous to your schedule! To keep the indirect and support activities from hijacking your time, schedule them during your low-energy periods of the day. *And* during the time the 11 a.m. Rule is likely to sabotage your day. After all, what better time to devote to serving your customers than when your customers are most likely to be contacting you? These strategies help keep peak performance slots reserved for DIPA — and DIPA only. (See the earlier section "Turning time from enemy to ally" for details about adjusting your schedule to your peak performance time.)

Time Blocking: A Way of Life for Winning Salespeople

In my company, Sales Champions, we offer many valuable time-management tools to the sales professionals we coach. But figuring out how to time block, our program alumni tell us, is the most life-changing. *Time blocking* is prescheduling your day's activities in segments of time. When the concept of time blocking clicks in for salespeople, it not only increases their sales success, but it also influences all aspects of their lives. When they apply time blocking to workout time, spiritual time, social time, children time, and relationship time, they often experience a positive shift that results in a healthier balance — a lifestyle that more accurately reflects their values and priorities.

For the telephone salesperson, time blocking is certain to take the process of task prioritization to the next level, leading to higher sales numbers and — perhaps — a career-improving change.

The first step toward effective time blocking is to grid your day into 15-minute increments. Why 15 minutes? For an effective salesperson, time is of great value — even 15 minutes can represent a lot of revenue and production. Losing even two or three of these small blocks could represent hundreds of dollars. As you work through this section and discover more about time blocking, you can use the schedule in Figure 7-2.

Real Estate Champions
Time Blocking Schedule

	MONDAY	TUESDAY	WEDNESDAY	THURSDAY	FRIDAY	SATURDAY	SUNDAY
6AM							
7:00							
7:15							
7:30							
7:45							
8:00							
8:15							
8:30							
8:45							
9:00							
9:15							
9:30							
9:45							
10:00							
10:15							
10:30							
10:45							
11:00							
etc.							

Figure 7-2: Block time in 15-minute increments for maximum effectiveness.

Achievement-oriented sales folks tend to follow the "squeeze-it-in" philosophy of scheduling: They cram everything they possibly can onto their calendar — and then some. It's important, however, to attack the process of time blocking in the right order, scheduling first things first. And speaking of first things first, Steven Covey, in his book of the same name, uses "big rocks" as a metaphor for people's most important priorities and values. (See the nearby sidebar "Putting the big rocks first" for more details.)

What are the big rocks in your life? Time with loved ones? A worthy cause? Your faith, education, or future plans? Providing for your family? Mentoring others? Whatever they are, it's critical to put your big rocks first in order to make time blocking work for you. That means identifying your most important priorities — not just at work, but in life — and blocking out time for them *before* filling in your day with tasks and activities that don't support those priorities. The following sections show how many may go about time blocking their week.

Putting the big rocks first

When Steven Covey and A. Roger Merrill used this story in their book *First Things First* (Simon & Schuster), they didn't cite the source. But its message is powerful and worth my re-telling it here:

One day an expert in time management was speaking to a group of business students. Standing before the group of high-powered overachievers, he said, "Okay, time for a quiz." He pulled out a one-gallon, wide-mouthed Mason jar and set it on a table in front of him. Then he produced about a dozen fist-sized rocks and carefully placed them, one at a time, into the jar. When the jar was filled to the top, and no more rocks would fit inside, he asked, "Is this jar full?" Everyone in the class said, "Yes." He said, "Really?"

He reached under the table and pulled out a bucket of gravel. He dumped some gravel in and shook the jar, causing pieces of gravel to work themselves down into the spaces between the big rocks. He asked the group once more, "Is the jar full?" This time the class was on to him. "Probably not," one of them answered. "Good!" he replied.

He reached under the table and brought out a bucket of sand. He started dumping in the sand, and it went into all the spaces left between the rocks and the gravel. Once more, he asked the question, "Is the jar full?" "No!" the class shouted. Once again, he said, "Good!"

Then he grabbed a pitcher of water and began to pour it in until the jar was filled to the brim. He looked up at the class and asked, "What is the point of this illustration?" One eager beaver raised his hand and said, "The point is, no matter how full your schedule is, if you try really hard, you can always fit some more things into it!"

"No," the speaker replied. "The truth this illustration teaches us is if you don't put the big rocks in first, you'll never get them in at all."

Block out the most important personal time

Whatever your personal priorities — workout time, prayer time, quiet time, family time, kids' sports events — block these into your weekly schedule first. Doing so gives weight to these activities and ensures that they won't be usurped by an obligation of lesser importance. There's nothing wrong with telling a client that you're not available for an evening appointment if you've scheduled that time for your family. You merely need to say that you're booked at that time.

Reserve days off

I personally believe two days off each week is best, but schedule at least one day — one *entire* day — off. This means no calls, no checking e-mails, no going through the mail, no working on a proposal. Time off is meant for relaxing and recharging. And a regular charging of your batteries is absolutely essential for your work productivity: The more re-energized you are after time off, the more you can focus on and achieve your work goals.

Block out evening time

By blocking out your nights each week, you help ensure a reasonable end to your workday. Of course, you sometimes need to put in extra hours or schedule an evening appointment. But make it something *you* control. You might, for example, leave Tuesdays and Thursdays open for appointments or to catch up on paperwork, and block out the rest of your evenings for family or fun time.

Schedule all other personal time

I work out every morning. I always block that time on my weekly calendar. Reading, study, yoga, or a pedicure — whatever your personal avocations or interests are — are important enough not to leave to chance. Don't assume, for instance, that you'll simply squeeze in the time necessary to read *Catcher in the Rye* for your book club. Schedule it.

Schedule direct income– producing activities

After you've scheduled your personal priorities and family time (see previous sections), you must then start blocking out work priorities. As I emphasize throughout this chapter, generating sales is the most important priority to the telephone salesperson. And in order to do so, the sales pro must do direct income–producing activities first (I cover these activities earlier in this chapter). Blocking 90 minutes for prospecting and an hour for lead follow-up each day is a good rule.

For most people, mornings are the best time for prospecting and lead follow-up. I advise scheduling these tasks first thing. That way, you don't put off your most critical activities until you're too tired to give it your best. If your best time mentally is in the afternoon, then block your direct income–producing activities there. However, completing them at that time will be harder, due to the 11 a.m. Rule that I discuss earlier in this chapter. You may have to fight harder for your protected prospecting time in the afternoon.

Add appointments

Not only is blocking out your existing appointments (frequently DIPA related) important, but also, you must develop a consistent structure to your appointment scheduling. This way, you can offer choices to your clients while still maintaining control over your own schedule.

For example, my typical sales presentation was no more than 45 minutes, so I made my appointments in one-hour increments, allowing 15 minutes of drive time between appointments. I set appointments at 3:15, 4:15, and 5:15 Monday through Thursday. On Tuesday evenings, I also had 6:15, 7:15, and 8:15 slots.

Because I operated with specific appointment times, I had more control of my schedule. Instead of asking a client when she could meet, I offered a choice: "Sue, which would work better for you — 4:15 on Monday or Tuesday?" If Sue said she couldn't get home until 4:30, I'd move her to a 5:15 slot.

Work in time to return calls

You can count on accumulating calls that must be returned, so block time daily. Schedule one time segment for late morning — allowing you to concentrate on the DIPA tasks without anxiety. You may also want to schedule another "return-call" block toward the end of the day to catch up on all the calls you may have missed during a busy afternoon. This block of time should be about 30 minutes. You want to try to keep the return phone call less than 10 minutes.

Schedule ongoing production-supporting activities

All administrative and customer-relations tasks require regular attention. Although I maintain that these PSAs are secondary to generating sales, they must still be accomplished. Scheduling adequate time to stay on top of ongoing service activities ensures that they don't get pushed to the schedule for the next week. And the next week. And the next week.

Your sales process and client servicing greatly influence the amount of time you spend in PSAs. Some salespeople do a lot of servicing. Some salespeople hand the servicing over to another department. The real truth is to invest as little in PSAs as you can while keeping your client happy. (I go over the basics of PSAs earlier in this chapter.)

Set aside time for staff

If you have direct reports, your job responsibilities include coaching and supporting others. Schedule the necessary one-on-one and meeting times to ensure you stay on top of staff productivity and performance. Block on your schedule brief daily "touch-base" chats with individuals as well as weekly meetings with the whole staff.

Take emergencies into account

 Some flexibility is essential in order to keep to a time block schedule. For every two to three hours of productive time per day, schedule 30 minutes of "emergency" time. In case an appointment runs late or some other glitch derails your day, you've got a half-hour leeway to get back on task.

Putting the "Now" before the "Later" with Daily To-Do Lists

Daily to-do lists help the telephone-sales professional meet sales objectives. Sometimes, you just don't have enough time in the day to get *everything* done. That's why it's necessary to identify which tasks are the most important. The process of organizing your to-do list in order of importance is called *prioritizing*.

Many people make daily lists, which is a good start. But as the day goes on, they get into trouble and don't even know it. Why? Because they see accomplishment as crossing off as many items on the list as possible. They measure success in quantity. But what really counts isn't how many tasks you cross off, but *what* you cross off. When creating a daily task list, put all the tasks in for the day. Don't just list the sales tasks, but the servicing tasks, as well.

The following is a powerfully effective prioritization system that can take your task list making to the next level:

1. **Write down all your tasks (in no particular order).**

   To set effective priorities, create your list as you normally would. Don't worry about which tasks are most important . . . yet. Concern yourself only with what needs to be done. This is the brainstorming stage: Just get it all down on paper.

2. **Categorize tasks according to their importance for the day.**

   Wait! Don't start prioritizing in 1-2-3 order. At this stage, you group your listed tasks in A-B-C-D-E categories according to these criteria:

   A: Items that have a significant negative consequence if they're not completed *today*

   B: Tasks that have a mild negative consequence if not completed today

   C: Actions that, if not done today, won't cause any negative consequences

   D: Tasks that can be delegated

   E: Items that can be eliminated

3. **Prioritize the tasks within the categories from Step 2.**

   Start with the A category and determine which item has the highest priority. Designate this as A-1, followed by the next most important item, A-2, then A-3, A-4, and so forth. Repeat this process for the B, C, and D categories. You don't need to prioritize the E category because you need to eliminate these items. Your list is now accurately prioritized, and you can start accomplishing each item, confident that if you run out of time at the end of the day, you've at least finished the most important items on your list. And, best off all, no negative consequences!

Don't expect to complete as large a volume of cross-offs as you may be used to. Because you're doing more important items, which likely take more time, you may not be able to get as many tasks completed. In my view, however, the measure of a great day is whether you achieve closure on all the A-category items. If you follow this system for a year and complete only the A items each day, you will see your production and income explode. How is this possible? Because the B, C, and D items quickly work their way up to As — and you *always* get the most important things done!

Questioning the status quo

My friend Zig Ziglar tells a story about a little boy watching his mother prepare a holiday meal. He asks her why she cuts off the end of the ham. She says this to him, "I don't know. My mother always did it this way." Now this 5-year-old boy (the reason I know he was 5 is that my son Wesley is 5, and he would say the exact same thing) says, "Let's call Grandma right now and find out why." So they call Grandma and ask her why she always cut the end of the ham off. Her reply? "The pan was too small!"

People often continue to do their jobs a certain way because "that's the way I've always done it." Sometimes the original reason for doing it no longer has any relevance. Critically questioning the status quo can help identify and eliminate needless tasks, freeing up your energy for more important activities.

Making Each Day a Time-Management "10"

A day that rates as a perfect "10" doesn't just happen. Oh, sure, a *can-do* attitude is important, but it takes a concerted effort to keep a productive day on track. Time management offers some valuable tools in constructing a high-scoring day.

Managing distractions and interruptions

Your best-laid plans can go awry when external forces scheme against the productive schedule you've set for yourself. Your office mate wants to tell you all about his weekend. Your phone keeps ringing. Your e-mail program signals that you've got more messages. The conversation out in the hall makes it hard to hear your prospect on the phone.

The best way to handle interruptions is to stop them from happening in the first place. Because the most critical time is DIPA time, it's helpful to establish some preemptive strategies during this period of your day. Just a few of the steps you can take to avoid interruptions include:

- ✓ Turning off your cellphone
- ✓ Asking the receptionist to hold all calls or forward them to your voice mail

> ✔ Turning off your e-mail program so the you've-got-mail icon doesn't distract you
>
> ✔ Signing out of your instant message program
>
> ✔ Closing your office door
>
> ✔ Hanging a Do-Not-Disturb sign on your door or cubicle entrance

Do whatever it takes to stay on track. In most cases, when you explain to your colleagues, clients, family, or boss that this is a critical production time for you, and you give them a specific time when you can get back to them, they're more than happy to let you be.

Keeping calls short 'n' sweet

Telephone sales is a numbers game: The more calls you make, the more money you can earn. So it goes to reason that the shorter the call, the more calls you can make. A good practice is to keep customer-service calls and PSA calls as brief as possible.

Tell your sales contact that you have another appointment in 15 minutes (and if you follow the advice on time blocking earlier in this chapter, you *should* have another appointment in 15 minutes!), but you felt it was important to get in touch as quickly as you could. This technique tells the person two things:

> ✔ That the situation must be resolved quickly (diverting unproductive chit-chat)
>
> ✔ That the client is so highly valued that you're making time for the call even with your full schedule

Assure the client that 15 minutes is more than enough time — and if not, you'll set aside time later that day to talk again. The truth is, however, I've never had to talk with the client later — we always manage to resolve the issues in the first call.

With prospects, you want to speak with the person directly — it's the only way to drive them to a face-to-face meeting or make the sale on the phone efficiently. But PSA calls are another story: Take advantage of voice mail at every opportunity. This allows you to answer questions without a time-consuming conversation. Of course, you want to give them the option to call you back. Here's a good script to use in that case:

"Bob, I know that you are very busy. I believe that this resolves the issue. If you agree, there is no reason to call me back. If you do need to speak with me, I will be available later today between 3:30 and 4:15. Please call me then."

Getting a head start on the next day

A perfect "10" day is born the previous day, created through strategic setup. At the end of your workday, take 10 to 15 minutes before you go home to review your calls for tomorrow. Who are the leads you need to reach? What presentation appointments are on your schedule? Are you prepared — or do you need to invest more time? For each call, make sure you have all the information you need on that prospect and that you have everything you need to answer their questions. This brief time investment to review, arrange, analyze, and create your strategy increases the likelihood that tomorrow will rate a "10."

"Seasonalizing" your schedule

Most businesses follow a predictable seasonal pattern of ups and downs. Maybe sales for your business are flat or declining as you approach the holiday season, or possibly, the holidays are your biggest time of the year. Breaking down sales results from quarterly or seasonally to monthly to weekly to daily also produces an enhanced urgency that results in better time usage. The daily focus on calls, contacts, leads, appointments, and presentations shows up first when a salesperson is off the mark.

Look at historical sales patterns for your company. Recognize that you may want to pattern your hours invested to match historical sales data. You may work longer hours in the high sales weeks and months and decrease your hours or plan for vacation time when sales are historically slow. I have traditionally taken off the last week of the year for close to 20 years. I found that sales were very low the last week of the year for my sales business. The return for the investment of time wasn't warranted.

At Sales Champions, each of our telephone salespeople has a specific annual income goal, reflecting a mix of products and services broken down by season. By factoring in the seasonal swings, our sales staff is more likely to stay on course. If the sales goals were spread out flat, some who merely hit the modest goals for a busy season would certainly face more challenge in making them up during the times when sales are more challenging.

Using your car as a classroom

One of my greatest vehicles for higher learning? My car. In my early sales years, I turned it into my learning classroom. Spending hours in my car every day was an opportunity to expand my knowledge and grow professionally. I was never in my car without a tape or CD playing. Not music, but rather lessons on sales skills, motivational messages, and advice from the sales world's most renowned experts.

I am a long-time supporter of the *auto*-university. Those of us in the world of sales tend to spend large quantities of time in our vehicles. Having an educational CD or CD series playing helps improve your learning curve as you're maneuvering your sales routes.

I'm convinced that the time I spent in my own auto-university is one of the key reasons I've achieved the levels of success that I enjoy today. You're success-minded, too, or you wouldn't have invested in this book. Turning your travel time into learning time enriches your long-term growth in addition to boosting your day's value to a "10."

Putting off procrastination

Falling into the procrastination trap is easy. Too many available working hours leads to a lack of urgency, which leads to the I-can-do-it-later syndrome. Defining a clear line between prioritization and procrastination is critical to making the most of your time. Setting precise deadlines — and adhering to them — stops procrastination in its tracks. For success-minded individuals, deadlines drive performance.

Think about what happens the week before your vacation. If you're like me, just prior to your getaway, you're typically operating on overdrive to cross off all the to-do's on your list. Why? You don't have an option. You don't have tomorrow to catch up. Your vacation deadline creates an urgency that enhances your focus, action, and intensity to a level you may rarely reach at other times.

Successful telephone salespeople apply that sense of urgency to all their deadlines. They resist the inclination to wait until a "better time" to pick up the phone. They won't permit themselves to make excuses to postpone. They treat all deadlines with the same importance as they give a vacation. They live by the motto, "There is no time like the present." They take action, and they do it *now.*

Continuing to call, even when you're down

Frustration. Stress. Burn-out. It's a fact of telephone-sales life: At some point in your professional work, you're bound to confront some "down" moments — times when you'd consider it a miracle to boost your day even to a "5." At these times, you may be tempted to give up on your time-management efforts, rationalizing that it won't do you any good to "stick with the program" when you're in the dumps anyway.

My advice when this urge hits? *Get on the phone!* Just pick up the phone and do what a telephone salesperson does — *call.* If you're feeling a bit insecure, then call your best clients. Hearing from satisfied customers is a sure cure against a case of the doubts. They're pleased that you're calling to check in on them, and *you* gain from a boost to your confidence. Even one or two positive calls to your best clients can turn the day from a big zero to something closer to a "10."

Linking rewards and deadlines

Working the phone for appointments and sales is hard, taxing, even grinding — sometimes for long stretches. Most salespeople go through a drought or slump at least once in a calendar year. Getting through the hard times can be tough, but rewards can help soften the angst. Not commission-based rewards — which come from successful sales efforts, of course — but personal incentives that motivate you to stay the course and get past the slump.

Personal is the operative word. What's an attractive "carrot" to keep *you* committed to your schedule? A day at the spa? A long weekend getaway? A new set of golf clubs? What are you willing to go the extra mile for? Choose a reward that's tailored to please *you.*

After you choose a reward, set short-term stakes. If the reward is too far away, it will lose its pull. The promise of a healthy retirement fund isn't going to motivate you to meet your daily objectives now. Instead, a reward that dangles just a week or month away is more likely to inspire you to make that additional phone call today — say, treating yourself to an evening of fine dining Saturday night. Reward yourself in small, meaningful ways for managing your time wisely and hitting deadlines and production goals.

Part III
You Make the Call!

The 5th Wave   By Rich Tennant

"I've revised my sales script. Tell me what you think."

In this part . . .

You turned to this part first, didn't you? After all, the call is the *heart* of telephone sales. And although making a phone call may seem pretty straightforward, consistently making sales calls that end in closes takes more effort than simply letting your fingers do the walking. These five jam-packed chapters guide you through the sales call.

In Chapter 8, I give you tips for getting past even the most militant gatekeeper. And even if you turn that bulldog of an assistant into your staunchest ally, you still have to get your foot in the door — so to speak — with the prospect. In Chapter 9, I show you how to develop and use a powerful opening statement that's sure to keep the prospect on the line.

But be sure: Successful phone sales isn't "show and tell." In fact, in Chapters 10 and 11, you discover that *asking* and *listening* are skills that serve you better than *telling* and *selling*. I also reveal the best questions to ask in order to get a sale. And all that asking and listening is leading up to your big scene (give me a drum roll, please): your sales presentation. Chapter 12 holds the secrets for sliding seamlessly from your supporting role as prospect confessor to center stage, including the keys to effective delivery.

Chapter 8

Getting Past the Gatekeeper

. . . .

. . . .

*T*here I was, outside the castle gates — the drawbridge closed tight. The moat was filled with crocodiles; the parapet armed by legions poised with arrows and cauldrons of boiling oil. And inside the keep, the treasure I sought was secure in an impenetrable tower, guarded by the ruler of the land. . . .

No, I'm neither a weekend role-player at a Renaissance fair nor am I playing a Medieval-themed video game. I'm describing how it can feel for me — and leagues of telephone salespeople — when calling a business to try to reach that all-powerful decision maker. You know — the one who can grant the key to the kingdom's riches. Problem is, I have to pass the gatekeeper to attain those riches.

Getting past the gatekeeper is a constant challenge in reaching high-level decision makers. Recognize this, though: The more difficult getting beyond the gatekeeper is for you, the less likely your competition has succeeded. This is great news. And, trust me, breaking through the gatekeeper gauntlet *is* possible. In this chapter, I share the best battle strategies, from finding secret passages that lead to the decision maker to employing the passwords that persuade the gatekeeper to let down the drawbridge.

Meeting the Three Gatekeepers

In order to keep you out of the castle, gatekeepers use all sorts of tactics, based on their individual position, experience, temperament, and relationship with the decision maker. Some, wearing "company policy" as a suit of armor, are hard as nails to get past;

others aim to derail you through disinformation; some may even disguise themselves as a decision maker, when all they're really empowered to do is to fool you into thinking you're making progress.

Typically, all gatekeepers fall into one of three general categories. By recognizing them, you're better equipped to circumvent their efforts to block your passage.

The loyal assistant

Secretary. Administrative assistant. Personal assistant. Executive aid. Even office manager. Gatekeepers with these titles invariably have direct-report status and work very closely with the individual you seek to reach. Each sees it as her mission to keep callers from intruding on the boss. A loyal assistant frequently labels "intrusions" according to her own definition. The longer this individual has worked with the boss or company, the stronger the loyalty factor — and the greater the challenge to get past her.

The mid-level manager

Often, you make it past the initial gatekeeper — the loyal assistant — only to run into another gatekeeper. The assistant commonly directs you to someone with a title, someone who may report to the decision maker you want to reach, but who *doesn't* have the authority to buy your product or service— usually some type of mid-level manager.

Mid-level managers are less driven by personal loyalty and more concerned about whether they look good. They're on their way up, on their way down, or stuck. If you can persuade the mid-level manager that your service or product is the key to her advancement — or the salvation to his demise — you'll have a strong advocate who can help you reach the decision maker (see the section "Enlisting the Gatekeeper as Your Ally" later in this chapter for more info).

Here are some clues to help you figure out which direction the mid-level manager is headed:

✔ The manager on the climb is your most likely ally — you're presenting a new and innovative idea that may save or make the company money, which will make him look good.

✔ Managers on the way down — or out — are more challenging. Supporting something new isn't what most managers on the decline are focused on. If you do manage to convince them, you *must* gain audience with the higher-ups. Why? If the down-and-out manager presents your case, you run the risk that:

   • His reputation will taint management's view of your product.

   • His delivery may not position your product in the best light.

The imposter of importance

Ah, the toughest gatekeeper of them all — the employee who projects importance and power far beyond what she really possesses! She may insist that you deal directly with her: send *her* all your information and make the presentation to *her.*

The more she insists you deal with her the more likely she is an imposter of importance, especially if when you ask her for her title, she hesitates to tell you. She is often trying to come up with some title that sounds more important than the one she currently possesses.

When you suspect you've encountered an imposter of importance, you must probe, clarify, repeat, question, and even confront, if necessary, as to the exact parameters of her role. Find out the answers to the following questions:

 ✔ What does she typically do when a salesperson asks for her boss?

 ✔ Does the boss usually agree with her decision?

 ✔ How much weight does her opinion carry?

 ✔ How does she advise you to proceed?

 ✔ Even ask her outright if you had misinformation — is she the decision maker?

Her responses may need further dissection. Imposters often create gray areas with phrases such as, "I am involved," "I have a hand in," "I wield some influence," or "I have some responsibility." When you hear responses that need further interpretation, feed them back for clarification by using phrases such as the following:

"What do you mean by _____?"

"Can you clarify _____?"

"Can you give me a little perspective on _____?"

An imposter often backtracks, contradicts, or continues to be vague. If you're talking to the *real* decision maker, you should get clear-cut responses that confirm authority.

Enlisting the Gatekeeper as Your Ally

The gatekeeper can stop you dead in your tracks, so it is wise to turn him into an internal advocate if you can. You will find techniques to do just that in this section.

Making a good first impression

Your first call to the gatekeeper is a little like trying to land a glider: You can't circle back for another pass. With that initial call, you set the stage for the resistance level on future calls. If you're dismissive, you may crash and burn. If you come off as trying to *schmooze* the gatekeeper, you'll get the "sleazy salesperson" treatment.

Although you may feel as if gatekeepers exist to make your life difficult, keep in mind that they're bombarded daily by a legion of vendors, clients, employees, and strangers — all trying to gain audience with the person they work for. The gatekeepers may also receive the message from these people (and possibly even their boss) that they aren't important. Your ability to treat the gate-keeper with respect and reinforce his value, and — after all, he is *very* important to your efforts — can open doors.

Three techniques to convey your respect of the gatekeeper can be employed in the first phone contact:

> ✔ **Say the person's name.** This signals that you recognize him beyond the role of assistant or employee. Use his name in all conversations and follow-up calls. If you're not good with names, add this critical detail to the prospect record. (See Chapter 3 for details about keeping an accurate database of call activity.)

✔ **Promote the gatekeeper.** Even if you know the title is "secretary" or "assistant," refer to the individual as "office manager" or "executive adviser." This communicates that you recognize his critical role in the workings of the company. Using these titles reinforces the gatekeeper's value *and* reduces the likelihood that he'll push you off with the "I'm just the assistant" ploy.

✔ **Ask for help.** By soliciting the gatekeeper's help, you say, "You're important to me" and "I rely on your knowledge," both positive and ego-boosting messages. Plus, the more you can glean from her, the more effective you can be after you reach the decision makers. You're transferring and admitting the power position that she currently has. It conveys respect.

Digging for information

Questions for the gatekeeper are one of your best tools for prying open the gates that lead to the decision maker. Use the initial opportunity to establish, first, whether you're reaching the right person, using questions such as the following:

> *"Does Mr. Jones usually handle decisions regarding _____?"*
>
> *"Who do you normally work with to provide _____?"*
>
> *"If you were me, how would you approach Mr. Big?"*

Then fish for a little more detail to help tailor your efforts to the individuals (both the gatekeeper *and* the decision maker) you're working with. Some questions secure more information so you can build a more spot-on presentation. Some may reveal shortcuts or alternate routes to reaching the decision maker. Some are designed to involve the gatekeeper and elicit support, and others simply keep the gatekeeper on the line a little longer. However you use them, the following questions are bound to garner more info for you to better do your job:

> *"I know it's challenging to anticipate his every move, but when might be a good time to call him back?"*
>
> *"Is she usually more available in the morning or the afternoon?"*
>
> *"I would assume he is like most successful _____ and comes in early in the morning."*
>
> *"You certainly know her well. How does she approach decisions such as _____?"*
>
> *"If you were in my shoes, what would you do?"*

If you get stuck, focus on results. Instead of talking about the copiers you sell, zero in on desirable results: Ask the gatekeeper what goals are important to the decision maker. Point out how you have a solution that results in more effective presentations, greater office productivity, and money savings. A responsible gatekeeper will surely want the boss to hear about that.

Always get the gatekeeper's extension number. Why? The boss's extension is often one digit more or one digit less than the gate-keeper's. This information allows you to attempt to reach the decision maker directly — your best bet is to try before or after official work hours, in hopes of catching the boss when the gatekeeper is out.

Asking for help

Believe it or not, when asked, most people are only too eager to help. Recruiting the gatekeeper as an ally instead of an adversary is an extremely under-utilized but effective technique for getting through to the decision maker. Enlist the gatekeeper's support with lines such as

> *"May I ask a favor of you?"*
>
> *"Can you help me out?"*
>
> *"I would really appreciate your assistance."*
>
> *"I know you are extremely busy, but could you advise me?"*
>
> *"I know your time is valuable, and I hesitate to ask because of that, but . . ."*

To pack this tactic with added punch, be sure to tack on the gatekeeper's name to the beginning of your request, as I explain in the earlier section "Making a good first impression."

Providing an out

I consider this method a *master* technique. One of the most reliable ways to elicit the help of gatekeeper is to offer an "out." I call it the *pressure release* technique because it takes the pressure off the gate-keeper by allowing him to say no. Here's how it works — you say something like:

> *"I understand if you can't, but is it possible to . . .?"*

Of course, the beauty of this technique is that giving the individual permission to refuse your request makes him all the more eager to grant you the favor. The best pressure release statement is, "I understand if you can't." Link this with, "I have a favor to ask," and you've got a virtual battering-ram's chance of getting in the door. Odds are good that the gatekeeper will drop his defenses and let down the barriers.

Avoiding Sidetrack Sabotage

One of the gatekeeper's most trusted methods of sabotage is to throw decoys in your path. Gatekeepers have an arsenal of these diversions. You may be hit with one on your first call and bombarded with different ones at each subsequent effort. It may even start before you get to the gatekeeper — the receptionist may be in on the subterfuge, too!

If you get sidetracked at the front door, here's a tactic to get past the receptionist: When asked to hold, respond by saying something like, "Holding for Mr. Jones, please." Most phone systems re-ring the receptionist after a caller has been on hold for some time. A busy receptionist may believe she has "screened" your call earlier and then simply put you through to the decision maker! Look out for the following common decoys as well.

"Send us your brochure"

This brush-off is a favored ruse among those who like to avoid confrontation. It allows the gatekeeper to postpone, diminish, or avoid rejecting you outright. The gatekeeper appears to be opening the door, but in reality he knows that few salespeople actually follow up. And if they do, an envelope is a lot easier to deflect than a person.

This method only works if you, the salesperson, allow it to work. Or you can turn the tables and use the gatekeeper's decoy as an opening to collect more information about the decision maker's needs by using the following method:

> *"The truth is, one of the reasons for my call is to be able to send more information to Mr. Jones in the near future. I wouldn't want to waste Mr. Jones's time by sending something that doesn't apply to your needs. Can we take another few minutes, so I can ask a few more questions about _____?"*

This technique moves you away from "send me your brochure" and back to your fact-finding mission (for more on this, see the section "Digging for information" earlier in this chapter).

"Mr. Decision Maker is busy right now; can I take a message?"

One would hope Mr. Decision Maker is busy doing something. Although your prospect is unlikely to be flossing his teeth when you call, be prepared to hear this type of response. What might you not be prepared for? If the gatekeeper has anything to do with it, Mr. Decision Maker may be too busy to *ever* get your message.

One of the primary duties of the gatekeeper is to protect the boss from unscheduled intrusions. Although, technically, the gatekeeper *takes* the message, the likelihood is slim that the gatekeeper will actually *give* the message.

To keep your message from being written in invisible ink, you may need to employ this strategy — respond to the request in this way:

> *"Sure, but before you take the time to do that, can I ask you a few questions to make sure that Mr. Jones even needs to call me back?"*

What you're saying is, "I'm giving you the power to decide whether I call back again." Now, you will, of course, call back again. But if you use this technique successfully, you can often move from a message to an appointment with the boss.

However, if this first technique doesn't work and the gatekeeper continues to press you to leave a message, ask for a time and date when you can call back and be assured of reaching the decision maker instead of simply leaving a message for a return phone call. Make it as difficult as possible for the gatekeeper to find an excuse to refuse your request. Ask for a small amount of time: 15 — even just 5 — minutes. Check out the following examples:

> *"I can appreciate that Mr. Jones is busy. You sound like the person responsible for handling his schedule. Does he have an opening of 15 minutes on Wednesday or Thursday when we could talk?"*

> *"I understand his schedule is full; mine is full, as well. In the interest of saving time, is he available on Thursday in the morning or afternoon to speak with me for 15 minutes?"*

Before you hang up, see whether the gatekeeper will tell you what's scheduled after your phone appointment. Knowing what comes next gives you a sense of whether the call could be extended — or whether the call must be kept to a certain length. Later in the call, you can impress the prospect with your respect for her time with comments such as the following:

> *"I know you have a meeting in a few minutes, so could we finish our call* _____ *or* _____*?"*

Another Gatekeeper: Using Voice Mail to Your Advantage

Many executives use voice mail to screen out callers. Inept and unscripted voice mail messages don't generate return calls. Leave a bad voice mail message, and you can anticipate an even greater buildup of the ramparts.

But just as you can turn an executive assistant into your ally, you can use voice mail to *your* benefit. Just think: Even if the live conduit in the company refuses to pass on your messages, you can count on voice mail to deliver a well-crafted message — *exactly* as you want it delivered. I provide some guidance in the following sections.

Following five steps to a powerful message

Just as effective *live* conversations with sales prospects are built of important component parts, the voice mail message must also be carefully constructed, as you find out in the following sections. Even though you may serve customers with varying needs, you can easily come up with a basic voice mail template you can customize, of course, when you have insider information to tailor it.

Here are some crucial guidelines for a productive working relationship with voice mail:

- ✔ Keep your messages 15 to 30 seconds.
- ✔ Be prepared. Have a script at hand; if you stumble, mumble, and bumble in the message, you're worse off than if you leave no message at all. I can't overemphasize how important being prepared really is.

✔ Take advantage of voice mail features such as the replay-and-rerecord function.

✔ Ramp up your energy level to deliver with passion and enthusiasm. (If you sound like a sleep-aid commercial, delete and repeat!)

✔ Smile when you leave voice mail messages. It can't sound like the 50th message that you have left today.

Provide your name, rank, and phone number

Launch the call by identifying yourself. State your name, company, rank, and phone number. Because of unreliable reception quality of voice mail, speak with greater clarity in your voice. Relay this critical information slowly and carefully. If the recipient must replay the message several times to decipher the details, well . . . she probably won't do it.

Construct an attention-getting bridge

Before diving right into the heart of your message, ease your way in with a one-of-a-kind warm-up phrase. Most salespeople say something like "I'm sorry I missed you." Don't you do it! Instead, try a fresh approach:

"It's a pleasure to leave you this message today."

"Since our last discussion. . . ."

"Since my last voice mail. . . ."

"I am certain you recognize my voice by now."

State your purpose — with an accent on benefits

"The reason for my call . . . " is an obvious but also extremely effective introduction to the crux of your call. These words signal that it's time for the recipient to tune in. At this point, you're presenting the benefits, the opportunity, and the critical details you hope will hook the prospect into returning your call and asking for feedback.

You want to spotlight *benefits* for the recipient, of course — benefits that you're at the ready to offer. Don't confuse *benefits* with your laundry list of products and services. The prospect already knows, for example, what an office equipment company sells. Instead of running through your catalog of products, offer results: for example, more just-in-time business opportunities because of faster turnaround, or 24/7 maintenance service means no downtime, ever. The individual who listens to your message ought to hear how your product or service can help boost sales, decrease costs, or increase productivity.

The objective of stating your purpose is to increase urgency. Here's an example:

> *"The reason for my call is to alert you to three strategic benefits we provide our clients: reducing duplication service costs; increasing quality in promotional and presentation materials; and increasing staff productivity with the walk-away feature on our machines. Which of these services is most important to you?"*

This segment of the voice mail message is what changes most as you make additional follow-up calls to that prospect (see the later section "Setting a six-call limit" for more information).

Specify a call to action

A compelling message also contains a call to action. Saying "I called; tag, you're it," just doesn't cut it. Be specific about the next step:

> *"Please call me back tomorrow between 10 and 3."*

> *"Please be on the lookout for an information packet I've dropped in the mail for you."*

> *"I will try you again tomorrow. If another time is more convenient, please feel free to call me at. . . ."*

Close the call

Restate your name, company name, and phone number at the end of your voice mail message. The recipient may not have jotted it down earlier, and this saves her the trouble of replaying your message. Then end with a sincere thank you. Expressing appreciation for her time is a solid strategy, showing courtesy and respect to the listener.

Setting a six-call limit

Through years of testing, research, monitoring thousands of calls, and analyzing my own track record, I've hit upon *six* as the magic limit for leaving sales messages on voice mail to the same prospect in a few weeks' period. When you go beyond this number, you're past the peak and looking at diminishing returns.

But by no means should you be leaving the same message with each call! If the prospect didn't call back after the first two "Sorry I missed you" efforts, what makes you think he will respond to the third, fourth, fifth, or sixth?

Develop your first benefits-oriented message, and then script five more messages that build on the previous efforts — with new detail, more benefits, and increasing urgency. With varying messages, you're more likely to hit the prospect's hot button.

Don't neglect to use the insider information you acquired through the gatekeeper or through your earlier research (see previous sections for more on this). If you can insert the insider information in the general scripting, the call-back rate climbs even higher.

Chapter 9

Opening Your Sales Call with Ease

*Y*ou may have heard the saying "You never get a second chance to make a good first impression." This oft-repeated axiom is never truer than when selling over the phone, where the full weight of your sales success hangs on your first words. You can't rely on your physical presence, the benefit of reading body language, or the ability to hold the individual with eye contact as you can when you make your case face to face. If you don't hook the prospect within your first few sentences, your odds of seeing the sale through to the close shrink faster than the time it takes your prospect to say good-bye or to hang up.

And as much as you want to think otherwise, most folks don't eagerly await the ringing of the phone in hopes of hearing from a salesperson — even if they really need and want certain products or services. When they stop to answer the phone in the middle of a busy day, they're not likely to be receptive to a message that translates as, "I want to sell you something."

Of course, *you* would never start a sales call in that manner. But, in so many words, that's exactly what many common opening-statement formulas convey. The message you *do* want to impart is this: "You're looking for a solution and I have it." No matter the situation, the product or service you sell, the size of the company you approach, or whether you're selling to individual consumers or businesspeople, if you can zero in on the need and benefit of the prospect and craft a compelling opening that addresses that need, you've found a way to make that first impression a positive one. And this chapter shows you how.

Living with the Seven-Second Rule

It's a law of sales physics: From the beginning of the call, you have seven seconds to give the customer a good reason to stay on the line with you. Therefore, your opening statement must be *great* at the very minimum. Outstanding, world class, or stellar is even better.

Seven seconds isn't a lot of time. But, unfortunately, it's enough time for the prospect to formulate a rejection response. If your opening statement is less than great, you're likely to hear, "I'm busy"; "We already have one of those"; "I'm not interested"; "We are happy with our current supplier"; or "I'll get back to you if I need it down the road."

How do your prospects know they won't be interested in your offer? They don't. But they do know that you weren't interesting enough for them to want to explore the possibility. They drew that conclusion based on your less-than-great opening statement. To make the first seven seconds something special, this section helps you get off on the right foot.

Never assume

I don't have to tell you what happens when you assume. But all too frequently, salespeople do just that. They assume that the prospect is familiar with their company and what it offers. They assume that the prospect remembers them, whether they've met once or many times. However, studies on recognition indicate that it takes more than six contacts before a prospect remembers and recognizes a salesperson.

No matter how many times you or someone from your company has talked to a prospect, always clearly introduce yourself and your company — even if you shook hands with the prospect last week or talked on the phone yesterday. Sure, it takes up some of those precious seven seconds — but stopping in the middle of the opening statement to remind the customer who you are and what your company does eats up a lot more time.

If you're taking over someone else's call lists, don't assume that the prospect remembers the previous salesperson. If you open with, "John Jones left, and I am taking over." You will likely hear, "John who? What company?" The better approach is to treat the call as a cold call and allow the prospect warm-up time to connect the dots. After you get past the opening, you can remind the prospect that John used to be the company representative.

Make your voice music to their ears

In that first seven seconds, the prospect makes a judgment of your intelligence, professionalism, and knowledge by the sound of your voice and delivery of your message. He establishes a mental picture. If you open those seven seconds with power and value, he visualizes a capable, accomplished salesperson and treats you as such.

When you talk to another person, your words only account for 7 percent of your ability to communicate, but the modulation of your voice makes up 38 percent. Without the visual component — which comprises 55 percent — you're working at a distinct disadvantage when you sell over the phone.

 You can succeed in conjuring that professional image, compensating for the lack of the visual component, by training yourself to maximize your modulation. Pay close attention to the following areas when you practice and deliver your opening statement:

- ✔ **Pace:** A plodding dialogue does nothing to generate enthusiasm or interest. And if you're as hyper as a Dalmatian, you risk wearing the prospect out. Moderate a reasonable pace, but be sure to incorporate variety. Slow down in places to emphasize a point, and vary the position and length of your pauses.

- ✔ **Tonality:** Avoid being monotone, at all costs. Practice moving from a power delivery with a strong tone to a softer, patient delivery. Varying your tone adds interest to your presentation and helps highlight key points. Using tonality effectively helps convey enthusiasm, believability, and passion.

Scripting an Opening Statement

In order to have a great opening, you can't just wing it. You want your opening to be great. In order to do so, you need to script it and deliver it word for word. With the entire presentation resting on those seven quick seconds, you can't afford to wing it. This section helps you draft an effective opening.

Including six important aspects to your seven-second opening

A powerful opening statement must contain six key components. Each step is critical to launching a positive sales call. To prepare an opening that can lead to a close, draft your statement on paper, using these six parts as your outline.

Step one: Greet the prospect by name

The sweetest words in any language are those of one's own name. When you say the prospect's name, she homes in on your voice as quickly as a cat perks up its ears at the sound of the can opener.

Don't undo all your good work by mispronouncing the name. Do the recon necessary to verify the pronunciation ahead of time. If the name is tough to pronounce, either call in advance to find out how to pronounce it by listening to the prospect's voice mail or ask the receptionist to pronounce it. If you butcher it, you waste valuable seconds being corrected — and alienate the prospect in the process.

Step two: State your full name

Often in the frenzy and stress of hooking the prospect, salespeople rush through their introduction with only a first name — especially when they've met or spoken to the prospect previously. Make sure you tell the prospect your full name. If you write out your full name as part of your script, you remember to say it.

Step three: Identify your company

Just as with your full name (see the preceding section), don't assume that the prospect is familiar with your company or what it does. Make sure you state your company's service in a jargon-free, easy-to-understand fashion. Don't assume that the prospect knows acronyms or complex terms. Initially state your service offering as if you were speaking to a novice.

You can also add what I call a specialty statement after giving the name of the company. A *specialty statement* tells the prospect your area of expertise or the area you're known for. Set yourself apart even more by incorporating a benefit into the specialty statement. (This quick singular statement isn't to be confused with the benefit statements in step five where you deliver multiple statements.) Check out the following examples:

- ✔ We specialize in reducing payroll costs.
- ✔ We specialize in rapid radiator repair.

> ✔ We specialize in selling high-end eastside real estate properties at the best value.

Check out the section, "Building Your Elevator Speech" later in this chapter to help you develop a quick, but thorough, speech about your company in case the prospect wants more background info.

Step four: Explain why you're calling

It's time to get to the point. You're now going to reveal why the prospect is taking her time to talk with you. The easiest way to get to the point is . . . to get to the point! "The reason for my call is . . ." should be put right in your script.

Keep your focus on the prospect. On one hand, the reason for your call is to make your sales quota by the end of the week. But that is irrelevant to your prospect. Cast your "reason" in a way that is meaningful to her. For example, "The reason for my call is our new cable package offers 30 percent more channel selection that what you're currently getting."

Step five: Link in a benefit statement

The *benefit statement* is added to your reason-I'm-calling statement. You're now approaching the seven-second cut-off: If the benefit statement isn't tuned to WIIFM, you lose the listener. WIIFM is the

The power of specialization

One of the best words you can use in describing your company or yourself is *specialist*. It positions you as an expert. People want to work with the best, and *specialist* implies that you're more experienced in this particular field than others. Ultimately, it shows that the prospect has a low risk when choosing to work with you.

When you define yourself as a *specialist,* this also tends to focus your efforts as a salesperson. Instead of being all things to all people, your potential for sales success actually increases when you narrow your area of expertise. Be sure to sell those strengths in the specialty statement of your opening (see the section "Step three: Identify your company" for more info). What does your company do better than anyone else? What are the core competencies, core focus, or core components that set your business apart?

When you're positioning yourself or your company as a specialist in an area, it doesn't mean you can't offer other products or services outside your defined expertise. You can always recommend an alternative if the prospect doesn't want your specialized offer. But when you sell your best first, you increase the odds of opening up a strong and long-lasting relationship.

radio station that plays in our brains 24/7. It stands for *What's In It For Me?* If your benefit statement doesn't address that listening audience, you run a good chance of turning off your prospect.

The less contact you've had with the prospect, the more critical the benefit statement. But even if you're making a follow-up call with an established client, playing WIIFM is always music to a prospect's ears. Here are some examples of effective benefit statements:

- ✔ "We've had considerable success in reducing payroll costs in mid-sized companies like yours."

- ✔ "We've achieved significant performance increases for our clients through our scheduling software that they now use."

- ✔ "We've seen our clients reduce their weight by more than 15 percent, on average, in just three weeks."

Step six: Add a close or bridge

. . . Five, four, three, two. . . . The time has come to wrap up the opening statement as you close in on the seven-second marker. But you don't want the road to end here, so you make your conclusion a question or a bridge so that continuing the conversation is natural and easy.

If you choose to close with a question, use it to establish some form of commitment. Ask for an appointment, for example:

- ✔ "Let's set an appointment to talk. Which would work better for you — Wednesday or Thursday?"

- ✔ "Our next step would be to meet. Do you have time this week, or would next week be better?"

The *bridge* is a softer approach, linking the benefit statement with the close by asking permission to explore further. Although the question close infers more certainty, the bridge places some power into the prospect's hands, which often makes her more comfortable to proceed:

"Until we invest a few minutes together, I don't know if your results will be the same, worse, or better than those of XYZ Company. Would you be willing to spend a few minutes together to see?"

"Bob, I am not sure at this juncture if I can help you, and you are not sure if I can't, so let's spend a few minutes together to find out if you could benefit from our product."

Engaging the prospect

When you're establishing communication without the benefit of a visual or physical connection, any technique that can help you reach through the phone and connect with the prospect is bound to smooth the way. Add one of these to your opening for extra impact:

- ✔ **Drop names when appropriate.** Name-dropping takes a bad rap, but it's a tactic that works in the business world. If you can mention a respected friend or colleague or even a prominent person in the industry, you earn the prospect's attention and reduce resistance. For example:

    - • "During a conversation with Fred Smith at FedEx last week . . ."

    - • "Just the other day while visiting Microsoft's headquarters . . ."

    Mentioning a competitor of the prospect's company can also work as a doorstop, but you must do it carefully. Referring to a leader in the industry — a company that surpasses the prospect in sales, stature, longevity, and brand recognition — is best. The prospect perks up at the possibility of discovering the secrets that the competitor is so successfully using.

- ✔ **Use manners.** The words "thank you" are magic. I know when I pick up the phone and hear, "Dirk Zeller, I want to thank you for . . ." I tune in for more!

    A perfect opportunity to say thank you is when the individual is already a customer or has purchased in the past. You may be following up with someone who bought over the Internet or through former sales agents. Instead of the typical, "I see you bought _____ from us, and I would like to sell you something else," launch it with a thank-you: "I'd like to thank you for your recent order. I see we had the opportunity to provide you with toner and copier paper."

Putting it all together

More than a few salespeople are intimidated by the task of crafting an opening statement. Coming up with an introduction that captures the prospect's interest can seem daunting. And, indeed, your seven-second speech may take hours of wordsmithing — and many more in practice, fine tuning, and evaluating. I'm here to help. In this section, I put together a fill-in-the-blank statement for you. Use it as a framework for your own customized openers.

I even provide a list of word suggestions (see Table 9-1 for some examples) so you can plug in the best description for your particular needs. Use these words or explore through your thesaurus to find your own. I suggest you continually work to expand the chart to include as many as 20 or 30 words in each category. Then you'll always have the right words at your fingertips.

Table 9-1	Words to Use in an Opening Statement				
Shrinking Verbs	*Negative-Result Nouns*	*Expanding Verbs*	*Positive-Result Nouns*	*Call-to-Action*	*Closing Phrases*
Reduce	Challenges	Enjoy	Profits	Evaluate	That work for you
Lower	Troubles	Enhance	Sales	Analyze	That will help you
Modify	Waste	Expand	Income	Discuss	That would be of value to you
Decrease	Costs	Maximize	Productivity	Explore	That would interest you
Eliminate	Expenses	Increase	Time		
Cut	Hassles	Aid	Savings		

Use the following outline and word list from Table 9-1 verbatim to jazz up your existing statements or to prime your mental pump when creating your own. Break down the fill-in-the-blank statement into its parts:

1. *"Hello, [name of prospect], I'm [your full name] with [your company's name]."*

   Easy enough. Just remember to verify the correct pronunciation of the prospect's name before you call.

2. *"The reason for my call today is, depending on your experience in [specialty area], there is a probability we can aid you, like we have [name drop], with [shrinking verb] your [negative result noun] while also [expanding verb] your [positive result noun].*

In the bracketed *specialty area,* briefly describe what you and your company offer customers. In the *name drop* brackets, plug in a name familiar to the client — whether an admired industry professional you both know or a prestigious client that the prospect may relate to.

Now, you get into the mini grammar lesson! In brackets, you see the phrases *shrinking verb, negative-result noun,* and *expanding verb.* Basically, this sentence highlights the benefit that you can provide, by showing how you can turn an undesirable situation into a positive one for the company. Thus, the *bad* verb and noun versus the *good* verb and noun. My list in Table 9-1 gives you some common words you can choose. You should come up with something like, ". . . we can aid you in *reducing* your *expenses* while also *maximizing* your *productivity."*

3. *"If you have a moment, I'd like to [call-to-action phrase] your situation to see if this is something [closing phrase]."*

   Finally, you're ready for the wrap-up, incorporating a *call-to-action* phrase with a *closing phrase.* For example, ". . . I'd like to *discuss* your situation to see if this is something *that would be of value to you."*

By using this script, you have now constructed an effective opening statement.

Delivering a Knock-Down-the-Door Opener

Writing your opening statement (see preceding section) is only half the task; delivering it effectively is just as important. The way that you write is entirely different from the way that you speak. So what looked great on paper now has to be brought to life to be sure it also *sounds* great. You want to sound confident, professional, knowledge-able, and helpful — in essence, be the expert. This section shows you how to rehearse your opening, how to determine whether it's effective, and how to make adjustments to it.

Rehearsing for the real thing

Before you pick up the phone and try your opening, you want to practice. Investing the time to rehearse and practice your state-ments put the words to the test. Does your introduction sound natu-ral? Persuasive? Is your opener attention getting? Intriguing? Is your description of your company's focus clear? Do your words present a compelling case to explore further? You know only if you test them.

In order to rehearse your opening statement, follow these steps to ensure your opening doesn't fall flat:

1. **Find a coworker, friend, or partner to role-play with you.**

   Go through your script a few times and then ask for feedback.

2. **Take the suggestions and adjust accordingly, and then test again.**

   In this go-round, focus on the words rather than your delivery. Check out Table 9-1 or a thesaurus to adjust your script.

3. **After you tweak the opening based on the feedback you receive, practice the delivery alone.**

   When doing so, vary the tone and pace of your voice to so you're more interesting to listen to. Recalibrate the emphasis points and downswings as necessary.

4. **After you feel comfortable with the opening, role-play with another salesperson or your sales manager and ask for more feedback.**

   Try delivering the script with a few variations: maybe slow the pace in one delivery or emphasize different phrases in another. Ask which version sounded best.

5. **Apply the feedback you receive and record and listen to your opening.**

   This step separates the top salespeople from all the others. Hearing yourself allows you the closest thing to objectivity you can get in evaluating your delivery. And listening to your recorded self is actually closer to the way your prospects hear you on the phone. It shows you how you really come across. The recording device demonstrates, unfiltered, how your prospect hears you.

   When listening to yourself for the first time, don't do it at the office! Take the recording home and, before you turn on the tape, pour yourself a glass of wine. You're going to need it — you probably won't like what you hear!

6. **Then make the necessary changes and test again.**

   Adjust the emphasis points, play with the tone, change the words you're using, or just spend some more time practicing if your delivery needs work.

Your opening is a work in progress. Professional golfers are always tinkering with their swings in hopes of improving their scores. Likewise, a salesperson can benefit from tinkering with the opening statement. And sometimes you may stumble upon an unconventional twist that increases the effectiveness of your openers.

You not only want to rehearse your opening before you start making calls, but you also want to revisit it again and again during your sales career to fine-tune your opening. Perfecting your opening statement requires patience and commitment to ongoing improvement. When I'm asked how long it takes to become an outstanding salesperson, I reply, "Forty-five years, and I'm still working on it." Focus on getting better with each day.

Measuring your effectiveness

Because the purpose of an opening statement is to open the door with the prospect, you can consider your opener a success if it gets you to the presentation level. You can measure the success rate, then, of your opener with the *contact-to-appointment ratio,* which means measuring how many contacts you made (in which you reached and spoke to a live person) against the number of appointments you scheduled.

A high close ratio, say 7 appointments out of 10 contacts, means your opening statement must be pretty convincing. A more disparate ratio — 1 out of 10 — indicates your opener may need some fine tuning (for tips on how to do this, see the preceding section).

Don't make the mistake of using your sales numbers as a gauge; too many variables come between the opening statement and the close to rely on that factor. Stick with the contact-to-appointment ratio.

The objective of your opening statement isn't beautiful prose, but results. If you ever watched golf champ Lee Trevino swing, you would swear the big banana arc of his golf shot would never work. It worked well enough, however, to win him six major championships in golf. The same is true for your opening statement. If it's not pretty, but it's effective . . . who cares!

Dodging Kiss-of-Death Openings

Before you even begin the sales process, a kiss-of-death opening statement can bury your chances in less than seven seconds. Why? Kiss-of-death starts create resistance and shut down receptiveness. They result in high levels of, "I'm busy now," "Not interested," and "Don't call me; I'll call you." You want to avoid such starts like the plague. But what does a kiss-of-death beginning look like? Here are a few examples to avoid at all costs.

Ask for just what you need

I coached a financial-planning client who was consistently getting shut down during his opening statement. Immediately after identifying himself, the cold-call prospect would reply, "Not interested," or something along the lines of "Fred Jones at XYZ Company handles our money."

I asked him how long he thought he really needed on the initial call to pique the prospect's interest and have a shot at booking an appointment. "A couple of minutes," he said. Well, you can imagine that it took us some time to agree on a length that we both felt may work. With effort, we got it down to 37 seconds.

And that's exactly what my client asks for from his prospects: 37 seconds of their time! The results have been amazing. He has doubled the number of presentations he's making. Is the 37 seconds unorthodox? A gimmick? Sure —but it works.

Inviting "no" responses

If you give the prospect an opportunity to say "no" in the first few seconds, you find your opening statement aborted and your sales call derailed. Consider carefully any content that allows for a response. For example:

> *"My name is Bob. I sell widgets. May I take a few minutes of your time to talk with you about them?"*

This statement practically says "no" *for* the prospect. When you ask anything remotely close to "Do you have time to talk?", expect to hear a hang-up click in response. To make matters worse, this statement is me-centered: *"My* name is . . ."; *"I* sell . . ."; and "May *I.* . . . "

Here's another deadly lead related to inviting "no" responses:

> *"I sent you a brochure about XYZ Brand widgets and was wondering if you got it."*

Sure, he got it . . . and he's already thrown it away and forgotten about it. This scenario is lose-lose: If you don't hear a "no," then you get something along the lines of, "I may have seen it, but had no interest in it." That forces you to divert your efforts into over-coming an objection. Giving the prospect this power is another kiss-of-death move that would need a jaws-of-life solution to save it.

Putting on the sleaze

I've done my best not to bring up the image of the sultan-of-sleaze salesman. This mostly undeserved stereotype emerged in the 1970s when verbal judo techniques were practiced by a few. You can just picture him, can't you? Leisure suit, gold chain, open collar, and pinky ring. But even more insidious are the tactics this image evokes: a fast-talking, strong-arming, sign-at-whatever-cost image that has resulted in more damage to the salesperson's reputation than *The Godfather* movies have for Sicilians.

When you're speaking to a contact for the first time, the last thing you want to do is to conjure up this scary image. (Remember, no second chances to make a first impression.) But certain wording can make you come across as the sleazy salesperson. For example, "If I could show you a way to reduce your inventory costs, you would want to hear more, wouldn't you?"

 Tie-down endings such as ". . . wouldn't you agree?" attempt to entrap the prospect into saying yes. The underlying message is, "You'd have to be an idiot to disagree." It may have worked back in the '70s, but businesspeople have had a few decades to recognize the signs of sales sleaze. If you're lucky enough not to get an immediate hang-up, you spend the rest of the sales process trying to win back trust.

Avoiding "And how are you today?"

First cousin to the sleaze lead, this opening, "And how are you today?" just screams to the world that you are a salesperson — and not even a good one. Many salespeople open with this question because they believe it helps build rapport. But these days, "How are you today?" has even less relevance and resonance than the *Star Trek* Vulcan salute.

 We have a money jar in our Sales Champions sales department. When anyone hears another salesperson executing a poor opening statement, a dollar goes into the jar. But if someone uses "And how are you today?" it's $10. That's how much I hate this opening.

Let me share with you a few reasons why you don't want to use this opening statement:

> ✔ **It's not genuine.** Be honest with yourself. You really don't care how they are — and they know it. To really engage the client at that level, your heart and brain need to be connected and caring. And that's too much to do in the first seven seconds of your relationship.

✔ **It's devoid of creativity.** This opener is so lacking originality that you not only won't grab the attention of your prospect, but you'll also dull her mind and push it to auto-pilot. You're getting awfully close to the "no" switch.

✔ **You open yourself up to a cold-water response.** This type of response from the prospect is one from which you can't possibly come back. For example:

- "My department didn't meet quota for the third quarter in a row, and I could get fired."

- "My wife just served me with divorce papers."

- "I have a terrible headache."

Oh, sure, you can find dozens of ways you can reply. But none can get you back on the sales track.

If you're calling a current customer or someone you know fairly well, "how are you?" may be appropriate. But be prepared to listen — and hold off your sales opening for another call.

Building Your Elevator Speech

Can you effectively convey what you and your company do beyond your job title and list of services? A powerful, clear, and succinct explanation has great value to you as a salesperson. Having such a description prepared and at hand provides a ready summary from which you can pull. Among its many merits, your elevator speech serves as the foundation for your opening statement.

The term *30-second elevator speech* is age-old jargon in the sales profession that describes your explanation of what you or your company does. The statement should be brief enough to deliver in the time it takes to ride an elevator — about 30 seconds, or 100 to 150 words. In today's marketplace, however, I don't believe you're granted even 30 seconds — it's quickly shrinking from elevator ride to revolving-door entry! This section points out some helpful tips to assist you in drafting your elevator speech.

Accentuate the positive

Part of building a good elevator statement is cogently conveying what your company does. However, what you sell isn't enough. Often, the prospect doesn't know anything about your company, doesn't want to know, has never bought anything from your company in the past, and doesn't expect to buy anything in the future. You can reverse this by conveying your business in terms of *benefits* to the prospect. For example:

"I'm Bob Smith with ACME Adhesives. We are an all-in-one adhesives group that specializes in the plumbing industry."

 At Sales Champions, one of our primary services is coaching. Trust me; no one wakes up in the morning wanting to buy coaching. However, they *do* want the benefits we provide through coaching: more time off, higher sales, increased income, growing repeat and referral business, and more prestige because they're the leading salespeople at their firm. *This* is what we sell — not coaching. What are you providing and selling?

Going beyond your job title

No matter your job title (whether it's salesperson, account executive, vice president of sales, or certified financial planner), this label doesn't describe who you are or what you do. You want your elevator speech to be crystal clear in what you do. Describing what you do for your clients, rather than giving your title, allows you to clearly communicate the *benefits* that you have to offer. Relying on your job title to parlay that information could, in some cases, mislead the prospect or be totally meaningless.

For example, say your job title is sales consultant and your responsibility is to acquire and serve new accounts. In your prospect's work environment, the *sales consultant* title is carried by administrative or support staff, individuals who possibly even report to your prospect. That title doesn't mean anything to your client.

But if you give the client some concrete info about what you do and how it can benefit her, then she can appreciate much better what you have to offer. Take a look at a couple examples:

- ✔ Instead of copier salesperson: "I'm a document specialist who creates efficiencies and cost savings for companies through proper utilization of office equipment.

- ✔ Instead of long-distance salesperson: "I'm a communication specialist who increases and enhances performance of companies through advanced communication technology."

Setting yourself apart

You can also use your elevator speech to stand out from the competition. In addition to focusing on what you *do* rather than who you are, here are some other tips for making a lasting and positive impression:

✔ **Review corporate materials.** Study *all* of your company's materials, including consumer brochures and single-product promotions, annual reports, media kits, marketing pieces, press releases, the corporate Web site, news articles about the company, outlines, corporate sales memos, and annual reports. Then, from what you've absorbed, answer these questions:

- What is our area of specialization?
- What are the top-ten claims or areas of emphasis?
- Which of these pieces clearly describes what we do?

✔ **Put on customer-colored glasses.** When you can see your business through the eyes of your customers, you're better poised to position the salient information that matters most to them. What must the prospect hear to understand what you do and the benefits she will receive?

✔ **Tackle the problem in a sales meeting.** Gather the input of other sales colleagues in the company. An effective exercise is to call a meeting and ask each person present to craft an answer to your "What does the company do?" question. Give them a short time limit — less than two minutes is preferable. You want their honest gut reaction to that question. Then review the statements together.

I find it best to write them for all to see on a board. Don't be surprised if the responses are all over the map. You may wonder whether you all even work for the same company!

Work together to select the best answers, and combine related descriptions to whittle down the list. After some culling and editing, you may come up with one or two that everyone likes. Then role-play the statements to further test the elevator speeches. Ask yourself:

- Does it sound right?
- Is it compelling enough?
- Does it accurately describe what we do?
- Is it too long?

Take the time to edit it, practice it, and play with it until the delivery is comfortable.

✔ **Get feedback from a trusted client.** After you polish and practice your elevator speech, consider calling your best clients and testing it. Ask them the same questions you asked of yourself and request their honest feedback — no soft-pedaling!

Chapter 10

Getting Out of the Answers and Into the Questions

Silver-tongued. Fast-talking. Able to sell snow to an Eskimo. Expressions such as these are often used to describe salespeople. The traditional image portrays salespeople as using the gift of gab, the ability to *talk* people into buying anything.

In reality, sales doesn't work this way. Like the proverbial horse to water, you can lead a prospect through a sales presentation, but you can't make him buy. As a sales professional, you don't talk a customer into buying, but, instead, *question* the prospect into recognizing that *you* have the answer to his needs.

Oh, sure, you still run through your sales presentation. But before you offer your solutions, you lead the prospect to the obvious conclusions through your deftly crafted and choreographed questioning process. Oftentimes, not meeting your sales goals is a sign that your questioning skills may need a tune-up. This section can help you draft the right types of questions to turn around your sales.

Questions show you care

The sister company to Sales Champions — Real Estate Champions — provides education, coaching, and training to real estate professionals. In the rare instances that sales calls make it past the gatekeeper to my office, I find that at least 40 percent of the salespeople launch right into their "pitch" without asking a single question. Within one minute, the fact that they don't know anything about Real Estate Champions is clear.

I usually stop the caller in midsentence and ask, "What do you think my company, Real Estate Champions, does?" I hear some vague, garbled, uncertain response about real estate sales. I politely say "Thank you" and hang up. I don't want to buy from someone who demonstrates a total lack of interest in my business's true needs. It's clear to me that this sort of individual cares only about making a sale.

Understanding the Importance of Asking Questions

A top salesperson helps match a tailored solution to a prospect's specific need. In order to pinpoint that need and customize your sales presentation, you must have information: the who, what, when, where, how, and why of the need; the decision-making process; previous experience with other providers; and how this prospect is differentiated from others. And asking questions is the route to knowledge.

The more questions you ask, the more information you gather. And, just as in any field or profession, the more information you have, the more effective you are in your job. When you're talking or telling, you only reconfirm what you already know. When you're *asking,* you open up yourself to discovering something new. This section explains why asking the right questions is vital to you having a good call or a hang-up.

Building trust through questions

At the early stages of your dialogue with a prospect, in order to get off on the right foot, you want to build trust with the prospect and to lay the foundations of a mutually beneficial business relationship. Just as you develop positive *personal* connections, you know that you make a better impression when you focus on the other person rather than talking about yourself.

Creating the E. F. Hutton effect

Television viewers of the 1970s and '80s may recall a series of commercials featuring the stock brokerage firm of E. F. Hutton. In each spot, a buzzing crowd halted all conversation as people strained to listen in on an investment discussion. "When E. F. Hutton talks, people listen," is how each commercial concluded.

Making a declaration that's powerful enough to stop the conversation — or at least intrigue the listener to hear more — is the intent of this approach: Instead of asking permission to question the prospect — you *announce* the importance of what you are about to do. For example:

✔ *"Bob, I have some very important questions to ask you. Do you have a few minutes?"*

✔ *"Bob, there are some critical issues I'd like to ask you about. Is now a good time?"*

The words *very important* and *critical* catch the prospect's attention and generate curiosity, resulting in the lean-in, high-alert response that you want.

Use this approach with care, however. From this setup, the questions you launch had better be meaningful to the prospect, or the call could be over in less than a minute. If you ask questions about the prospect's current supplier of products or services that you're trying to sell, you have asked a bad question. You just asked a you-centered question rather than a them-centered question. The focus of the call is not about you at this juncture; it's about the prospect.

By asking questions, you create an interesting dynamic. Even though you're controlling the conversation, you shift the spotlight on the prospect. And even though the prospect is revealing more than you are, your potential customer leaves the interaction with a clearer perception of *you.* "Boy, that salesperson was sure insightful and service oriented. I can tell that company will give my business the attention I want."

Asking permission to ask

Before you jump into a deluge of questions though, you want to ask the prospect if you can ask her some questions. Believe it or not, *asking permission* to ask questions is effective and shows the prospect that you respect her and her time. By allowing the prospect the *choice* of answering your questions, you frame the opening dialogue and launch it on a positive path.

Here are some ways to ask permission that I have found to be effective:

> *"Bob, would it be okay if I ask you a few questions about your business?"*

> *"Bob, would it be alright to spend a few moments asking you questions about your company?"*

> *"Bob, could we review some questions I've prepared, so I understand your department needs?"*

By showing this courtesy, you're also more likely to gain the prospect's agreement to reschedule the conversation if this time isn't convenient.

Give the prospect a clear idea of how much time you need for questions, keeping it to ten minutes or less. If you reach the ten-minute mark and you're not done, you may ask for a few more minutes — or suggest scheduling another appointment with more time to talk. Don't continue without permission; the prospect may feel that you pulled a bait-and-switch.

Qualifying through Questions

Having spent more than 20 years of my life in 100-percent commission sales with no salary base, company car, expense account, and so forth, I'm fanatical about knowing the opportunity cost of a prospect. When you get paid only for results, you do everything you can to zero in on prospects most likely to offer a high return on your investment of time and energy.

Qualifying is one of the most important sales stages during which to use questions. When you qualify, you're determining the needs, wants, and desires of your prospects. Certainly, to make a sale, you need to know those factors. During qualifying, however, you also assess and evaluate the probability of making the sale and determine the size of the sale. Great salespeople are extremely effective qualifiers of prospects.

Gathering information about the client's unique needs, gauging the urgency of the need, getting a sense of his decision-making power — these are all benefits of the qualifying phase of your call. This section gives the lowdown on each aspect of qualifying.

Getting the prospect to open up

As you prepare your questions, you want to pose queries that provide you information and allow the prospect to share his needs and desires. When asking questions, you basically have two types of questions to ask:

- ✓ **Open-ended questions:** These types of questions generate details, information, facts, experiences, and opinions — these are the questions that bring you the knowledge you need to effectively qualify a prospect. Make sure you use numerous open-ended questions during your call.

  A couple examples of open-ended questions include

  - What are the most significant challenges you are experiencing in your division or business right now?

  - If a widget company like ours could provide additional service and value to you, what would that look like for you?

  Prepare a list of open-ended questions that connect with the product or service you're selling. Be sure to plan open-ended questions in advance. You don't want to "wing it" with open-ended questions. (Check out the next section for more on asking open-ended questions.)

- ✓ **Closed-ended questions:** These types of questions elicit a simple yes, no, or maybe answer. Closed-ended questions have their place in the sales presentation. However, you want to use them sparingly. Some examples include

  - Do you see yourself using our service?

  - Have I demonstrated our value well enough for you to consider purchasing?

You can use closed-ended questions in trial closes that test where you are in the sales process. You can also use them to confirm information that has been shared to make sure that you understand the prospect's needs and desires. They are also used effectively in final close statements before you take the order.

Not just the facts, ma'am

When you ask your open-ended questions, you're not only looking for facts. You also want a fuller, more-dimensional rap sheet on the individual: Emotions, feelings, values, and ideals as they relate to the business at hand and problems that need solutions are all critical in order to know the prospect's modus operandi. And open-ended questions that elicit these particulars are of the utmost importance.

Why and how questions garner much of this information. At a minimum, your questions should identify *why* the prospect is considering action or change and *how* they measure, gauge, consider, or evaluate proposals or a long-term relationship. Consider asking the following questions:

> *"Why are you considering a change?"*
>
> *"Why do you feel you have a problem in this area?"*
>
> *"Why have you done business with these companies in the past?"*
>
> *"Why is the timing right now?"*
>
> *"Why are you considering this company?"*
>
> *"How will you make the decision?"*
>
> *"How did you typically make decisions of this magnitude in the past?"*
>
> *"How will you evaluate the proposals?"*
>
> *"How will you weigh the priorities you have outlined for me?"*
>
> *"How would you gauge a long-term, successful relationship with a service provider like me?"*

You ask these types of questions to determine timeframe, decision process, and the odds of you having a reasonable chance at earning their business. If you can't get favorable responses that offer you a reasonable chance to win new business, you may be forced to find another prospect and move on.

Checking Your Prospect's DNA²

Knowing the prospect's DNA² (desire, need, ability, and authority) is paramount to your sales success. If one or more of these four factors are out of line, you may not make the sale or — at the very least — you'll find the process lengthier than you'd like.

The only way to find out the DNA² is to ask questions. In this section I look at a prospect's desire, need, ability, and authority to place the order with you.

Uncovering that object of desire

Desire relates to the prospect's motivation to do something — the greater the desire, the more motivated the buyer is to take action. A high level of desire often means a shorter decision-making period and less concern about price. Clearly, a prospect with desire is a great prospect for you.

You want to add questions to your plan that help you determine the prospect's desires. The best sign for strong desire is that the prospect has a plan. She knows her requirements for service and time to make a decision and has quantifiable expectations that you can uncover as you ask the right questions. Your questions should be timeline focused. You want to know how quickly she will make the decision and if the decision is imminent.

Some example questions include

> *"How long have you been considering changing suppliers?"*
>
> *"What is your timeline to make the change?"*
>
> *"If we could provide you with what you're looking for, what would the next steps be?"*

Don't mistake interest level for desire. Often, an individual who eagerly engages in the sales process may be at the exploratory phase — gathering information just as you are. This type of prospect may give himself away by expressing unrealistic expectations. For example, an "interested" real estate prospect may suggest selling his home for $50,000 more than it's worth and buying a home for $50,000 below market value. In truth, this person — though interested in the real estate climate — doesn't have a high desire to get out of his home and into a new one. He's simply testing the waters.

Working on a need-to-know basis

The quantifiable void between where the prospect is now and where she wants to be defines the prospect's *need* for your product or service. Your job is to get a precise measure of this void — the more exact your figures are, the easier you can successfully respond to the need. And, of course, the bigger the need, the more certain the sale. Some example questions include

> *"How large a problem is what we are discussing today?"*
>
> *"What do you feel is the cost of this problem in lost revenue to your company?"*

"If you could design the ideal solution, what would it look like?"

After you identify the need, the next step is to gauge its size and significance. "How painful is this problem?" and "What are the costs?" are focuses for good questions. The bigger the problem and the bigger the costs of the problem, the larger the desire. Ask what it's costing your prospect in revenue, efficiency, labor, waste, customer service, and repeat business. Also ask "Is the potential sale an already budgeted item?" and "When is the proposed implementation scheduled if you do go forward with a purchase?" Asking can help you determine if she is merely information gathering or really going to take action.

When you devise questions, you want to get the specifications in terms of numbers: hours saved, production increased, dollars reduced, and amount of new revenue created. Instead of accepting vague answers like "It would be worth a lot" or "I could save a fortune," probe for specifics. Some examples include

- ✔ How many dollars?
- ✔ How much time?
- ✔ How big an increase in revenue?

With these answers, you can demonstrate how your service can satisfy the prospect's need. For example, you discover that the prospect has a budget that is $1,000 below what your office copier costs. You also find out that the company makes an average of 50,000 copies a year. Because your machine would reduce print costs by one cent per copy, you can show how, over the course of just two years, the machine would pay for the additional hit on the budget.

Assessing financial ability

The prospect may have the desire and need for your product, but *financial ability* is essential for you to make a sale. That's why it's important to ask about money at the question stage, in order to determine whether budget is a barrier. Some examples include the following:

"Is this type of purchase in the budget?"

"Will you be using working capital, or do we need to establish a payment plan for a purchase like this?"

"Do you usually lease or purchase these types of investments?"

Just because you receive a negative response to any of these questions doesn't mean the discussion is over. Further questions can help you determine when and how the circumstances might change — you may even be able to come upon some creative payment possibilities. Questions such as these help you to make those determinations:

> *"Is there another budget area you could use to make the purchase?"*
>
> *"Is there enough value in the purchase to override the budget?"*
>
> *"Could we explore some financing solutions?"*
>
> *"When does the next budget cycle commence?"*

Financial limitations are the most common objection used to derail a sale. A skillful salesperson can use questions to help recognize when budget is played to evade and when it is a legitimate reason for not moving ahead. Check out Chapter 13 for more info.

Measuring authority level

The final element of DNA^2, decision-making authority, is essential to bind the other components into a formula that ensures sales success. Desire, need, and ability can all be in place, but they don't matter a whit if you're talking to a person who can't say "Yes."

Don't assume that just because the company representative is willing to talk to you, he's in a position to make a decision. Lots of employees like to project a "big-cheese" image, when, in fact, they have little authority.

Questions such as these can ferret out the *faux* decision makers:

> *"Are you the sole decision maker with regard to this purchase?"*
>
> *"Is there anyone else who will have influence over this investment?"*
>
> *"Is there anyone else involved that I should send the information to?"*
>
> *"Is there anyone else who should attend the sales presentation?"*

Nothing is more frustrating and ineffective than to get through your presentation and have someone say, "Well, I'll pass this information on to my boss. He's the person who will make the final decision."

Now, you're relying on how well this intermediary can make your presentation for you. I guarantee that it won't be done as well as you would do it.

Past the Qualifying Round: Asking More Questions

So your questioning tactics worked to qualify the prospect and determine her desire, need, ability, and authority. Are you ready to move on from the questions and into the answers? Not necessarily. Questions are also a great tool to position yourself to build your case before you go into your presentation. This section helps you address questions after you've qualified your prospects.

Circling the problems

The questioning process is guaranteed to raise what salespeople euphemistically like to call *challenges*. You may also know them as objections, roadblocks, or problems. Whatever you call these hindrances, uncovering them is imperative, so don't shy away from asking the questions that bring them up.

And then, after you uncover these problems, be prepared to ask *more* questions. Before you fly in like Superman with a solution, keep asking questions until you can see the problem from all sides. Don't leave it to chance that your first reading is complete. The solution may be 180 degrees different than either you or your prospect first imagined. Ask questions like:

> *"What sort of solutions have you tried in the past to resolve this problem?"*
>
> *"Why do you think these efforts didn't solve the problem?"*
>
> *"What do you see as the most logical solution?"*
>
> *"Have you ever tried _____?"*
>
> *"In your unique situation, do you think _____ or _____ would work best?"*
>
> *"If you found the perfect solution, what would it look like to you?"*
>
> *"How does your boss see the problem?"*

By deftly asking these questions, you can effectively come to a solution that pleases the prospect and puts you in prime position to be the hero. After you're there, you can tie the sale up with questions like:

> *"Do you see this as the most logical solution?"*
>
> *"Is there another answer that neither of us has thought about yet?"*
>
> *"Have the other people or companies come up with similar recommendations as I have for this problem?"*
>
> *"If they differ, how do we differ from them?"*

You're ready to close if you get favorable responses to these questions. Turn to Chapter 14 for more.

Checking for intention

The questioning process typically gives the salesperson a fairly accurate read on the prospect's intentions to buy. But asking outright isn't only admissible, but also wise. At this point, you don't have to be as direct as "Can I have your business?" Instead, you can take the prospect's temperature with questions like:

> *"Do you see yourself using a service like mine?"*
>
> *"Could you see yourself doing business with my firm in the near future?"*

Remember to anticipate responses and be prepared for any answer so that you can follow up appropriately. In the case of a yes answer, you can ask questions like the following to keep the ball rolling in a positive, productive direction:

> *"Under what circumstances would you see that happening?"*
>
> *"What are the steps we need to take to make that happen?"*
>
> *"If I draft a proposal, would you be willing to review it?"*

The follow-up question to a no response is straightforward: "Why?" Or, to be more specific, "Why do you feel there aren't any circumstances that would enable us to work together?" You can often guide the prospect to the sale without knowing why you're being stopped, slowed down, or detoured, but the word *why* is one of the most powerful tools a salesperson has to use. By asking why, you're prompting the prospect to explain his logic, decision, or action, getting you to the root of the problem, challenge, or barrier.

The power of why

One winter when my family vacationed in Palm Desert, California, my 5-year-old son, Wesley, woke up one morning and decided he was going to open a lemonade stand. We were staying on a golf course, and he saw a ready market for his product among the golfers coming off the green behind our condo.

Wesley and I went to the store and bought lemonade, cookies, and paper cups, as well as construction paper and felt pens to make a sign. Later that day, Wesley's lemonade stand opened. When he spied the first group of players to come our way, I could barely contain him from approaching them before they finished putting. I held my breath as he launched into his sales presentation. Then I heard one of the "prospects" say no. I prayed in my head, "Please don't let him get discouraged."

But before I could complete the thought, I heard him ask, "Why? It's really good lemonade; it's refreshing, and I made it myself." These guys were no match for my 5-year-old. They were the first of many people to buy from him that day. He made more than $22 in lemonade sales before he ran out. You can learn a lot about sales from a child who isn't afraid to ask the big sales question: "Why?"

How to Get Better Results: Five Strategies

The questioning phase is critical to the sales process. But it's not all that difficult when you follow five basic strategies to help you form questions. These aren't "steps" that must be taken in a certain sequence; rather, they're helpful avenues that can improve your results and help you get to the next phase of the process more successfully.

Know your goal

You've heard it before: If you don't know where you're going, any path will take you there. And if you don't set your sights on the purpose of your call, your questions are untargeted and likely to generate useless information.

Determine, before punching in that phone number, what you want to accomplish with this particular call. Are you trying to generate a lead? Get a referral? Create an appointment? Convey information? Make a sale? Know where you want to go so you can ask the questions that will take you there.

For example, say you're calling a lead to discover how the company goes about making a purchase decision. You can then dispense with queries that you'd ask to close the sale and tailor your question to reveal the decision-making process.

Narrow the focus

When forming questions, simplify and focus your questions to a narrower point. Questions that are too broad based and general may be difficult for a prospect to answer or at least summarize in a way that's helpful. The prospect may not even know how to *begin* answering questions like "What do you look for in a supplier?"; "How do you choose a vendor?"; or "What do you expect from this type of service?"

If, for example, you want to know what the company looks for in a provider, try asking the prospect to share past experiences:

> *"What were the determining factors you used in selecting your current vendor?"*

> *"What were the factors that made you terminate your relationship with your previous provider?"*

Tap into fantasy

Often, prospects have difficulty defining exactly what it is they want or need from a provider. Instead of asking a prospect to tell you what kind of company he wants to work with, get him to tap into his imagination.

For example, have you ever heard a single friend try to describe the type of person she wants to meet? "Oh, I don't know . . . someone nice, with a sense of humor. Nice looking. I guess I'll know when I meet him." Yet if you ask her which actor or celebrity she finds most desirable? "George Clooney," she says without missing a beat. Or if you tell her to describe the perfect first date: "We meet at a park and stroll past flower gardens as we're lost in conversation. . . ." Well, you get the idea.

Try the same technique with a tongue-tied prospect.

> *"If we could create the ideal situation, what would it look like?"*

> *"If you had the perfect _____ designed for you, what would it have?"*

"If you could design the perfect solution to the problem we are discussing, what would it have?"

Focus on benefits before features

Results-focused questions help identify the bottom-line benefits the prospect is seeking. For example, instead of hammering on about the features of your widget — such as improved design, smaller size, or fast performance — ask questions that pinpoint the results that are important to the client. If you find out that she's looking for a widget that can cut production time in half, you can then focus on the fast-action features of the widget rather than the slim, streamlined look.

Questions that uncover the desired benefits may include:

"How will you define outstanding results?"

"What will cause you to know you received good value?"

"How will you measure a successful result?"

Present a choice

If your prospect resists answering direct questions, you can ask questions that offer choices. This technique is a gentler way to extract information, one that is often used for 3-year-olds establishing their independence ("What do you want for breakfast today — cereal with a banana-and-raisin face or cowboy eggs?").

Instead of pointed questions such as "Bob, where are you getting your widgets now?" or "Bob, what is your budget for this project?" you can ask questions in a way that the prospect has a choice between two answers, which creates a feeling of control. For example:

"Bob, are you getting office supplies from XYZ Company or ABC Company?"

"Is your budget for this project more or less than $1 million?"

Avoiding Question Quicksand

Salespeople can make a handful of missteps during their questioning. In the heat of the moment of working with a prospect, falling back on these mistakes is easy. When you don't know what to say or where to go next, that is when slip-ups surely rear their ugly head. This section highlights some question situations you don't want to get stuck in.

Sounding like a survey

Often, inexperienced salespeople are directed by their sales managers to stick to the script. It's fair advice. But a combination of nervousness and unfamiliarity with the process often results in a detached and robot-like effect when you follow the script too closely. Although scripts are essential for every salesperson's success, you want to avoid coming off as if you're conducting a survey. (Check out Chapter 4 for developing a script.)

Invest time, in advance of your calls, to familiarize yourself with the script and anticipate the possible responses (not many new ones are out there). Then use feedback-response techniques to create a sense of dialogue with the prospect. Don't jump into the next question, but instead, react to the prospect's response, using words like *great, fantastic, terrific, ouch,* or *I'm sorry.*

Then replay the response. And remember: Feed back the prospect's response; don't parrot the exact words the prospect used. Here's an example of a good feedback response:

> *"Mr. Jones, I'm hearing that you have concerns about the cost of replacing your copier with the newest, high-tech versions. Is my understanding correct?"*

This type of feedback helps create a connection and moves you away from sounding like prerecorded, automated blah.

Asking GIGO questions

When querying your prospect, you want to stay away from GIGO questions. GIGO is a computer term from the 1970s that stands for "garbage in, garbage out." It refers to the truism that if you input bad information, your output will be bad information. Likewise with the questions you ask during your sales call: Bad questions result in worthless answers.

What makes for a bad question? Avoid anything that may open you up for negative observations of your company, queries that are so general they simply won't elicit a meaningful response, and questions that may generate questions that you aren't prepared to answer. Here are a few GIGO questions to avoid:

- Do you have any questions for me?
- Do you need anything else from me?
- Is the product or service you're currently getting acceptable to you?

These questions lead nowhere and almost assure you a response that you don't want . . . a negative one.

Avoiding a premature presentation

When a prospect throws up a stall, question, concern, or objection, your knee-jerk reaction may be to leap into presentation mode in order to counter the concern. Resist at all cost! This is a diversionary tactic on the prospect's part (whether she realizes it or not). If you fall for it, you're sure to get off-course.

You shouldn't take lines such as "I have a concern about . . ." or "I don't know if you would be right for us" as an opening for objection-handling techniques or benefits-and-value discussions. Instead, these are openings for a professional to deliver more questions to uncover more information. Respond with:

> "If we can take a few more minutes so I can find out more about your concerns, I will be better able to combine my responses to what will be most beneficial to you"

> "With your permission, let me ask you a few more questions, so I can really understand your situation and so I know I am making the correct recommendations for you and your company."

The only way to get back on track is to ask questions at this point. Asking the right questions can help turn around your sinking ship.

Chapter 11

Mastering the Art of Listening and Silence

*M*any salespeople like to listen . . . to themselves. Chances are, you've followed a career path in sales because family members and friends have always told you that you have the "gift of gab." Reaching out to strangers, initiating conversations, and making others comfortable are indeed qualities that make for great salespeople. But more important — *much* more important — than the gift of gab is the gift of *listening*.

In any situation involving a salesperson and a prospect or client, one party is more important than the other; one individual carries the more critical information, relevant experience, and valuable opinions and comments. ***Hint:*** It isn't the salesperson! The prospect or client holds the key to unlocking the secrets that lead to a sale. This is especially true for phone sales: Because the nature of the medium precludes the telltale signals of body language, you must listen even more closely for verbal messages and other sound clues (for instance, does the clicking of keyboard keys indicate the prospect is distracted by another project?).

Why is listening so important? The answer to *why* is this: more sales, shorter sales cycle, higher conversion of leads, and more referrals. In this chapter, I show you the link between listening and better sales results. And after you understand the importance of the *why*, the *how* becomes much easier. The more you can orient yourself to listen, the more you'll see sales results mounting up.

Honing Your Listening Skills

Proactive, type-A, energetic, action-oriented sales professionals may have difficulty imagining themselves as listeners. After all, listening is so *passive*. Don't you have to do something to make a sale? Absolutely! You have to listen.

Listening is an *active* behavior. It requires much greater focus than talking — you expend a lot of energy to capture, record, process, and catalogue the data you pick up when listening. So discard any notion that what I'm talking about is defined by "doing nothing." Listening effectively isn't easy work. Holding yourself back from blathering can be a struggle. Asking good questions and shutting up for answers is a challenge. But this kind of hard work pays off in a big way.

Listening is also a *smarter* way to work, for through listening — not talking — you can discover with more certainty the prospect's wants, needs, expectations, timeframe, desires, motivation, authority to take action, and financial ability. This edge enables you to transition to your sales presentation more confidently and increase your chances for a close exponentially. (See Chapter 12 for details on executing powerful sales presentations.)

 Effective listening brings about an interesting bonus for salespeople: As you exercise your listening muscle and gather more information to turn prospects into clients and better serve your customers, they perceive that they're getting to know you, as well. They begin to define you and your company as caring, trustworthy, professional, and reliable. You have opened the door to a quality, long-term service relationship! And it's all because you kept your mouth closed and listened.

In the following sections, I share some tips for sharpening your listening skills, and I steer you clear of a few mistakes that may block effective listening.

Three secrets of effective listening

As I say earlier in this chapter, listening is an active sport. And it's all the more challenging because listening demands extreme attentiveness and mental acuity while keeping your mouth shut and allowing someone else to hold the floor. (Ever wonder why you're so exhausted after one of those all-day business seminars? Despite the fact that you've been sitting for nearly eight hours, your brain has been working overtime capturing and processing all the information.) Three listening practices, however, can be considered the steroids of the phone-sales league (except that they're totally legal!).

Always take notes

You don't need to be a stenographer to be effective at note taking. Just jotting down key concepts, problems, issues, and company info directly from the prospect will do. The act of taking notes forces you to stay focused on the prospect and what he is saying. Your mind is less likely to wander or jump to what you want to say next.

Tell the prospect that you're taking notes to better work with him. Here's a sample script:

> *"Mr. Smith, I'm taking notes because I don't want to miss anything and need this critical information you are sharing with me to better serve you."*

By telling Mr. Smith in advance that you're taking notes, he appreciates that you're so interested in what he's saying that you don't want to lose a single thought. He thinks, "This guy is different than the other salespeople." Also, he is more understanding when you ask him to repeat something or slow down or give you a moment, like in the following script:

> *"Mr. Smith, I am sorry, but my shorthand needs a little help. I want to clarify the information on _____. Could you please go over that again, so I can get it on paper?"*

 If you have a customer relationship manager (CRM) software program to help you capture prospect information, I suggest typing this data into the CRM while you're listening. A *CRM* is the software you use to store your contacts' and prospects' information. Examples of CRM software would be Act, Goldmine, or Salesforce.com. Using a CRM means you don't have to re-enter information later from hand-written notes — that's double entry and double the work. Again, your prospect is likely to hear the clicking of your keys, so be sure to explain that you're entering notes into the software program as he talks.

Ask more questions

The person asking the questions is the one in control of the conversation. The asker is the receiver of information. And information, as you know, is power. You won't learn anything by talking — you already know all that you know. "Even a fool appears wise until they open their mouth," goes an old proverb. Project your brilliance through the questions you ask.

> ## Get 'em to spill the beans
>
> If I want to communicate with Wesley, my 5-year-old son, all I have to do is ask questions and the floodgates open. He tells me about his day, how he felt, what was awesome, what other kids did, what he wants to do tomorrow, how much he loves me, and so on. I get all this information simply by asking a few questions. Wesley, like most other human beings of any age, wants to share, but shares much more when prompted by questions.

Having trouble getting started? Let me share with you a few very effective general questions you can use to prompt the speaker. These basic queries jump you out of the "stall" position and move your listening and discovery process forward:

- *"Can you elaborate on that?"*
- *"Can you give me a little more perspective on that issue?"*
- *"Can you explain to me how this works?"*
- *"Can you review that again for me?"*
- *"Bob, I'm not quite sure what you mean."*

See Chapter 10 for more details on questioning your prospect or client effectively.

Move to instant replay

If you've done the first two steps correctly (see previous sections), you will be granted the third step. At this point, you want to verify that all the detail you've captured is correct. The only way to do that is to review and summarize what you understood the prospect to convey. Check out the following sample script:

> *"So, Bob, let me see if I am on the right track. You are wanting to increase your communication between departments in your company. You feel that having an intranet would be a big step in accomplishing those goals. Being able to send video messages that you can record from your desk and send to your employees in your offices is the U.S., Europe, and Asia would be a big plus for you. Is that correct?"*

Don't repeat word for word what the prospect or client said. Some prospects will become offended or feel that you are using a sales technique on them. Your job is to summarize accurately and interpret what you heard — not act like a myna bird. Do, however, try to use the same jargon for specific industry trademark and company terms; this act shows you have done your homework.

When you engage in "instant replay," your prospect often does one of these three things:

✔ Confirms that your understanding is correct.

✔ Corrects your instant replay.

✔ Gives you new and additional information.

All these outcomes are good — with any one of them, you know you have it right when you hang up the phone, plus you may have gotten bonus information. Typically, the detail a prospect or client adds after the instant replay is the really important stuff. You made it past the surface issues and now have insider information that your competitors may not have been savvy enough to unearth.

When a prospect adds information at the replay stage, you must repeat this step. Yes, it's time for another instant replay. Run through your summary again, with the new details this time, and conclude with a phrase such as:

✔ *"Do I have it right?"*

✔ *"Bob, am I on the right track?"*

✔ *"How does that sound?"*

Picking up nonverbal signs

In a face-to-face sales situation, a prospect's body language communicates a vast amount of information. But how about over-the-phone sales efforts? Although you can't see nonverbal messages such as eye blinking, head nodding, and clock watching, you can still tune in to unspoken signals that indicate interest, rejection, boredom, and other responses. The nonverbal signals can give you an indication as to how you are doing and where you are in the sales process. And your listening skills are what help you pick up these signals.

Listen for background noise. Taking a pause (check out the section, "Using the pause to your benefit" later in this chapter) may be helpful — it's hard to detect what's going on around the prospect when you're talking. You may hear another person interrupting your prospect with a question, detect the muffled sound of the prospect's hand cupping the phone, or pick up on the squeak of a chair as the prospect leans back. You may hear the click of keys on a calculator and surmise that she is adding up the numbers you're sharing — a sign that the prospect may be ready to buy!

If you pick up signs that you have lost the prospect or she is bored, one technique to get her back on focus is to start a statement with her name. By inserting her name before a statement, you gain three to four seconds of attention; you better make what comes next good.

Three mistakes that block listening

Sometimes, one of the best ways to master a skill is to find out how *not* to do it. In doing so, you apply the 180-degree theory to success. When approaching the sales situation with listening in mind, sales-people must work to avoid the following three common reactions.

Overpreparation: "I've got this nailed"

Rehearsing scripts and dialogues definitely aids in a smooth deliv-ery and response during sales presentations (see Chapter 4 for the basics on using scripts). But you *can* have too much of a good thing: When you prepare to the point where you're too focused on your script and responses, you run a high risk of losing your listening focus. You're so tied to the script that you're ready to lurch forward with the next line — and miss the nuances that ought to be shaping your next line in order to make the script come alive.

"What?" you may be thinking. "Dirk has hammered on scripts and dialogues and thorough pre-call preparation for numerous chapters, and now he's changing direction?" I'm definitely not changing direction, merely waving a caution flag.

By all means, practice, practice, *practice* your sales script! But, remember, the sales call isn't a performance in which you're the star. If anything, think of it more as improvisational theater: You're a skillful and prepared professional who is poised to respond to any scenario tossed your way. Imagine an actor thrown into a pie-throwing comedy scene and reciting Hamlet's soliloquy. Something similar can happen if you listen with one ear and use most of your brain to call up your next stock answer. You may miss some critical information that could help you close a sale.

Butting in and showing off: "I'm the expert; just ask me"

When you're more focused on what you're going to say next, you miss a critical opportunity to hear some valuable information. Maybe your mouth is shut and you're mumbling the appropriate "um-hmms" — but all the while, you're looking for openings to flex your mental muscles. You're channeled on opportunities to butt in and show off how prepared and knowledgeable you are about your client's needs, rather than really *hearing* your client's needs.

Of course, you're eager to move the process along, closer to the point when the client says, "I'll take it!" You want to show the client how much you know. But this eagerness can shut down your sense of hearing — and possibly lead to cutting off the client in mid-sentence. Just keep in mind that what the prospect has to say is always more important than what the salesperson has to say.

Try applying the three-second rule. You wait three seconds to respond to a prospect's questions. It insures that you have time to formulate your response and also not interrupt the prospect.

Leaping into your pitch before listening: "Enough about you; how about me?"

A close cousin to the "I'm the expert; just ask me" scenario (from the preceding section), this circumstance results when you stop listening to the client because you're intent on finding an opening to leap into your pitch. Your radar is picking up only the cues that may serve as your entrée into the presentation.

I despise the term *sales pitch,* but when salespeople fall victim to the enough-about-you syndrome, this is exactly what the sales presentation turns into: They home in on any signal that tells them the prospect is ready to bat, and then start the wind-up and throw their pitch. To resist the urge to leap into your pitch, be sure to pause or take a deep breath before you respond.

Prompting More Dialogue through Silence

Earlier in this chapter, I establish that *not talking* is one of the salesperson's greatest strategies for successful selling, and I help you sharpen your listening skills. Another important telephone-sales tool is the effective use of complete silence during your sales calls. In the following sections, I show you some silent tactics for encouraging a prospect to open up and yield more information that you can use to close the sale.

Using the pause to your benefit

The difference between great and good is very little. As little as a fraction of a second for an Olympic swimmer. In telephone sales, as well, the smallest detail can separate the champion sales professional from the many good salespeople out there. In selling, instead of inches and seconds, greatness is measured in words — and how they're used . . . or *not* used.

Sometimes, the brief seconds that pass after the prospect stops talking can be the small difference that elevates a sales professional from good to great. When you've just wrapped up running through one of the benefits of your service, allow the silence to linger before diving into the next benefit. You want your prospect to feel the full weight of your information before you ask for the order.

Sure, allowing that dead air to linger can be scary. Silence in the middle of a conversation feels awkward and uncomfortable. Your instinct is to fill it up, but the pause is a powerful tool for the salesperson. During that sound void, your prospect may volunteer an opinion or reaction. To a salesperson, such volunteered details are extremely important. What a prospect says *after* answering a question from you can be infinitely more valuable than the initial response. The pause gives the prospect time to consider and process your information. If you step into the pause, you invalidate or weaken your last question. More often than not, you'll be rewarded when you use the pause and wait for the prospect to offer more crucial detail.

Here's an example of a conversation between a salesperson and a prospect that effectively uses the pause:

> **Prospect:** *"We made a decision to go another way."*
>
> **Sales Rep:** *(pause)* *"Oh?"*
>
> **Prospect:** *"Well, not completely another way. Orders have come down from above to hold off and analyze a little further before we finalize training budgets for next year."*
>
> **Sales Rep:** *"I see."* *(pause)*
>
> **Prospect:** *"When we are released by the upper management in 30 days, you have a good opportunity to be part of next year's budget. Between you and me, you have a high probability of being a preferred trainer, but you will need to wait this out before we can discuss details."*

The salesperson discovered that what seemed like a "no" was really just a delay. He went from a-decision-to-go-another-direction status to preferred-trainer status in a few minutes. The salesperson kept the dialogue going by pausing and not talking. The prospect did the rest.

The power of the pause

Arthur Rubinstein, the world-famous pianist, was once asked how he handled the notes so masterfully. He responded, "I handle the notes no better than many others, but the pauses . . . ah! That is where the art resides." Like a brilliantly played piece of music, your sales presentation can also evoke emotional responses, simply by the way you handle the pauses between your words. Let the power of the pause take over. Rubinstein would let the note resonate throughout the hall. Let your questions and information resonate over the phone.

Reading between the lines

You'll encounter situations in which your "I see" prompts and carefully placed pauses don't elicit more info. When that occurs, read between the lines. To yourself, ask the following questions:

- ✔ Was my presentation off?
- ✔ Did I miss a need that was expressed?
- ✔ Is the timing off?

You don't have much time to evaluate — you want to keep the flow of conversation moving. To get between the lines if they're blurry, ask the prospect these questions:

> *"Bob, what did I miss?"*
>
> *"How do you feel about that?"*
>
> *"Is there anything that can be done to reverse your decision?"*
>
> *"Where do we go from here?"*

The ability to read between the lines is a skill you develop over time. As you become thoroughly familiar with your product or service and its clientele, you develop a sixth sense about the invisible messages that can be summoned by your prompts, pauses, and — when necessary — your questions.

Chapter 12

Executing Powerful Presentations

In This Chapter

▶ Stacking up the building blocks of a winning presentation

▶ Giving the presentation

▶ Driving home the delivery

*T*he sales presentation: It's an art, a skill — some may even say a science. However you define it, the effectiveness of the sales presentation — particularly for the telephone salesperson — is the apex in the process of transforming a prospect into a customer. A powerful sales presentation doesn't just happen. It's orchestrated, honed, and formulated. You can't just go off the cuff or by your gut, and you don't get bonus points for spontaneity or being impromptu.

Throughout the sales process, you've discovered the importance of putting time and thought into every step. Those preparations all lead to this point: the *sales presentation.* In this chapter, I walk you through the structure of a solid presentation and explore how to approach the presentation process in two distinct scenarios. I also share valuable tips on delivery.

The Fundamentals of a Dynamite Presentation

The sales presentation, like a sturdy building, consists of individual components that fit together to support a solid effort. Each building block plays an important role — leave one out and the presentation may wobble or even tumble down. But don't worry; none of the components of the sales presentation are that complicated or difficult to acquire. This section adds them up.

Starting with a qualified prospect

To deliver the *best* sales presentation for a particular prospect, you must have gone through the qualification process *before* your presentation. Unqualified prospects are like the kernels that don't pop into popcorn. If you can identify those kernels ahead of time — you can weed them out of the bag before you stick them into the microwave. Or cook them longer to get them to pop.

Qualifying prospects is, in essence, prescreening to determine their likelihood of buying. By gathering answers to key questions, you can flag those individuals who probably won't "pop." Or if you discover what the barriers are, you might be able to butter them up in a presentation that better addresses their unique needs. (For a step-by-step walk-through of the qualifying process, check out Chapter 10.)

Letting the prospect know what's coming

Don't you hate meetings where there's no agenda, no clear purpose, and no hint as to how long you're going to be held captive? Meeting hosts who walk you through the agenda, on the other hand, help establish expectations among the attendees. You know that as soon as you check off each item on the handout, the meeting is over. This knowledge puts you at ease and, chances are, you'll be engaged and even participate more as you anticipate each point on the list.

Apply this preview strategy when opening your sales presentation: At the get-go, guide the prospect through the points of your plan to establish a sense of the timeframe, content, and order in which you plan to discuss the content.

Your presentation really begins after your opening statement to grab the prospect's interest. It occurs after you have qualified the prospect to ensure a presentation can be made. If your sales cycle involves more than one sales call, the presentation usually happens after the initial call, during the second call or later. That timeline allows you to use the agenda approach.

Adding value for the prospect

Your presentation should be packed with value — after all, you intend to sell a product or service that helps the prospect save money, make money, achieve business goals, have a better quality of life, or solve an existing problem. However, you want to give the individual something valuable that he can take with him and use later.

If you've asked enough questions in qualifying (see "Starting with a qualified prospect" earlier in this chapter), you can add value through your consultative recommendations. Realize that you're a fresh set of eyes, ears, and cognitive thinking that can be the right combination to break through a tough challenge that's stumped the prospect and his company for years. Whether it's a series of economic findings that influence business decisions, insider news about changes in the industry, or new strategies to increase sales or reduce costs, the operative word is *value.*

Solving the prospect's problems

In essence, people buy solutions to their problems. Your mission, if you choose to accept it, is to demonstrate how your product or service solves the problem better, faster, cheaper, or more thoroughly than any other possibility. In order to do that, you first want to *quantify* the prospect's problem.

Quantifying begins with qualifying — your questions should've determined the cost of this problem to the prospect or company — in terms of budget, revenue, time, materials, labor, and other factors. Then based on that information, you're armed to present your solution.

You may base your solution on cost — yours is cheaper than the competitor's or the current provider's. But you're wiser to offer a solution that

- ✔ Reduces labor
- ✔ Shortens production time
- ✔ Increases output
- ✔ Requires fewer employees
- ✔ Demands fewer resources

Keeping it short and to the point

A sales presentation needs to be exact and to the point. You can't expect a sales prospect to hang in there with you for longer than 20 or 30 minutes. At that point, the ability to pay attention plummets dramatically — no matter how charming and personable you are. (Even sitcoms last only a half-hour.)

Don't play the cost-cutting game

Emphasizing lowest cost to solve your prospects' problems may be hazardous to your wealth, at least if you plan to get rich on sales commissions. If you're inclined to focus on cost in your sales presentation, just remember the old sales adage: "Value = Benefits – Cost." You're wiser to *increase the benefit* to the prospect, so the *cost* issue is overshadowed and a greater *value* is perceived.

No business in the world operates on lowering cost — or they shouldn't. A growing company always zeroes in on increasing sales or productivity. Your job in the sales presentation is to show how you can increase the client's productivity or sales — not sell the cheapest widget in the industry.

You don't need any more time than 30 minutes if you've qualified your prospect, kept your purpose in mind, and set your agenda (see the preceding sections). If you're attempting to present enough info to persuade the prospect to meet with you face to face, your phone call should take less than 15 minutes.

To help keep your presentation short and to the point, remember the following pre-planning pointers:

- ✔ **Be sure to know, before the day of the presentation, who will be present so you can research and prepare.** By knowing who's attending, you can gear your presentation toward those individuals.

- ✔ **Take roll at the beginning of the call.** Doing so alerts you who's actually in attendance. You want to demonstrate professionalism and organization.

- ✔ **Make sure you engage everyone in attendance.** You want to interact with each person and ask for questions or concerns.

  The exception to this rule is the support staff who are there to record the conversation and keep notes, unless the person is the gatekeeper who helped you. Then you want to engage that person and recognize him for his role.

Building your credibility

The best way to firmly establish your credibility is to know the prospect and the prospect's company. Chapter 4 tells you where and how to dig up background information about the company. This detail puts you in good stead throughout the sales process, but especially during the sales presentation.

From this information, you can shape your presentation accordingly. For example, if you discovered on the corporate Web site that one of the company's core values is environmental responsibility, you can emphasize how your product is made from 100-percent recycled content. This point illustrates that you have a good understanding of the prospect's unique needs and, therefore, are a credible source for an effective solution.

 Another method of conveying credibility is offering names of referrals from satisfied clients. Why? You can assure the prospect all day and night that using your product brings success, but the testimonial from someone who's already had a successful experience with your company speaks volumes more. "If it can work for that guy," thinks the prospect, "it'll work for me."

Making Your Presentation

Many companies have a pre-scripted sales presentation that all salespeople are required to follow — to the T. In other firms, the script may be an outline with wiggle room for customized conversation based on the salesperson and the client.

Whether you follow a word-for-word script, are guided by a basic presentation framework, or you're completely on your own, I firmly believe in a planned presentation model. In other words, *follow a script, of your own making or otherwise.* You may skip over critical points if you don't have the script written out and rehearsed.

Although scripts differ, all should

- ✔ Address the prospect's unique circumstances
- ✔ Show a solution to the prospect's problem
- ✔ Highlight the key benefits your product or service offers
- ✔ Establish your credibility as the solution to the prospect's problem

But the particulars and the choreography of the presentation are determined by a number of factors. This section highlights two different ways you can make your presentation.

Moving into a one-step sale

What you sell determines the complexity of the sales presentation process. If, for example, you offer a fairly straightforward product or service that's familiar to the prospect — and one that isn't considered a significant investment — you may expect to step from *prospecting* to *qualifying and information gathering* to *sales presentation* to *close* in a single call. Common one-call products and services include long-distance services, cable television plans, office supplies, and Internet services. The following sections detail what you need to know to make a successful one-step sales presentation.

Transitioning to presentation

You can only wrap up a one-step sale if you can do it in a reasonably short amount of time. You want to move from the qualifying question phase into the presentation as quickly and efficiently as possible. As soon as you've gathered enough information and raised the needs, wants, and concerns of your prospect, you can prepare to dive into the presentation.

How do you know when you're ready to move from questions to presentation? Listen carefully for these signals:

 ✔ When the prospect identifies a need to take action

 ✔ When the prospect quantifies a desired result

To move along the question-to-answer process, ask questions like these:

 ✔ Have you been considering a change?

 ✔ What specifically is causing you to consider a change?

 ✔ Is this a recent consideration, or have you been thinking about it for some time?

 ✔ If there were a solution to this problem we are talking about, how valuable would that be to you?

Reviewing the situation

Before you leap at the chance to move into your presentation, stop and take just 30 seconds to a minute to confirm what you discovered. It's easy to get excited when you have a prospect leaning your way. But taking the time to summarize and repeat helps ensure that you understand the prospect's need clearly. You might start with the following script:

> *"Bob, so I am confident I know what your needs and wants are, let me summarize our discussion thus far. . . ."*

> *"Bob, to be certain we are on the same page, let's review what we've talked about thus far. . . ."*

> *"Bob, let me make sure I understand and that we are working together on this. You want . . ."*

Steering clear of a wreck

Who can anticipate all the possible scenarios that may derail your presentation? Maybe the prospect is pressed for time. Maybe it's clear that the prospect is distracted or keeps allowing interruptions. Maybe you just can't get her off a particular sticking point that she refuses to back down on.

When you find yourself heading for a wreck, don't keep driving toward the close. Change course — and fast. Put on the brakes and set up a second presentation. It's easy to turn a one-step presentation into two steps, especially when it raises your odds of closing. You can use scripts like the following:

> *"Bob, just so you know, I typically meet with the client twice. The first meeting is to determine your goals and objectives, and the second one is to review my recommendations."*

> *"Bob, in order to provide you with the best service, I usually go back to my office and prepare my analysis of your situation, and we will talk again in a few days for a short meeting. Would Thursday or Friday later this week work for you?"*

This fallback gives you a chance to collect the other decision makers if needed, align with a better timeframe, create solutions for their concerns, and even have your sales manager help you if needed.

Now and later: The two-step presentation model

Whether your sales cycle is more effective with a two-step presentation or you have made the switch to a two-step model because of road blocks erected by the prospect, you must commit to it. A *two-step model* is when you fact-find, probe, question, and qualify the prospect in one call. You then independently research, evaluate, and prepare for a second appointment to make a presentation of your conclusions and benefits to the client, ending with a close.

The first step has only a trial close to confirm a presentation appointment and potential conditions of service and satisfaction of the prospect. The second step is the actual presentation where you are closing for the signed agreement, purchase order, or whatever mechanism you use to secure the order.

If your product or service is more complex or costly, the questioning phase is almost certain to be a first step, followed by a more formal sales presentation. Some other situations in which the sales presentation is singled out as its own meeting include

✔ When your product or service is complex and requires in-depth explanation and information

✔ When your product or service is a high-ticket item

✔ When you've run into objections at the initial sales presentation that require further work on your part

✔ When you discover some information you didn't have in your initial presentation that requires you to reload

✔ When you discover in your initial presentation that more people are involved in the decision-making process

✔ When a face-to-face presentation is critical to the close

Nothing is wrong with a two-step model when desires, needs, abilities, and authority are determined in the first step. You should have enough benefits to pique the prospect's interest to secure the second appointment when the real presentation and closing will be conducted.

Prepping at the question phase

In step one of the two-step presentation, you're on a fact-finding mission, doing company recognizance. You want to find out what the prospect's problems, challenges, needs, wants, and desires currently are, as well as internal processes for making changes, decision making, and more. You want to explore the typical process of changing vendors of suppliers. How do they go about making big decisions? You find this info out by asking questions.

When you know from the start that you'll be scheduling a dedicated presentation meeting, it's a good idea to demonstrate some benefits and value at this point so the prospect is interested in hearing more. Don't give it all away on this call. The key is giving enough so the prospect wants to find out more.

Booking the presentation

After you complete the exploratory phone call, landing the appointment for the presentation is critical. Don't hang up the phone until you book it! If you end the call without the appointment, you may lose your opportunity. Now that the prospect has hung up without further commitment, he may simply dodge your future attempts at contact, or, worse, he may do business with someone else before you have the chance to schedule. Setting the presentation for a separate time allows you to prepare more effectively because you can devote time to organizing all the benefits and results for an organized and professional delivery.

To snag the presentation appointment, avoid asking in a way that allows the prospect to say no. Try *assuming* that you'll meet and offer some choices on times. For example, look at these scripts:

> *"Bob, there is no doubt in my mind that these new copy machines would provide you what you need. Would Wednesday or Thursday next week work better to meet and discuss your options further?"*

> *"Fred, I am convinced, after spending this time with you, that our widget could help you reduce your production costs by at least 18 percent. Would Thursday or Friday later this week work better for you to meet and explore the benefits more thoroughly?"*

The most challenging part of the two-step model is setting an appointment and determining whether it should be a telephone presentation or a face-to-face presentation. The securing of the presentation appointment is the toughest step and is where most salespeople fail.

Locking in a Successful Delivery

Whether one-step or two, over the phone or face-to-face, all successful sales presentations are driven by your delivery — the intangible qualities that make your presentation rock-solid. You can work with an A-plus presentation outline, but if your delivery lacks the qualities in this section, your effort can flop as badly as Hamlet's soliloquy performed by a parrot.

Staying in control

Controlling the presentation is a delicate effort. You want to be loose enough to respond to and fine-tune your prospect's questions, but you don't want your carefully crafted presentation to be derailed. This tragedy can easily happen if

- ✔ **You lose your place:** Your prospect leads you down a rabbit hole, and you neglect to leave breadcrumbs to get back to your point.

- ✔ **You respond to objections before establishing value:** You've just started your presentation and the prospect jumps in with an objection about an issue that you plan to cover later.

When your prospect jumps into the presentation with questions, objections, or a call for closure, diplomatically wrestle back control of the conversation. Don't be a drill sergeant, but *do* try something like this:

> *"I am glad you asked that question; I normally answer that type of question at the _____ stage of my presentation. Would it be alright if we talked about it then?"*
>
> *"I go over those exact issues when I talk about _____ in my presentation. Could we wait until then, and if you have further questions after that discussion, please ask me."*

If you or your company has truly designed an effective presentation process, follow it. The more you deviate from it, the lower your sales may be.

Showing conviction

If you expect to convince people that you have the answer to their needs, you'd better believe it yourself! If you're not behind what you're selling, believe me, your prospects will figure that out. Conviction is something that's hard to fake. If you're in a sales job where you're selling something you don't believe in, I'd advise you to get out of it fast and find something you *do* think is worth sharing with others.

After you come to the self-awareness that you *do* believe in what you sell, the next step is to be sure you convey that conviction in your presentation. It's hard for me or anyone else to tell others how to sell with conviction, but I can guarantee you that the stronger you believe in what you're doing, the easier it is to communicate in your sales presentation.

Expressing enthusiasm

Allow me to share a timeworn sales adage that says it all:

> *"Enthusiasm is to selling as yeast is to bread; it makes the dough rise."*

Enthusiasm sells! A presentation without enthusiasm isn't worth watching. If your "show" doesn't grab your prospects, they turn you off — even if you don't realize it. So be sure your positive attitude about your offer shines through.

Like conviction (preceding section), enthusiasm is a hard thing to fake, so include a little pep talk to yourself as part of your preparation efforts.

If you can maintain your enthusiasm for your product, working through the bumps along the road to a close is easier. For example, you may have to deliver some bad news to the prospect — the price is higher than he'd hoped or the delivery can't be made as early as requested. If you can impart your enthusiasm for how happy the client *will* be with your product, that "bump" is just something that's gotten over quickly.

Exhibiting confidence

Confidence for most people, including telephone salespeople, comes from a history of positive results. But even if you're new to your current sales job or even new to telephone sales period, you can tap into positive experiences from previous jobs and even non-work-related successes.

When I entered the sales field, I knew that my edge was my personal confidence. Mind you, I had no sales experience, and as a new sales-person, I was no better than any other newbie. I was clueless and didn't know diddly-squat about selling. I did know, though, that I had an extremely high level of self-confidence that came from years of athletic success in professional racquetball. I knew that I was a winner, and that attribute came across in my sales presenta-tions. Don't get me wrong; I still had to work plenty hard to succeed (my sports experience gave me plenty of exposure to hard work), but that extra shot of confidence leveraged my efforts exponentially.

In coaching thousands of salespeople over the last few years, I have discovered that one of the most challenging times is the advent of a new year. It's almost as if, when they tear the page out of the calendar that reads December, they forget about all the success they had the previous year. They lose confidence because they perceive that they are starting over again from ground zero.

My advice? Work in a New Year's resolution to record and review your victories over the past year — and further back. By document-ing these successes, you'll have them at the ready as you prepare for the next sales presentation and need a little boost.

Communicating assertiveness

Top salespeople are assertive. They ask for the client to commit to something, whether that something is merely to review the material they're sending, to set an appointment, to review their budget, or to buy the recommendation. These salespeople don't leave a sales opportunity without assertively asking for action.

Some salespeople shy away from this boldness because they equate assertiveness with aggressiveness. But they're not the same thing — and being assertive doesn't mean being rude or pushy or forceful.

Assertiveness is affirming your belief and conviction in your offer. And, believe me, your assertiveness arms your prospect with assurance that the decision to do business with you is a wise one.

One strategy is to tell the prospect at the beginning of your presentation that you're going to ask for the business at the end. You don't have to use a hard-edged statement. You can be simple, friendly, and informative — but be straightforward. Check out these examples:

> *"At the end of my presentation, provided we're all in agreement, we'll finalize the paperwork, so I can begin to work for you right away."*

> *"When we conclude in _____ minutes, I will know enough about your needs, wants, and desires, and you will know enough about how our _____ will assist you in reaching your goals and objectives that we both will be able to make a decision at that moment to either work together or not. Does that sound fair?"*

Another assertive technique is to use a simple summation close and connect with a statement of your belief that the prospect should act on your recommendations now, or that you believe that you offer the best solution, or that you personally guarantee their satisfaction. Check out these examples:

> *"Bob, I know that we can provide the _____ and _____ and _____ that we discussed and you want by end of the month. There is no question in my mind that this is the right decision for you and your company; let's get started so we can meet your time line."*

> *"Bob, it's clear that you have done a lot of research on your software problem, because you want the software to be _____ and _____ and _____. There really is no company that can deliver those with no risk on your part except my company XYZ software company. Let's get the paperwork out of the way so we can make this happen for you."*

Part IV
Going for the Close

In a chance meeting prior to their singing careers, Carreras, Domingo and Pavarotti all worked at the same call center.

"Whoa, whoa, fellows. Tone it down! What are you tryin' to do, impress someone?"

In this part . . .

*O*bjections: the bane of the salespersons existence, right? A surefire sign that you're going to hang up without a sale? Guess again. This part covers some of the most challenging situations phone salespeople — both newcomers and pros — confront, including addressing objections, closing the sale *now,* and turning a failed sale into future potential.

In Chapter 13, I identify the most frequently cited objections and introduce you to my six-step process for defusing them — as well as your *fear* of objections. Chapter 14 unlocks the secrets to successfully obtaining a client's commitment and closing for the order *now*. And if you don't get the sale — because sometimes you won't — I give you some ways to keep your foot in the door. Believe it or not, sometimes you can transform these "failures" into a future sale, if you follow the advice in Chapter 15.

Chapter 13

Overcoming Objections

. . . .

In This Chapter

▶ Defining objection

▶ Identifying the most frequently used objections

▶ Getting ready for objections

▶ Knowing how to deal with objections in six simple steps

. . . .

*O*bjections are a fact of life in the sales world — a natural part of the process. The novice salesperson may see them as a sign that something is wrong with the prospect, the product, or the sales pitch. Not only are objections completely normal, but also they're *healthy* and often work to your advantage.

I considered titling this chapter "Embracing Objections," or "Welcoming Objections." Some of you may think "Avoiding Any Prospect Who Has Objections," may be a more-fitting name. But the more comfortable you are with the sales process, the more you view objections not as a barrier to the sale, but as an opportunity to provide the prospect with *more* reasons to buy.

In this chapter, I define and identify the most common objections that prospects throw out at salespeople. I explain how to prepare for this resistance, and I offer a surefire strategy for handling any obstacle, turning it from a stumbling block into a home-team advantage. So instead of responding like a deer caught in the head-lights when you're hit with an objection, you can leap at the chance to turn a challenge into a close.

Recognizing a Sales Objection for What It Really Is

When a prospect starts lobbing objections your way, you can easily translate this as, "He doesn't want to buy." Naturally, you perceive such resistance as a stall or a barrier — an expression that the individual doesn't want or need your product or service.

What exactly is a sales objection and how can you clearly identify one? When a prospect says, "I want to think it over" or "the other supplier will do it for less" or "you're too inexperienced," you have just heard an *objection*.

But instead of seeing an objection as a rejection or a "no," understand it for what it really is: a request for more information, an appeal for the knowledge to justify to the prospect that buying your product or service is the right thing to do, and an opportunity for you to offer clarification regarding the details the prospect is questioning.

The objection is a signal that the prospect *is* interested — so interested that she's carefully considering what issues must be addressed before proceeding with a purchase. If the prospect wasn't interested, she wouldn't have anything to object to!

Eyeing Common Objections

Despite the infinite number of products and services sold over the telephone, the number of *objections* is relatively small. They may be worded differently, but scratch below the surface and you can find that most resistance reflects no more than a handful of concerns.

That's good news for the salesperson — preparing for and overcoming a few issues is an extremely manageable challenge. So take a deep breath; this section highlights the two most common objections you encounter. (Figure out how to handle these objections later in this chapter.)

Cost

The number-one objection you hear as a salesperson is about price. Are you surprised? Probably not, because you may have had the same reaction when a salesperson called you on the phone. In fact, an objection about price can show up in many different forms:

- ✔ "I can get it cheaper elsewhere."
- ✔ "I can't afford that."
- ✔ "It's not worth that much money."
- ✔ "I'm only prepared to pay half that amount."
- ✔ "I just don't have the money right now to pay for it."

No matter how the prospect phrases it, understand this: This objection isn't really about cost at all — it's about value. Instead of hearing the message, "It costs too much," recalibrate your ears to listen for this message: "I'm not yet sold on the *value* of what you're offering." When price is the objection, value is the answer.

When you focus on the benefits of your service or product — whether reducing risk, ensuring long-term savings or profit, resolving a problem, or making life easier — you're building value. As that value adds up, the prospect finds it easier to make the decision to buy — and cost becomes a non-issue. This time-tested but true sales equation governs the results you'll achieve when encountering an objection related to price or cost of goods and services and ultimately value.

Value = Benefits – Cost

Here's how it works: Say you're presenting your business service to the owner of a company with a problem that's costing $100,000 a year in net profit. You can solve the problem — the cost for your service is $50,000. Without your guidance, the owner may feel that $50,000 is too high a price to pay for saving $100,000. You, however, skillfully direct the presentation to preempt that objection. You point out that the investment in your service is worth $1 million in his pocket over a ten-year period! That's a 100-percent return on the money he invests.

Timing or delivery

Another common objection you may encounter is about timing or delivery. A portion of selling is being there at the right time. You must make sure before you make a presentation that you understand the prospect's timing in making a decision. You don't want the wrong timing. By questioning the decision maker as to the timing of the decision or the delivery of service in the qualifying process, you can lower the odds of being faced with timing and delivery objections. (Check out Chapter 10 for more info on questioning.)

For example, if you're making a sales presentation to a prospect whose decision to purchase new office equipment and the decision won't be made until the forth quarter of the year due to budget timing, but you want to make a full presentation in April, you can ask appropriate questions and make enough of a presentation to keep in the running but avoid engaging in the full sales presentation.

The problem with timing could also be a delivery problem or delivery delay. The two sweetest words after someone is down to the final decision are *right away!* After people make a decision to use your product or service, they want it right away, right now, or even yesterday. Don't allow your sales to be thrown off by delivery problems or delivery delays.

You can also have a plan already in place or in development for rush orders. Some companies charge more. Others have a contingency plan. If possible, work through these situations with the operations team ahead of time to make sure there is a plan in place to handle immediate sales.

Preparing for Objections

One of the secrets to overcoming objections in the sales process is to *always* expect objections. Because a handful of issues come up about 80 percent of the time (see the previous section, "Eyeing Common Objections"), you can prepare for them simply by anticipating these frequently raised challenges. This section helps you create a battle plan for objections.

Rehearsing responses to resistance

Perfecting your delivery of effective responses to objections requires practice and role-playing. In order to be prepared for objections, you first want to be sure you're familiar with the most commonly raised objections to buying your particular product or service. Then, a few times weekly, deliver your boilerplate response in your office, as you drive, or with a coworker or spouse.

Don't practice with your prospects; practice *before* you talk to them. To be truly prepared, you want to memorize, rehearse, and internalize *multiple* ways to overcome each objection you're likely to frequently encounter.

Uncovering objections before your presentation

The best way to prepare for objections is to uncover potential objections before they occur. The more you discover about the prospect ahead of time, the fewer objections you encounter during the sales appointment. In many situations, you have opportunities to gather this information prior to the sales presentation.

If the sales process is a two-step process, then you may have a preliminary phone conversation with the prospect in which you can ask questions. Perhaps the leads you're working with have already been qualified, and this information is included in the database. However you gather it, the more key questions you have answers to, the better you can anticipate this individual's objections.

Before your presentation, you want to ask questions covering five areas:

- ✔ **Problem/need:** Attempt to pinpoint what problems or needs the prospect has that can be solved by your product or service.

- ✔ **Experience:** Probe into the prospect's history of using a service or product similar to yours, the current provider, and the consumer's level of satisfaction with that provider.

- ✔ **Time frame/motivation:** Explore the urgency of the prospect's need, the level of interest, and when he's planning to make a decision.

- ✔ **Budget/price:** Get a reading on what the prospect expects to pay for your product or service. What does she consider too much to pay? What has the prospect paid in the past?

- ✔ **Expectations:** Gauge what needs or wants the prospect expects will be met. What level of service does he anticipate? What measure of quality?

The prospects' responses to these preliminary questions help answer the questions that in turn help you predict potential objections during the sales process — your inquiries to the prospect help you find out the answers to the following:

- ✔ How's the customer going to make the decision?

- ✔ When does the customer plan to make a decision?

- ✔ Does the customer have the authority to move forward?

- ✔ What does the customer want or need?

- ✔ Is the customer able to afford the product or service?

- ✔ Is the customer strongly motivated to act?

- ✔ How does the customer judge a successful sales outcome?

- ✔ What competitors is the customer talking to?

- ✔ What are the possible threats that may raise objections?

- ✔ What objections has the customer raised already?

When you know the answers to these questions, you encounter fewer objections. You're also ready for the most likely objections, so you can prepare professional, confident, and objective responses.

Delaying objections until the end

Objections raised at the wrong time can put a premature kibosh on your efforts. If the couple you're talking to about a timeshare week in Florida has the chance to throw in, "It's not in our budget," before you've had a chance to convince them that this opportunity is so valuable that they can't afford *not* to buy, you have a greater challenge trying to get your derailed presentation back on track. Price objections in particular tend to come up early, before you've built enough value. The best tactic is to delay the objections until later in your presentation.

Early on in your conversation with a prospect, ask permission to hold any questions until later in your presentation. Explain that you're likely to address their queries at some point in your talk, and that you plan to spend as much time as they need after you've finished.

If you e-mail, fax, or mail the meeting outline in advance — or even simply hand out the agenda if you meet face to face — you're more likely to get buy-in of the hold-all-questions tactic. If the prospects raise an objection, refer to the agenda and assure them that you'll address all their concerns at the designated point:

> *"I thoroughly cover that concern in Step 6 on the outline. Would it be okay if we talked about it then?"*

Rarely do prospects insist, "No, I want to talk about it now."

Handling Objections in Six Easy Steps

No matter how much you prepare for objections, you still have to face an objection or two before you close in on the finish line. When you do encounter objections, you need to know how to deal with them in order to overcome them. Handling objections is a six-step process. Follow the tried-and-true formula in this section in the proper order for best results.

Step one: Pause

The pause is a powerful thing. And when it comes to telephone sales, its powers have even greater potential. Figure out how to work the pause, and you discover one of the salesperson's most valuable strategies. Its benefits are numerous. The pause can

✔ **Give you time to gain control of yourself:** When you hear an objection, your instinct may be to leap into defense mode and pounce on the prospect with a quick response before she's even done speaking. Interrupting a prospect in mid-objection is the whale of all sales mistakes. The caller can perceive this act as aggressive or pushy and immediately want to end the call. The pause only needs to be a moment — a few seconds.

✔ **Create a tension and a shift of control in your direction:** The pause can generate some discomfort that effects a shift of control, bestowing the "pauser" (you) with a greater measure of power than the "pausee" (the prospect). Taking a moment to collect yourself gives *you* the edge.

✔ **Give you a chance to hear the prospect:** In addition to allowing the prospect a chance to think about his reactions, the pause allows you time to *hear* the prospect — not only to listen to the words spoken but also to make sure you understand the real objection. For more on listening, check out Chapter 11.

Pauses work best if you use them following something significant the prospect said. Keep pauses to about two to three seconds.

Step two: Acknowledge

Whether you believe the prospect's objection is valid or ridiculous, he must feel that you respect his objection, that his view carries weight, that you heard the objection, and that you understand it. This action demonstrates that you care about the prospect's feelings and best interests more than you want a sale.

Acknowledging the prospect's objection isn't the same as agreeing with the prospect. Here are just a few ways you can acknowledge — none of which requires agreement:

> *"I can see where that might cause you concern."*
>
> *"That's really a terrific question. I'm glad you asked it."*
>
> *"I understand your concern in this area."*
>
> *"Thank you — it's really important that I understand your concerns."*

Another effective technique is to link a probing question to the end of your acknowledgement statement. By asking the prospect a question, you convey your concern and build trust. Some of my favorites include the following:

> *"I understand your concern in this area. Tell me, why do you feel that way?"*

"I can see where that might cause you concern. Can you tell me more please?"

"I can appreciate your hesitation. Did you have a previous bad experience with a salesperson?"

This technique links this acknowledgment step (Step 2) with the next step (covered in the next section, "Step three: Explore") in a single script technique.

Step three: Explore

The probing question tacked onto the acknowledgment helps segue into the third step. This step is the question-asking, explore phase in which you gather more information about the prospect's objection:

✔ What's causing the concern?

✔ Did a previous supplier deliver a bad product or poor service?

✔ Has the prospect had a negative experience with a salesperson?

✔ Is it from a horror story of a friend or colleague instead of a personal experience?

The "But" of the problem

But is a word that doesn't belong in the vocabulary of a telephone-sales professional. And *especially* in a conversation with a prospect who's raised an objection. Too often, however, the word pops up — particularly during the acknowledgment step, the point in which the salesperson recognizes and validates the prospect's concerns. This effort can do so much to close the gap between salesperson and prospect. And then the word *but* blows up the bridge of understanding.

For example, "I see where that would cause you a concern" is a great acknowledgment statement — so don't blow it by sticking a *but* at the end of it. The *but* negates everything you've said before, clearly saying to your prospect that "I see your point of view, but you're wrong" or "I see your concern, but I don't care; I just want to make a sale."

To get beyond the *but,* use *and* as the linking word. *And* is a more effective bridge. You still get your answer across without the negative sting. Some folks try to get around *but* by using the word *however.* I don't advise that tactic. In the end, *however* is just a *but* with a bow tie!

The exploration phase assists you in gaining a better understanding of the size, intensity, and emotion behind his/her objection. Knowing this info prepares you to effectively answer the concerns. The exploratory process can take a few questions or minutes. What you don't want to do is cut it short; let your prospect talk all they want. The more the prospect talks, the more quality information you will receive. You want to make sure that the prospect has an uninhibited chance to share her concerns at a deeper level.

Step four: Isolate

The fourth step separates the top salespeople from the merely *good* sales pros. The isolation phase is what gets you past the smoke and mirrors to your prospect's bottom-line barrier. In the isolation phase, you try to pinpoint what the real problem is. You attempt through isolation to find out all the problems, barriers, and objections right now, not later. Most customers prefer not to reveal the real problem — or they may not even recognize themselves what their true concern is. Your probing questions help you isolate whether the objection is based on logic, hesitation, fear, or caution.

Getting to the bottom of the customer's objection is absolutely critical — without this understanding, you're stalled and unable to move forward. In order for you to take the next step, you have to know what problems, challenges, feelings, expectations, and emotions are preventing the prospect from taking the next step.

The best way to isolate the true objection is to enlist the prospect's help. Use questions like these to measure if you've identified the concern:

> *"Suppose that we could find a satisfactory solution to this important concern of yours. Would you give me the go ahead?"*
>
> *"Is this the only reason that is holding you back from moving forward?"*
>
> *"Other than _____, is there any other reason you can think of that would cause you not to make this purchase?"*
>
> *"If this problem did not exist, would you be ready to proceed right now?"*

All these scripts are extremely effective in getting the prospect to consider your options, service, or product if the objection is resolved. Of course, you can't always meet demands in terms of price, service, or delivery. But at least you've isolated the problem and can now concentrate on building value — and still have a good shot at making the sale.

Don't be afraid to probe for answers. Salespeople are often reluctant to push for information because they fear that they'll alienate the prospect and lose the sale. But you can't lose what you don't have! Without asking the questions necessary to isolate the real problem, you're unlikely to dissuade the prospect's concerns.

Step five: Answer

After you isolate the specific objection, you can move into the answer stage. Your answer requires conviction and solutions. You must also inject confidence that your company and your products or services can help achieve the goals and objectives that matter most to the prospect. And your delivery must be enthusiastic. You have to be excited for the opportunity for yourself and them. Enthusiasm sells.

You should be developing answers to the most common objections for your product or service. Talk with your sales manager to see if she has standard responses pre-scripted for the most common objections that you face. Start creating your own file and track the answers you give and what works well.

Step six: Close

The close follows immediately after your answer. I go into the ins and outs of the close in Chapter 14. But in short, the *close* is the moment when you confirm the agreement to act. This chance is the time to be bold — to step forward with confidence and assertiveness. Your conviction that you have the perfect solution is then transferred to the prospect.

Most top-performing salespeople don't break between the answer of an objection and the close or at least a trial close statement. You want to answer, and then ask prospects to buy or ask them if they're in agreement now. Even a simple tie-down close of "does that make sense" at the end of your answer can do the trick as a trial close.

Move right into the close. Here are some effective closes:

> *"There is no question in my mind that the solutions we discussed are exactly what you need. Let's go ahead and get started now."*

> *"I am confident that you will be elated with this _____. It will perform exactly as we discussed today. Let's get this paperwork taken care of, so you can have it right away."*

Chapter 14

Orchestrating a Successful Close

In This Chapter
▶ Mastering the "close" encounters
▶ Implementing four proven closes
▶ Following up for future sales

*T*he close of a sale is a complex coming together of many separate elements. Your efforts to qualify the prospect, lead through a series of questions, conduct a presentation, and overcome the discord of objections all build up to that climactic moment of a successful sale.

But the close doesn't happen all by itself. Nor is it a feat that is done *to* the prospect; rather, it is working in concert *with* the customer's participation. And although you're not exactly performing solo, you're directing this collaborative effort — and it is up to you to step up as the conductor. Just as the maestro of a world-renowned symphony wouldn't drop his baton and let the orchestra finish up Beethoven's Fifth on its own, you must take the lead and guide the prospect to its harmonious conclusion. This chapter explains why the close is important, how you can put together a smooth, successful close, and what you can do to lay the groundwork for a successful business relationship.

Grasping What Closing Entails

The close is the culmination of all your hard work to link what you're selling to the needs, wants, desires, and expectations of your prospect. If you've followed the presentation (check out Chapter 12) and performed each step flawlessly, you may anticipate a natural crescendo toward resolution. Often, however, the ending is less apparent. Don't worry: This section offers a few secrets to move things along.

Closing: More than just the destination

Making a successful close is more than the last step you take with your prospect before everyone signs the deal. In fact, closing starts at the initial contact and carries forward with each step of the sale. If your skills are strong in prospecting, lead follow-up, qualifying, and handling objections, your odds of closing skyrocket. Each stage of the sales process concludes with a "close" that leads to the next stage.

Before you hang up the phone from the first call, you must make your first close — confirm that you're both ready to take the next step. Doing so may be that the client simply agrees to review and consider the information you've shared. Or you may schedule a follow-up appointment.

Even the qualifying stage (check out Chapter 10) ought to include a close. You're asking for his expectations and conditions of satisfaction. You can then execute a summation close to ensure you heard him correctly, such as in the following:

> "Bob, I want to make sure I have this right. You want a copier that copies 50 pages per minute, collates the documents, and has a stapling feature, correct? So, if we can provide that, will we have a basis for doing business together?"

The close, at any stage of the sales process, follows the same formula:

> "If I do _____, will you _____?"

Understanding the Biblical truth about closing

"Ask, and you shall receive." What a wonderful thought. But how true is it? I'm here to testify to its veracity — at least in the realm of sales. Let me put it another way, "If you don't ask, you shall not get the sale." When you're working on a close, make sure you ask for what you want.

Countless studies have shown that the number-one reason consumers give for not buying is that they weren't asked. Think about it: A fisherman who baits his line with his best lure, then props it against the beer cooler instead of putting it in the water, isn't going to come home with a net full of fish. Likewise, a salesperson who prospects, creates a lead, sends information, follows up, books an appointment, makes the presentation, but never asks for the sale

The power of ASC

At Sales Champions, we use the acronym ASC to refer to what we call Actual Sales Close. *ASC* is defined as a selling presentation (whether over the phone or face to face) that makes a definitive statement of value to the prospect and asks the prospect to take action — to buy — *now.*

Over a decade of coaching and training salespeople, I've discovered one undeniable truth: Top-performing salespeople rack up more ASCs in a week than other salespeople. Because they ask for the close more often, they're making more sales.

As part of our program, we require our clients to count and report their weekly ASCs. We compile and track these numbers among all our clients. Some companies have sales champions with dozens of ASCs each week. The bottom performers may bring in less than one per week, and the very worst average just one-half of an ASC a week. We affectionately call them "half-ASC" salespeople!

Your action plan for this week is to track your number of ASCs. If you focus on driving that number up, your income will go up proportionally with it.

will also leave empty handed. The salesperson invested time, effort, energy, and company resources, but failed to do the simple step of closing.

This truth is simply a matter of action-reaction. For example:

- *Action*: Eat three cheeseburgers and a full bag of potato chips and drink a gallon of soda each day. *Reaction*: Gain weight.

- *Action*: Ask for the sale. *Reaction*: Get the sale.

Okay, fair enough . . . you aren't guaranteed to get the sale; you may *receive* a different response, even if you ask. But I can guarantee this: If you *don't* ask, you won't receive.

Reading the signs and using a trial close

Frequently, sales success is a matter of timing. From time to time throughout the sales process, you may want to determine whether the prospect's open to the close. You do this through a technique called *trial close*. This technique can be applied in any of the sales phases.

In essence, a *trial close* is a test question that measures the prospect's receptiveness to buying, such as the following:

> *"If what we are discussing makes sense, will you be ready to move forward today?"*

> *"If we can deliver everything you want in our widgets, how soon would you want us to deliver them?"*

> *"Is this the type of service you are looking for in a financial planner? Is there anything that I am missing?"*

Pushing for a close too early can result in increased resistance from the prospect and even damage the relationship. Sometimes, salespeople miss the window of opportunity — when the prospect is ripe for action. The moment can easily pass, whether the client's enthusiasm has diminished or a competitor seizes the opportunity.

Keeping your ear tuned for signals that indicate closing time is near is critical; particularly if you're conducting business over the phone, pay attention to any deviation in speech pattern. The following could be a sign that the prospect is ready to buy:

- ✔ **Shifting gears:** When the prospect increases the speed of her speech, that can signal that she's ready to move ahead. Likewise, slowing down can indicate that the prospect is in the final deliberation before the buying stage.

- ✔ **Attention to details:** The prospect homes in on smaller issues, such as who to call for problems, delivery or service start date, and finance details. Treat any such questions as a positive sign that the end is near.

- ✔ **Finding fault:** New objections can indicate that the prospect is trying to reconcile any last-minute doubts before making a decision. Objections are requests for more information. To master objections in the sales process, turn to Chapter 13.

If you don't pay attention to the signs, you can jeopardize the whole sale. At worst, another salesperson that you're competing with for the business may get the sale because she was more effective at closing.

You can develop an unlimited number of trial closes for your product or service. When I was in real estate sales, I sat down and crafted 20 to 30. I practiced them regularly and delivered them with every prospect. I inserted the trial closes into each stage of my presentation. In fact, in some cases, after qualifying the prospect, I would sit down before my presentation and select the trial closes in advance. It wasn't by accident that I closed more than 85 percent of the presentations I made to prospects!

Battling closing phobia

No matter how swimmingly the sales process has gone, getting to the final reckoning point can induce near catatonia for a salesperson with fear-of-rejection issues. It's like proposing to your sweetheart on national TV — a potential kiss-off at its most personal.

Okay, first off, trust me when I say, "It's not you." Rejection is part of any sales job. You won't sell what you have to everyone. If *everyone* bought, you wouldn't be selling; you'd be taking orders. So pat yourself on the back for putting yourself out there and flexing your sales muscles.

Secondly, look at it this way: You can't lose what you don't have. And you don't have the sale until the ink dries and the money's in the bank. Don't invest all your emotional capital on this one, single event. Instead, take a deep breath, smile, and get out there and ask for the sale.

Reducing contract fallout

The best way to get a contract signed is with a face-to-face meeting. When you close over the phone, you can expect a greater level of transaction fallout. But if your business is limited to over-the-phone interaction, don't worry: With careful attention and more direct follow-up in calls and e-mails to make sure that the contract comes back and the deposit is made, you can keep your recidivism at a low level.

However, some customers get cold feet when the time comes to sign the contract. When this used to happen to a sales manager of mine, he'd say, "Murphy is going to get his." Referring to Murphy's Law, he anticipated losing some sales to this perverse truism that if anything can go wrong, it will.

But with careful management, you can avoid most of your closes being lost to Murphy. The secret is to offer a clear and easy process to the prospect:

- ✔ **Let the buyer know when the contract will arrive.** Giving them a date lets them know when to expect it.

- ✔ **Make sure you're aware of the process the buyer must follow in order to turn around the agreement.** Does he need a legal review? A sign off by executives? You don't want to have to waste time and redo the contract if it's not done correctly the first time.

✔ **Pin down how long the client needs to turn around the contract.** Doing so can keep everything on schedule.

✔ **Instruct the client to e-mail or fax a copy of the contract as soon as it is final and mail you the original copies.** You can keep everything moving without having to wait for the hard copy.

✔ **Set an appointment to talk to the customer after the contract should arrive in your office.** Follow-up is essential.

✔ **Consider using an overnight delivery service or electronic delivery of contracts.** Doing so speeds up the return of the contracts and reduces the contract fall-out rate.

These steps should reduce the risk of contract fallout. Because you've been crystal clear about the sequence of events, neither you nor the client should be uncertain about what's going on with the other side. By giving you a copy of the contract immediately, the buyer is less likely to back out. And by setting an appointment ahead of time, if the client *doesn't* meet the contract return date, the call gives you an opportunity to give a gentle reminder and also allows you to gauge the customer's satisfaction level with your sales process and service.

Wrapping up: Zip it or rip it

When it comes time to close, silence is golden. Zipping your lip after you've asked for the order is paramount to a successful close. It's time to put your new customer in the spotlight. After you've identified the solution to the need, led them to this crossroad, and asked the critical question, you owe your prospects the space to decide what is best for them.

The wrap-up begins with a closing question. The *closing question* provokes your customer to think, consider, ponder, or even struggle with a bit of discomfort. And that's not a bad thing. Your question puts pressure on the client — and pressure results in change; change creates action; and that action, as long as you stay out of the way, is the close of the deal.

Discovering How to Close: The Four Best Closing Strategies

Finding the best ways to close for your unique sales circumstances may take some trial-and-error testing. Books, CD series, DVD training, and seminars deliver infinite options and variations on themes. But *your* goal is to uncover those that work best for you.

You can't succeed with just one close style, nor is it feasible to manage an arsenal of 50 techniques. If you have high levels of competency and conviction in about a dozen or so closing techniques, you're well-equipped to handle virtually any sales situation.

I stick with the straightforward, time-tested closing techniques in this section. The more complex your closes, the greater the margin for error. The longer you talk in closing, the lower the probability of success. These four methods all involve asking for the order in a direct, clear manner.

Offering an alternative choice

When you offer an *alternative choice* with this closing strategy, you give the customer a sense of control. But the amazing thing is, by offering even just *two* choices, you increase the odds exponentially that the prospect will choose to buy.

The choices you extend must be calculated to produce a positive response either way. Okay, so you don't offer: "Would you like to buy this product, or would you prefer that I leave now without getting your commitment?" Instead focus on two options, such as:

- ✔ "Which do you like better — the ocean-view condo or the one with access to the pool?"
- ✔ "Do you prefer the granite countertop in black or gray?"

And you don't have to make the choice about the product itself. It can be about delivery, service agreement, or payment plan, such as in the following:

- ✔ "Will payment be through VISA, MasterCard, or American Express?"
- ✔ "Do you want to meet Wednesday or Thursday this week?"
- ✔ "Would you like your free gift to be the potato peeler or the apple corer?"

Offering an alternative is one of my favorite closes: It's simple, it works, and it's made me millions of dollars in sales. This versatile technique works at every stage of the process — you can use it for qualifying, trial closes, and presentations.

When using this close, don't offer too many choices. Limit the options you offer to three — two is preferable. If you give a prospect ten options, for example, he may spend too much time thinking about which to pick, or he may attempt to hybridize the possibilities and create an option you can't deliver.

Don't be too concerned about coming up with options you're certain the client wants. Pairing up the likely choice with a sure loser may even move along the close process more effectively than if the prospect has to think about it. For example, I've discovered that this strategy is very effective with children. My 5-year-old son, Wesley, loves choices. When I want something done, I give him a choice between doing what I need done or a consequence he won't want: "Do you want to clean your room or not ride your bicycle for the rest of the day?" or "Which would you prefer? To help clear the dishes off the table or not watch a DVD before you go to bed?" Inevitably, he chooses the task that needs to be accomplished.

Making an assumption

Although the prospect hasn't yet said, "I'll take it — I'm ready to sign and write the check," your *assumptive close* statement ever-so-subtly suggests that the sale is imminent and helps make the buyer more comfortable with that outcome. Assumptive closes are often verbal (you are in telephone sales, right?); here are some examples of assumptive closes:

- ✔ "Are you looking to put your in-ground pool in the southern corner of your lot?"

- ✔ "Will you use your hybrid for daily commuting as well as your long-distance trips?"

Note that I refer to the product as "yours." I've already *given* ownership of the item, making it all the easier for the client to imagine having it.

If you're closing face to face, you can also deliver a *nonverbal* assumptive close. Taking notes on a formal document can be very effective in reinforcing the client's acceptance of the sale. As you ask questions and gather information, you can begin filling in the agreement form or the sales order. If the client expresses hesitation, you can explain why you are doing what you are doing. You can easily make the following script work for you:

> *"I want to take notes to make sure I have everything you want down correctly, so there isn't anything that is missed. Is that alright with you?"*

I would suggest that, even if the final sale comes over the phone rather than face to face, you make notes on the contract, as well. That way, you keep the notes all in one spot, and then you also have built-in trial closes with any agreements in terms of delivery dates, execution dates, specifics of what they're receiving, who the parties are in the agreement, and so on. You can find numerous ways to engage and close on the prospect.

Another way you can use the assumptive close: You can soften an assumptive close with opening phrases and even link an assumptive close with an alternative of choice close (see the preceding section); check out the following examples:

- ✔ "This is not meant to rush you. If everything we have reviewed thus far makes sense, how soon do you want delivery of the new copier?"

- ✔ "Not to be assumptive, but if everything we have discussed so far is on target, would you want the 8400 model or 9400 model?"

Taking a test drive

The *test-drive close* is a cousin to the puppy-dog close — most often used on the domestic front: "I just knew you'd love him after you saw him playing with the kids. But, honestly, honey, if you don't think we can take care of a dog, we can take him back to the pound." You know darn well that puppy's here to stay.

The *test-drive close,* however, comes with a guarantee: a full refund if the prospect isn't 100-percent satisfied. When your prospect expresses a clear desire for the product but hasn't yet committed, offer him a test drive. Check out the following script:

> "Mr. Jones, why not give the 8600 model a try? If you are not delighted, you can call me personally, and I will handle your return and refund. Can you get a pen and paper? My name is Bob Smith, and my phone number is 555-1234."

At any stage of the sales process, your personal guarantee is one powerful tool. When employed with the test-drive close, you and your prospect have little to lose — and lots to gain.

Going with a sharp angle

The *sharp-angle close* is one you use only in rare situations, but it can be highly effective. With the sharp angle close, you put the prospect in an "if" situation. Pull this one out of your arsenal when the prospect throws a conditional commitment at you. For example, the client states that she would buy if only you could deliver by next week. Now, this type of request may be a stall tactic — she may be tossing it out because she thinks it's an impossible request. But if you can meet her demand, you'd be surprised how often these situations turn into sales.

Check out the following conditional commitment and response from the salesperson:

> **Prospect:** "If I decide to buy long-distance service, I'd need it switched by the end of the month."

> **Salesperson:** "If I can guarantee that we can switch you before the end of the month, are you prepared to do business together?"

If you don't know whether you can perform by the specified date, you can use this type of response:

> **Salesperson:** "If I could guarantee that we can switch your service by the end of the month, and I am not certain we can without confirmation from servicing, are you prepared to move forward with our agreement?"

Strengthening the Sale: The Follow-up after the Close

You did it! From first call to final agreement, you got the sale — adding another victory to this month's sales goals. All that hard work paid off and now you're ready to take some well-deserved R&R.

But before you adjust the lounge chair and add the mint to your julep, you have a little more work to do. Sure, you got the client's commitment, but the curtain hasn't fallen on this act yet. Plenty of things could still happen to unravel all your efforts. By taking a few measures to shore up the deal, you reduce that risk.

Your follow-up steps offer another benefit: You set the stage for a long-running show with this customer. By strengthening this particular sale, you can look forward to more sales and even an ongoing stream of business referrals. This section can help you fortify your relationship with this prospect and ensure the buyer doesn't back out from the sale.

Insuring against buyer's remorse

Buyer's remorse is a fact of life. It's the feeling of the buyer questioning what he just bought. You've experienced it yourself — and if you're like most people, the higher the price tag, the harder the punch. "What have I done?" "How can I get out of this?" "I made a big mistake!" "I should have said no." Adding fuel to the fire are friends, coworkers, bosses, spouses: "You did what?"

Buyer's remorse can set in the minute the ink is dry on the order — or build over time as the customer second guesses his decision. A top salesperson takes immediate action to counter the insidious effects of buyer's remorse. To insure against buyer's remorse, the following can help.

Affirming the purchase

After you complete the sale, the first thing you may want to do is turn in the order. Get it up on the big board to advertise your success. Line up for your commission check. But hold off until you've completed the most important task: affirming the purchase.

Reassure your new client by congratulating him on his wise decision. For example:

> "Bob, I want you to know that you made a great decision in buying the 8600 model. It's exactly what your company needed to increase the productivity of the staff and improve the quality of your reports to your clients."

Be sure to insert some of the benefits that were most important to him when you were discussing the sale. Remind the purchaser of the key reasons he made this decision. When a "you-did-what?" person challenges him later, he'll appreciate the refresher from you.

Saying the magic word

Before you turn in the sale, you don't want to overlook the most fundamental courtesy — saying thank you for the customer's business. You can keep it simple, such as the following thank you:

> "Bob, I know that there are other options available to you besides our cable television service. I want to thank you for selecting us to provide that service to you. It was my pleasure to help you."

Some of you are in highly competitive sales arenas in which the consumer has many choices. Recognizing this and expressing your appreciation for the business reassures your new client that he made the right choice. For example, on virtually every flight I take, the flight attendant thanks the passengers for choosing the airline and acknowledges that they could have chosen another carrier to fly to their destination. Salespeople should remember that this practice applies to their industry, too.

Staying in touch

Although few salespeople keep in regular contact with their clients after the commission check has been cut, *your* efforts to do so promise to set you apart from the others. When you consider how much you invested into the relationship to earn the client's business, nurturing that connection only makes sense, and maintaining your relationship means locking in that client for life. Staying in contact doesn't take much: Occasional check-in calls, updates about enhancements or new services, or even birthday acknowledgments don't demand much more than dropping a card in the mail.

Schedule it

While the sale is fresh in your mind, you won't have much difficulty remembering to call the client to confirm on-time delivery and complete satisfaction with the product. But once that success is a distant memory, you may find the stretches between contacts gets longer and longer.

Don't let that happen: *Schedule* those regular follow-up calls, whether once a month or four times a year. Plug them into your calendar just like you do the weekly meetings with your boss.

Stay ahead of the game: "Thinking of you"

If you feel like you don't have a good reason to call — no new products to sell, no updates or enhancements — look at providing your clients with added value based on their interests. Keep in touch with your clients to show you're aware of their interests and thinking of them. Doing so shows professionalism.

For example, say your customer is an avid golfer. You may want to procure some passes to a prestigious course, tickets to a popular golf tournament, or a subscription to a golf magazine. The fact that you're doing this post-sale carries a lot of weight and certainly ensures that she'll remember you.

You can also stay on top of developments in her industry: forward articles of interest, send congratulations on positive company press or awards, or serve as "corporate intelligence" and report news about competition (as long as the competition isn't a client, too!). These efforts send the message that you're thinking of your client and always looking out for her interests.

Be sure to include in your mailing your latest catalogue of products or a new product brochure. They're more likely to get noticed in this added-value mailing than if you'd sent them solo.

Chapter 15

Moving Forward When You Don't Land the Sale

*R*ejection comes with the sales territory — even for the best salespeople. But dynamite salespeople *don't* equate the loss of a sale with *failure*. Just because you don't land the sale doesn't mean you've lost the prospect forever. In fact, dealing with the emotional whammy is one of the most critical factors in getting past sales rejection.

My best advice is to let go of attachment to the outcome. The more time and effort you invest in the prospect, the more devastating the rejection may feel. Getting over a hang-up on your initial sales call is easier than putting in weeks of work and hearing a "no" at the eleventh hour. I'm not suggesting that you cut and run if you don't tie up the sale in short order or that you refuse to give the effort your 110 percent, however lengthy the process. But be aware that the emotional gut punch could be more powerful — so be prepared to repeat the mantra, "Let go of attachment to outcome."

By following this approach and staying "in the moment" throughout the process, you're more likely to stick to the right steps — preparing and giving a dynamic presentation, overcoming objections, and effectively closing — that bring success. And if you don't make this particular sale, well, you'll know that you did your best. You're in it for the long haul. So the next time you hear "no" from a prospect, tap into your inner wisdom, accept the outcome with grace, and move forward. In this chapter, I share tactics for conceding graciously and retaining connection — which increase the likelihood that this loss will lead to success down the road.

Sticking to the Seven-Step Recovery Program

When you lose the sale, the first steps you take can help you conclude the process with professionalism and dignity. By adhering to the seven steps to closure in this section, you also build bridges for an ongoing relationship and increase opportunities for future business, as well.

Step one: Gather information

Even in the face of defeat, valuable information could lead to further sales opportunities. Although rejection often feels personal, in most cases it isn't. The prospect has specific business reasons why he made a particular choice. The more you understand what led to that decision, the better prepared you'll be to sell successfully in the future. Most prospects recognize and appreciate your efforts and are happy to answer your questions regarding their decisions. (Truth is, they may feel bad about saying no — this gives them an opportunity to assuage some of that guilt!)

Ask permission to pose a few questions, explaining that you want to do a better job in the future. The more information you gather about your performance, your company's performance, your products and services, the prospect's decision-making process, and the company's future needs, the more likely you'll parlay this "failure" into future success.

Here are some questions that may result in insightful answers:

> *"Where did we fall short in securing your business?"*
>
> *"Did I say or do anything that influenced the sale away from our company?"*
>
> *"If you were me, what would you have done differently?"*
>
> *"Do you see an opportunity where we might work together again in the future? What would that be?"*
>
> *"Is there anything else that I can do for you?"*
>
> *"May I contact you in a few months just to touch base and see how the solution you chose has worked out?"*

Step two: Express your disappointment

In an effort to remain upbeat in the face of rejection, salespeople may risk coming off a little too glib. A too-cheerful acceptance may translate as, "No big deal"; "I wasn't really expecting to get the sale"; or "Your business is not that important to me."

You *don't* want to leave this message behind. A sincere, clear expression of disappointment, on the other hand, can communicate that the prospect is, indeed, important. This doesn't mean whining or pouting or attempting to lay guilt. When done properly, your declaration communicates an admirable level of caring and commitment.

After listening carefully to the prospect's explanation, try a response along these lines:

> *"Well, I must confess I'm disappointed to lose your business. I believe we can meet your objectives and exceed your expectations. I respect your decision and wish you the best success. And if you find that your circumstances change and you need services such as ours, I look forward to any opportunities to serve you."*

Step three: If you can't say anything nice . . .

Later in this chapter in the "Avoiding the Three No-Sale Sins" section, I advise you to squelch the urge to badmouth the prospect's choice. In fact, at this stage, don't make *any* negative remarks, whether a slam at the prospect's judgment, a criticism of the values of her company, or a crack at the competition.

More importantly, seek out some positive things to say. I know, easier said than done, especially if you have strong conviction about your product or service — as you should. But you can find plenty of ways you can compliment without compromising. For example:

> *"I appreciate how much thought and effort you've put into your exploration process and know you've made this decision after careful consideration."*

> *"This process has made it clear to me how committed your company is to its values and convictions. I know that any company would be proud to earn your business."*

By saying something nice, you avoid the natural tendency to go negative when you hear bad news. You also avoid your reaction to begin the sales pitch all over again. You also position yourself as a professional with integrity.

Step four: Before hanging up, open a window

As a telephone salesperson, you're always in the process of preparing for the future — and that doesn't stop when you're coming off a no sale. The future is always brighter when you open a window. *Opening a window* simply means giving yourself a future opportunity to make a sale. As you wind down your conversation with the prospect, take these steps to keep the window open:

- **Ask permission to check back in a few weeks.** By doing so, you may discover that the prospect is now dissatisfied and looking for a new provider.

- **Ask to contact the prospect periodically.** "Can I call you in a month just to see how you are doing?" The larger the account, the more frequently you want to be in touch.

In most cases, the call back should happen between 30 days and three months. That timeframe is soon enough that the prospect hasn't forgotten you, but far enough out that you're not a pest.

- **Encourage the prospect to call you any time.** "If I can be of assistance to you in the future, please don't hesitate to call." Doing so shows that you're available to be of service.

Step five: Send a personal note

Thank-you notes aren't appropriate only for wedding presents and job interviews. Send a handwritten personal note to the prospect that got away, and I guarantee that she'll remember your name (as well as the fact that the salesperson who got the business didn't send one). This most-effective technique evokes professionalism and courtesy.

You don't have to say much. Simply express your appreciation for the opportunity to vie for their business. Mention your regret that you didn't land the business, and close with a promise to stay in touch in hopes that you may serve them in the future.

Step six: Deliver added value

Just because you didn't get the business doesn't mean you don't have as important a relationship with this prospect as you do with your clients. Treat your no-sale "clients" with the same attention you give the others —differentiate yourself from your competition and, likely, the company your prospects are currently using.

Recycle some of that knowledge you gathered during the sales process and put it to work providing added value. For example, forward articles of personal or professional interest. Recommend books or seminars. Alert prospects to relevant resources, products, and services. By showing the prospect an extra value, she may consider your business in the future.

Step seven: Just do it!

If, during your final communication with the prospect, you committed to doing something — whether calling, mailing an article, or forwarding information on a new product — make sure you do it! Following up and sticking to your word communicates that the prospect is as important as any other client.

Blowing off this sort of commitment is easy — you didn't land the business, so why go to the trouble? You're busy enough serving those folks who are paying your commissions, right? However, don't downplay the importance of this person.

Your no-sale prospects are highly qualified prospects. After all, you made it to the final round before you got the gong. So your investment in them is likely to offer a high return. If you're a good sport and don't go off and pout, when this prospect needs this service or product again, he'll remember how you followed through.

Finding Follow-Up Openings

When you view your lost prospects as future clients, you can see the value in maintaining a relationship with them. But challenges come along with the package. For one thing, because you *aren't* doing business with them in the present, you have fewer opportunities to make contact and build your relationship.

So your challenge is to *seek out* follow-up openings. It may take a bit of effort, but the opportunities certainly exist. Following are three arenas to explore — my advice is to go for a mixed-use plan that calls on all three.

Checking in with a service checkup

If the prospect said yes when you asked permission to follow up from time to time, you have the perfect opportunity. A service checkup allows you to take a reading on how satisfied the prospect is with his service and whether he has any new needs. Basically, you want the answers to these three questions:

- ✔ "How is the purchase of your competitors product or service performing?"
- ✔ "Are you getting exactly what you need and expected?"
- ✔ "Is there anything I can do for you?"

You'd be surprised at how much business these checkups can garner when you call on a regular basis. Make the commitment to call with a service checkup at least every quarter.

Keeping current with new products

Although your primary objective is to open the door and make a sale, a number of secondary benefits are uncovered — even if you don't land the sale. Chances are, your company rolls out new products or services periodically — providing a perfect excuse for contacting former prospects.

Updating them about your firm's new offerings may permit a peek at how the competition is performing. You're also demonstrating that your company is effective at bringing new products and services to the marketplace. By partnering with you, the prospects assure themselves a spot on the cutting edge.

Even if the prospect isn't in the market for one of your products, she still may like your product. If so, you can also ask for referrals: Does she know anyone within her company or industry who may benefit from your new product or service? Getting these names can provide more prospects.

Extending a social invitation

Even if your newest products aren't pertinent to the prospect's needs, or your service checkup turns up no opportunities (see the preceding sections on these topics), the social engagement is always a means to renew a connection. If you collected any information on a prospect's personal interests, you can use this knowledge to create an opportunity. For example, ask that Thai-food fan to lunch at the new Thai restaurant. Invite the former college athlete-turned-business executive to a ballgame. Let the theater-buff purchasing manager know you have two extra tickets to the city's hottest new production.

 This strategy is especially effective if you're selling personal professional services — real estate, insurance, financial planning, and so forth. Make sure the account value is large enough to warrant this additional investment of time. You wouldn't want to do this if you were selling $100 widgets — unless the prospect could buy thousands of them.

Avoiding the Three No-Sale Sins

Despite efforts to move on from "no" with your positive attitude intact, the sting of rejection often triggers a less-than-positive response. Awareness goes a long way in helping you avoid these three knee-jerk reactions to rejection.

The last thing you want to do is to retaliate or burn any bridges when you get a no answer. The best response is to stay professional and thank the prospect for his time. You also want to avoid doing any of the following no-sale no-nos.

Hitting instant replay

When you get a no answer, the very last thing you want to do is try the sales pitch all over again. When you do, all the prospect hears is "You'd have to be a total idiot to say no to my proposal, so I'll give you the benefit of the doubt and assume you just didn't *hear* my presentation. Let me start from the beginning." Attempts to save the game with a Hail Mary pass are pretty transparent.

This approach shows little respect for the prospect or the sales process. It smacks of desperation and a self-focused obsession on commission. You're better off keeping your mouth closed and listening respectfully. This way, you not only avoid turning off the prospect, but you may also learn valuable information that could help you regain the client at some point. You may be able to use this valuable information to find a solution that would get the prospect to say yes.

Switching to deep-freeze mode

Silence is golden, but the silent treatment can tarnish your professional image. When the prospect gives you a no answer, you don't

want to give the silent treatment. I've seen a lot of salespeople —
in an attempt not to express disappointment or frustration —
suddenly cool toward the client and clam up. The silence is often
preceded with a tight-lipped "Fine."

More than 20 years in sales have exposed me to countless instances
of the deep-freeze treatment. But in truth, 18 years of marriage have
taught me the real meaning of "Fine." When my wife, Joan, uses that
word, I can assure you that whatever I said or didn't say — did or
didn't do — is most certainly not "fine." It's a signal for me to take
immediate action to make amends for whatever I said — or didn't say.

No doubt, your prospects have the same clear reading of the word
fine. But unlike me — a model husband — they will take immediate
steps to divorce themselves from the situation. You're better off to
express your disappointment in a calm and respectful manner than
freeze your prospects with the silent treatment.

Knocking the competition

In a last-ditch effort to save the sale, desperate salespeople often
turn to bashing the company or service the prospect has chosen.
Sure, you know all sorts of sordid details about this company —
it's in the best interest of the prospect to let him or her know
exactly what they're getting into. Certainly, after they have this
insight, they'll switch to a company they can trust — yours, right?

Don't count on it. Although you may be successful in spoiling the
sale for your competitor, you're likely to damage your own reputation. Most people know sour grapes when they see 'em.

But what's the worst damage done? When you knock the company
your prospect has chosen to work with, you convey that you don't
think she's competent to make a good business decision. And who
wants to work with someone who thinks they're incompetent?

Part V
Increasing Your Sales

The 5th Wave   By Rich Tennant

BRINKLEMAN
FINANCIAL SERVI

WINNING

"I think you're still giving away too much for the close, Ms. Lamont."

In this part...

*I*nside every successful telephone salesperson is a human behavioral expert — an individual who can size up a prospect quickly and know exactly how to best communicate. This part gives you the tools you need to analyze your clients' behaviors and to understand and maximize your own unique sales style.

In Chapter 16, I help you discover your selling style and how to better utilize your natural gifts to increase sales. In Chapter 17, I demonstrate how to zero in quickly — within minutes — on your prospect's behavioral style through the tone and strength of voice, inflection, and even word selection in order to build trust faster, communicate more effectively, and sell in less time. Lastly, in Chapter 18, I tell you how to harness your emotions, maintain an optimistic attitude, and wield the self-discipline necessary to stay on the path to success. You hear athletes talk about being "in the zone," a place where all the shots drop and putts sink with little effort. Well, salespeople can get into the zone, too — and I show you how in this part.

Chapter 16

Exploding Your Earnings through Behavioral Selling

*U*nderstanding behavioral style can dramatically improve all your personal interactions, whether you're talking to your father or son, your friends, or business customers. The good news is that you don't have to be a doctor of psychology to master behavioral selling. You just need to know something about the DISC profile, which classifies behavioral styles into quadrants and helps you identify individual styles and how to communicate most effectively for that style. Equally important, DISC can help you identify and optimize your *own* behavioral style.

Sound complicated? It isn't. This chapter walks you through the nuts and bolts of DISC, helps you identify *your* behavioral style, and shares the importance of adapting your style to increase your sales.

Getting the Lowdown on DISC

Everyone reacts differently to any given situation: Say you're in a meeting to hear the bad news that your company earnings are down. If I were there, I might demand facts, numbers, and possibly hurt some people's feelings by my direct approach to finding the source of the problem. You might launch into a pep talk, pat the others on the back, and assure everyone that this is just a hiccup. Another attendee might latch onto a finance report, poring over every detail and attempting varying analyses. And someone else may simply sit calmly, taking in the responses of the others before speaking up.

These are examples of varying responses, defined within a behavioral model known as the DISC model. According to the DISC theory, a widely followed behavioral model — adopted and modified by numerous behavioral-modeling programs — each person exhibits one or more of the following behaviors in varying degrees:

- ✔ Dominant
- ✔ Influencer
- ✔ Steady
- ✔ Compliant

These four factors blended together create the make-up of your behavioral style.

Before diving deeper into DISC, you must rid yourself of two ideas before you make any wrong assumptions about people:

- ✔ **No behavioral style is better than another.** In truth, each style carries with it strengths and weaknesses, opportunities and challenges. In sales, some styles have a higher probability of achieving success, but each one — given the right product line, willingness to perfect sales skills, and commitment — can achieve success.

- ✔ **Most people exhibit a combination of behavioral styles, with one or even two commanding the mix (called *primary behavioral styles*).** Very few people — less than 4 percent — score high in only one style.

Was *Wonder Woman* a Dominant?

Humankind has been struggling to understand what makes people tick since the earliest times. And, since those earliest times, it seems that people have been dividing everything up into *fours:* Nearly 2,500 years ago, Greek philosopher Empedocles proclaimed that each personality is influenced by fire, water, earth, or air. His contemporary, Hippocrates, identified four temperaments: sanguine, melancholic, choleric, and phlegmatic.

In 1928, Harvard doctoral graduate Dr. William Moulton Marston published his landmark book, *The Emotions of Normal People.* In it, he established the DISC model, identifying four behavioral types: dominant, influencing, steady, and compliant. (Lest you assume Marston was a stuffy old academic, know that in addition to inventing an early lie detector, he's also the co-originator of the *Wonder Woman* comic strip.) Today, many behavioralists adhere to the DISC model or some variation of it — incorporating colorful foursomes from panthers, dolphins, peacocks, and owls, to guardians, idealists, artisans, and scientists.

A person's primary behavioral style is the style with the highest score when using an assessment instrument. It's the style that is most notable especially in pressure situations. The *secondary style* is another of the DISC factors that is a high score but not the highest score. It influences behavior to a lesser degree.

I dissect each behavioral style in the following section in this chapter for a better understanding of the DISC theory. I then help you figure out your style and how to use it to your advantage in the sales arena in the section "Figuring Out Your DISC Style."

D Is for Dominant

The Dominant person — in some DISC systems referred to as a *driver panther, organizer, guardian,* or *economist* — exhibits the characteristics that many perceive to be those of a leader. The High D is often described as:

- Aggressive
- Bold
- Competitive
- Confident
- Controlling

- Decisive
- Demanding
- Direct
- Results focused
- Risk oriented

I bet you're thinking that most of these characteristics describe a successful salesperson. And, indeed, they often do. These folks are invigorated by challenge and the feeling of accomplishment. This section provides a bit more about the Dominant.

What makes the Dominant tick?

Dominants are bottom-line oriented. They thrive when they have a clear, tangible goal, and they're in it — whether we're talking sports, stardom, or sales — to *win*. You find a lot of Ds in the sports world. Vince Lombardi's famous quote of "Winning isn't everything; it's the only thing" sums up life's philosophy for a High Dominant person. Dominants also love a challenge and are enthusiastic when the challenge results in an "est" reward: the high*est* salary, the big*gest* corner office, and so on.

I remember watching a *60 Minutes* interview a few years ago: Co-host Ed Bradley asked golf mega-star Tiger Woods, "If we played ping pong, would you want to beat me?" Woods responded, "No, I would want to kick your butt!" Then, Mr. Bradley said, "What if I won?" Tiger's response was classic High D: "We would play again until I won."

How does a D operate?

A Dominant thrives on results (see preceding section), but how does that play out in her life? Dominants are

- ✔ **Self-motivated, with a need to direct and control all situations that have an impact on them.** They can prefer to work alone rather than serve as part of a team. And if they're part of the team, they prefer to be the leader.

- ✔ **Focused on the destination, working hard to achieve their goals and eliminating steps they consider unimportant.** If you've ever said, "Don't ask how I achieved it; only notice that I did it," your core behavioral style is most likely that of a Dominant. (To find out more concretely, check out the section "Figuring Out Your DISC style," later in this chapter.)

- ✔ **Direct.** Some would call them forthright, straightforward, or to the point; others would describe them as curt or brusque.

- ✔ **Willing to work long and hard to make their plans happen.** People with a D behavioral style get to the office early, stay late, and pay almost any price necessary to achieve the success that they desire.

- ✔ **Quick, and expect others they work with to be as quick.** Your D boss wants to know your numbers; she's impatient when you attempt to explain the hows and whys.

What's the downside to Ds?

Fast-thinking, fast-talking, and fast-acting, Dominants can easily overpower or intimidate others. Dominants are by nature direct, aggressive, and to the point. Desire for immediate reward means that most Dominants prefer short sales cycles. When aggravated by stress, the High D can come across as egotistical, arrogant, too fast, not caring, out for the sale, a poor listener, and pressuring.

Dominants also tend to get bored easily and need the constant stimulation of a worthy challenge. A High-D salesperson often moves from company to company in order to seek out new challenges. In their efforts to control all factors that affect their success, Dominants often attempt to control other people as well, which can cause discord within a company. The good news is that when the battle's over, it's over. No grudges, no rehashing. For a Dominant, it's water under the bridge.

The High D has a primary fear of being taken advantage of. A High D must be convinced that he's getting a fair shake or a good deal before he's comfortable moving ahead. A High D also needs the straight story upfront. He's the type who walks into a car dealership and says, "Give me your best price." If he discovers that they didn't give it to him at the get-go, he walks out. The High Ds blind spot? His short fuse often has him exploding in anger. The fireworks go off, with little consideration for the aftermath, and sometimes he's surprised when others seem cold after one of his outbursts.

1 Is for Influencer

As the name implies, *Influencers* or *Expressives* are recognized for their contagious energy and enthusiasm, which can inspire others to action. Influencers typically make strong salespeople with characteristics that match the demands of the job. An Influencer may exhibit some of these qualities:

- ✔ Communicative
- ✔ Emotional
- ✔ Entertaining
- ✔ Enthusiastic
- ✔ Expressive

- ✔ Gregarious
- ✔ Optimistic
- ✔ Personable
- ✔ Persuasive
- ✔ Popular

When you channel the gift of gab, high energy, and powers of persuasion into a telephone-sales professional, you're reckoning with a powerful force. The Influencer makes things happen! Keep reading to find out more about the Influencer behavioral style.

Knowing what drives the 1

Influencers are *people* people. They enjoy working with groups as well as having one-on-one interactions. Influencers like a lot of attention, so in group dynamics, they tend to wind up angling for the spotlight. Being liked, being popular, and being recognized rank high with the I.

Optimism and can-do certainty make Influencers comfortable with the often high-pressure demands of a sales career. Their unbounded enthusiasm and desire for personal glory helps them reach sales achievements — especially if it earns them a gold plaque on the wall for all to see.

High Is are also drawn to the newest, cutting-edge, trendiest, most-exclusive products, services, and experiences available. They feel it's part of their image and that it affects the way others see them. A High I wants to be recognized by other people for her purchase or sound decision.

Spotting an Influencer in action

An I is the easiest of the four behavioral types to identify. Even in the midst of a crowd, look for the most colorful, most vocal, most expressive of the flock, and you've found your I. Influencer's command of language and strong verbal skills turn to his advantage in situations in which he must be persuasive. High Is are extremely social and personable; no surprise, then, that they excel at relationship selling.

One on one, Influencers exude the same amount of energy and optimism. They connect and build a high level of trust in others quickly and easily. In presentation mode, they bring energy, passion, connection, and trust. Influencers relish the presentation stage, and because of their remarkable verbal skills and personal demeanor, they excel at convincing even the most skeptical prospects.

For example, in your mind, replay some of the times you saw President Clinton on television. He's certainly the classic High Influencer. I don't think there has been as effective, friendly, persuasive, optimistic, and verbally persuasive of a politician in my lifetime.

Recognizing too much of a good thing

High Influencers can be bigger than life and sometimes overwhelming. Under fire, a High I can appear scattered, showy, lacking substance, out of touch, verbose, too familiar, self-promoting, and unrealistic.

High Influencers are also often highly emotional. Feelings and emotions can influence their actions heavily — often to the detriment of objective clarity. Focusing on the details — filling in the paperwork and adding up the numbers — just doesn't add up to a priority for an I. In fact, a High I may neglect most activities that don't involve social interaction or "fun."

Influencers tend to be trusting to a fault. They give their trust to people easily with out checking all the facts. Influencers as salespeople often trust that the prospect will do what they say they will do. They often count on sales that never come to fruition. In a sales situation, this trusting nature may put them at risk for major letdown when a sale fails to materialize as promised.

S Is for Steady

The Steady behavioral style is also known as a *relater* or *amiable* in some models. A Steady is rarely described as a high-pressure salesperson, but instead, sells on these other qualities:

✔ Good listener	✔ Predictable
✔ Harmonious	✔ Reliable
✔ Loyal	✔ Service oriented
✔ Patient	✔ Sincere
✔ Persistent	✔ Team oriented

Easy-going, laid-back, and low-pressure describe the sales style of the Steady, a style that often seems at odds with the traditional stereotype of the typical sales personality. For more on the Steady, keep reading.

Pinpointing what gets a Steady going

Steadies live to serve. They're driven to please and meet the needs of their clients and prospects first. They're extremely loyal to the people around them and are always willing to give help and support. An environment of collaboration and cooperation is the most comfortable place for the S.

The High S develops deep, long-term sales relationships, retaining clients for years and decades. The Steady is outstanding at maintaining, servicing, and expanding established accounts. High Steadies desire *completion* more than competition. They want to finish what they start and take a client through each step or stage of the sales process for their *own* fulfillment, as well as for the client's.

Distinguishing a Steady

If you want to see a Steady, look for the Energizer Bunny. This type sticks to the established sales strategy and cycle and keeps going and going and going. The predictable Steady sticks to the program, especially under fire.

Spotting High Steadies can sometimes be hard. They're behind-the-scenes operators, steering clear of center stage and opportunities for attention. That doesn't mean Steadies don't like working with people — in fact, they're very sociable, but in more of a what-can-I-do-for-you way, rather than a look-at-me way. Steadies treasure long-standing relationships and work hard to maintain them.

A High Steady is the type that sticks with her hairdresser of ten years — even though she's less than dazzled with her recent haircuts. The High S possesses unlimited amounts of patience for the sales process, feeling out clients' needs, wants, concerns, and hesitations. Although not dramatically emotive like the High Influencer, the Steady is empathetic and exudes a caring attitude.

Steady challenges

Although patience is a virtue, sometimes Steadies are steadfast to a fault, letting the sales process languish well past its productivity. Their lack of self-focus often translates to lack of self-confidence, and their discomfort with sudden change can paralyze them in times of upheaval.

The nature of the Steady is to proceed with caution when pressure increases. Steady salespeople are likely to contain their emotions and react slowly to a threat. They're uncomfortable with closing, especially if they sense any resistance, and will all-too-quickly hand over all control of the situation to the prospect. A High Steady in extreme can be viewed as uncaring, uncreative, slow to act, unable to change, afraid, inflexible, hesitant, and unconcerned.

The High Steady craves harmony in all interactions. She wants everyone to get along, work together, and talk it out. If a High S senses friction, her inclination is to flee. But to those she's connected with, a High S is a loyalist. Despite their strong commitments, High Steadies can come across as disengaged or uncaring because they tend not to express their emotions, and people may have a hard time reading them.

C Is for Compliant

The Compliant, also referred to as *rational* or *analytical* in other behavioral models, yearns more than any other type for quality and perfection. The High C doesn't match the traditional description of a successful salesperson, but many C qualities have a place in the sales world:

✔ Detailed	✔ Precise
✔ Diplomatic	✔ Process oriented
✔ Exacting	✔ Reserved

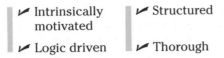

✔ Intrinsically motivated

✔ Logic driven

✔ Structured

✔ Thorough

Compliants' selling is fact oriented rather than emotional. They may be successful in commercial real estate, for example, where capitalization rates, cash flow, and other calculations and formulas determine sales success. In this world, investors are more numbers oriented in their decision making and they appreciate the strengths of a Compliant salesperson. Want to know more about what gets a Compliant going, how to identify one, and some of the pitfalls of being a High C? The following sections have your answers.

What puts a High C into high gear?

High Compliants aren't motivated by contests, recognition, rewards, and other incentives. They're there to compete with themselves based on the standard they've committed to meet — whether it's the company mission or the current quarter earnings goals. For High Cs, the focus is on the process and on achieving accurate and high-quality results — *not* on winning awards.

In any endeavor, having a clear grasp of all the details is important to a High C. For example, a High C wouldn't buy a new plasma TV until he's researched all the features and comparison-shopped with every store in town and on the Internet — even if it takes months.

High Cs thrive when they clearly understand the expectations and are given the time and resources to achieve accuracy and quality in their outcomes. They don't demand the sort of control that a Dominant does, but they crave control over the factors that affect their results.

How does a High C act?

Compliants, like Steadies, often fly under the radar. They can be quiet, reserved, and — although they're agreeable to team situations — often found working alone. Compliants are meticulous planners. The High-C salesperson painstakingly prepares for calls, questions, auxiliary information, and objections before picking up the phone. They're polite and courteous in their approach. For a sales manager, Compliants provide the fewest problems in regard to following the rules, procedures, and paperwork.

High Cs need to follow the process and be clear on their objectives. Naturally reserved and painstakingly thorough, they become more so under pressure, especially if they're being pressured to make a sudden change or break with the plan in any way. Under these circumstances, they turn to the procedures and carefully review the facts, the data, and the situation. High Compliants seek absolute accuracy. They often fear making the wrong decision and assess every situation thoroughly. High Cs often let their exacting nature lead to fear — a fear that they'll make a bad decision.

When Compliants turn uncompliant

Considering their moniker, Compliants can be the most difficult, contrary, and *uncompliant* of the four types. In fact, these High Cs are actually in compliance to a higher standard — one of thoroughness and accuracy at all costs. If they're pressed to compromise in a way that betrays these standards, they can become just plain belligerent.

Compliants, like Steadies, can be resistant to change and slow to adapt, especially from what they believe to be the right process or system. At their worst, High Compliants are viewed as perfectionists, unyielding to change, overly questioning, too sensitive, slow moving, nitpicky, pessimistic, and not focused enough on the results.

ANECDOTE

Watch out for Dominant Dirk

I'm naturally a High Dominant, and in a perfect world, I would prefer to engage in all situations in a High Dominant fashion. I like to give short, hard-hitting, direct, fast-paced, assertive presentations to prospects I've carefully qualified so I don't waste time. I also like to use assertive trial closes and straightforward objection handling (see Chapters 13 and 14 for more on these topics) that culminate in strong conviction-based closes.

That sales style works like a charm for me — as long as I'm talking to another Dominant. The High D loves that straight-to-the-point, just-the-results-ma'am, no-beating-around-the-bush approach. But for the 82 percent of the population who aren't Dominant, my communication style is likely to hit them like a category-5 Hurricane Dirk and push them into battening down the hatches or getting out of town when they know I'm coming.

If I want to reach my sales goals, I have to either limit my market to the 18 percent High Ds, or I must figure out how to adapt my selling style to reach the other 82 percent of the potential prospects in the world. If I limit my selling to Dominants (which would not be wise), I would need to dramatically increase my prospecting numbers to reflect my lack of adaptability in my approach and presentation.

Figuring Out Your DISC Style

Effective selling happens when competence and confidence connect. Most people have a higher level of confidence when they can tap into their own natural selling style: For one person, that may mean building a relationship (Steady); for someone else it may mean delivering an Academy Award–winning presentation (Influencer).

So when are you the most confident? Your style greatly affects how you interact with others and how you approach your sales goals. In the remainder of this chapter, I help you discover your own behavior style and — I hope — lead you to a greater understanding of who you are. With that info, I hope you can get a clearer picture of the way you work, so you can work with more confidence (and higher sales). (For more info about your prospect's behavioral style and why you need to understand it, check out Chapter 17.)

Know thyself; take the test

To be most effective in your communication efforts, you must first understand yourself. Then you can figure out how to adapt your sales style in order to effectively reach and sell to all behavior types. To advance your career by using the DISC model, you must take one action step right now — take the test!

To identify your primary behavioral style, go to the Sales Champions Web site, www.SalesChampions.com/FreeDISC, and take the free behavior-style assessment. It takes less than 10 minutes to answer the 12 questions, and you get the results back via e-mail within minutes. During the assessment, you answer questions that give you choices of words to decide if you're most like them or least like them to pinpoint your behavioral style. Then you receive a report with information about you and your behavioral style. This report points you in the right direction so you can begin to use your behavioral style to your telephone-sales advantage.

Reacting under fire

Based on your behavioral style, you tend to respond to situations in predictable ways. Pressurized situations bring on those responses faster and stronger. For example, if you're behind on quota, if it's the end of the month, or if you're talking to a large potential account, your natural tendencies are more pronounced.

Where do you score on the DISC test? Look at the sections earlier in this chapter that explain each behavioral style. None of the natural tendencies are inherently bad. But they can become a barrier to a sale if they're not aligned with the customer's behavioral style. And if the salesperson is under pressure, the behaviors can strengthen — thereby weakening the sales potential.

You want to be able to learn to recognize the prospect's behavioral style quickly so you can communicate more effectively. Your awareness of your own behavioral style allows you to know your natural reactions and tendencies so you can protect yoursef from overpowering your prospect with your strong behavioral characteristics that are out of alignment with theirs.

Recognizing your secondary style

Most people are amalgams of two or more behavioral styles. When you took the assessment exercise on the Sales Champions Web site (Oh, you didn't? Stop what you're doing and go to www.Sales Champions.com/FreeDISC), you identified your primary behavioral style, but I can virtually guarantee that you have a secondary style, as well.

Your secondary style can be determined by taking a more diagnostically complete DISC assessment that evaluates all four behavioral categories. It can help you analyze both high and low scores and their influences on your behavior. If you want to take a more complete version of the test, go to www.saleschampions.com/DISC to access a more extensive diagnostic assessment for a fee. Your behavior and how you react in situations is an amalgam of your high and low scores on the DISC model, although your primary style has the greatest control of how you react and what you do. The other styles apply force at times as well. To really understand yourself as a person and especially a salesperson, you need to know your whole self.

Chapter 17

Selling the Way Your Customer Wants to Buy

In This Chapter

▶ Figuring out what behavioral selling is

▶ Picking up on behavioral styles on the telephone

▶ Working behavior to work the sale

*T*he secret to sales success is simple: Figure out what prospects want to buy — and sell it to them. Believe me, it's a lot easier to give people what they want than to *convince* them that they want what you have to offer. The most effective telephone salespeople are skilled at matching their product or service with the prospect's wants and needs — and as a result, they enjoy shorter sales cycles, greater client connection, less resistance, and more sales.

Everyone has a *buying style,* a certain manner in which they're most comfortable "being sold." Just like some shoppers are more at ease buying through catalogs while others prefer to feel the merchandise, over-the-phone customers also have their style preferences. These preferences are shaped by the four behavioral styles described in Chapter 16.

In this chapter, I tell you how to shape your selling approach to your prospect's behavioral style. This art of selling in a manner the client is most receptive to is called *behavioral selling* or *behavior-based selling.*

Understanding the Power of Behavioral Selling

People exhibit their behavioral styles in everything they do. All you have to do is watch and listen. And what you discover can take you far in the sales world. Successful *behavioral selling* is persuading someone to take an action — or take an action faster — that results in a benefit by aligning your selling style to the prospect's behavioral style. The goal is to align your communication in a style or pattern that causes the prospect to hear and understand.

The key word in behavioral selling is *benefit.* If your offer doesn't benefit your prospect, and you try to sell to him anyway because you need the sale, you're not selling him something he needs. You're manipulating him into buying something. *Behavioral selling* isn't about verbal judo or about tricking, maneuvering, or manipulating a prospect into buying.

To more completely understand behavioral selling and what it means to you and your sales, check out the following three truths:

✓ **People tend to buy from others who have a similar behavioral style.** Behavior studies support the fact that people are most comfortable with others just like themselves. When you meet someone with a similar background, similar interests, and similar mannerisms, you tend to connect more quickly and experience a higher level of trust.

People buy from people they *like.* And they *like* others who are like themselves. So . . . if you want to make more sales, you have to be liked. And to be liked, you have to *be like* the person you're selling to.

For example, fast-talking, bottom-line Dominants can keep up with each other; data-focused Compliants share facts and figures to support their connection. (See Chapter 16 for detailed descriptions of the four behavioral styles and to find out what your style is.) When like styles are partnered, it makes the sales process smoother and easier.

✓ **Salespeople tend to sell to others who have a similar behavioral style.** Have you ever just clicked with a prospect on the first call? That's what often happens when you encounter someone who shares your behavioral style. And this ease in communication continues through the sales process until the successful close. The fact that the close ratio for style-to-style sales is much higher than in those situations with a different style comes at no surprise. You're more likely to make a sale when you and the prospect understand each other.

✓ **Salespeople who adapt to the prospect's behavioral style increase their sales significantly.** You can't rely on the first two rules to carry you to sales success. Consider these numbers:

- 18 percent of the world's population is a Dominant.

- 28 percent of the world's population is an Influencer.

Look for the clues

I have been studying, teaching, and coaching behavioral selling for almost ten years. I learned and perfected the skill by observing everyone I met or talked to and taking mental notes of the way they communicated: their pace, tonality, conviction, vocal volume, and choice of words. I watched newsmagazine shows such as *20/20, Dateline,* and *60 Minutes* to study the behavioral styles of interviewees and interviewers and catch the differences between, say, Barbara Walters's style and that of John Stossel or Ted Koppel.

But the interviewers' approaches weren't determined by their behavioral styles *alone.* The best interviewers adjusted their discussion based on the behavioral style of the interviewee.

- 40 percent of the world's population is a Steady.

- 14 percent of the world's population is a Compliant.

For the sake of illustration, say that you're a Dominant: You can guarantee selling to another Dominant, but you'll never successfully close the other three styles. This means, then, that the highest close rate that you can expect is 18 percent. Or, in order to increase your close rate, you must limit yourself to approaching Dominants only. Either way, you're not giving yourself very good odds of success. If, however, you can change your style to complement the behaviors of others different than you, you open your universe of potential.

When *you* adapt your selling approach to allow for the behavioral style of your prospect, your chances of success shoot up, based on my experiences, by 25 percent to 50 percent.

Recognizing Behavioral Styles Over the Phone

Selling over the phone does challenge your ability to zero in on behavioral styles — clues in facial expression and body language are often key in distinguishing Dominants from Steadies and Influencers from Compliants. But picking up on a prospect's behavioral style over the phone is far from impossible!

Three factors help you determine behavioral style without the benefit of face-to-face contact. When selling over the phone, you can successfully ID behavioral styles by tuning in to these helpful clues:

> ✔ Pace
>
> ✔ Tonality
>
> ✔ Choice of words

This section explains these three clues more in depth so you can identify them and use them to your advantage.

Keeping the pace

Pace helps you separate the four styles into "fast" and "slow" camps. *Pace* is the speed at which people talk. If they talk at 150 words a minute with gusts up to 200 words a minute, you're talking with a Dominant or Influencer. (You can figure this out within the first few seconds of your conversation.) Most of the time Steadies and Compliants are slow talkers and Dominants and Influencers are in the fast lane.

Behavioral style can align with job title

As you better understand behavioral style, you may find that simply by knowing an individual's job title, you can better pinpoint the behavioral style. It only makes sense that certain behavioral styles match certain jobs or occupations better than others. For example, the CEO or entrepreneurial owner of a company is highly likely to be a Dominant or an Influencer. Don't count on running into many Steadies or Compliants. The high-risk-tolerant D or I is better suited for this position. Dominants and Influencers also dominate real estate sales in high-priced resort areas such as West Palm Beach, Florida, or Aspen, Colorado.

If you sell to mid-level managers or provide technology products for the accounting of the company, you'll find more Steady or Compliant behavioral styles. Steady people become rooted in companies. They don't like risk or change, so they don't change jobs as readily as others. If you're selling products to accounting, you also see a higher concentration of Steady and Compliant behavioral styles because they like rules, procedures, systems, and processes. That would be the opposite of selling to someone who likes to bend the rules.

It doesn't mean you won't see High Steady or Compliant prospects in high-powered jobs like CEOs or as entrepreneurial owners; it only means you'll see less of them than in the normal population mix. Why they are less likely in those positions is fundamental to the risk and reward of the Steady and Compliant. The lower numbers in those positions are also contained in the lack of need for showy, ego-enjoyment items in their lives. The Steady and Compliant people don't need the latest, greatest, newest, fastest, or flashiest stuff. They're naturally more conservative with their money and possessions.

After you determine the rate at which your prospect talks, you can adjust your speed accordingly. Don't risk being labeled "slow" or "behind" because you're not keeping up with the Dominants or Influencers. Conversely, if you're talking to a Steady or Compliant, apply the brakes.

Tuning in to tonality

You can also identify your prospect's behavioral style over the phone by checking for tonality. *Tonality* is the force or intensity of your prospect's voice. It also relates to the friendliness and warmth in the tone as well. You can quickly narrow down a person's behavioral style through tonality.

For example, have you ever listened in on a conversation in an unfamiliar language? Even without watching the discussion or understanding a single word, you probably had a good sense of the relationship between the two: whether the two were romantic, angry at each other, or worried; whether one seemed to be the leader; and even whether you liked or disliked both, or one more than the other.

You were able to discern these factors because of the tonality of the conversation. And you can use tonality to help narrow down the behavioral style of your on-the-phone prospect as well. Table 17-1 lists key tonal characteristics of speech for each of the four behavioral types.

Table 17-1	Tonality and Behavioral Styles
Behavioral Style	*Tone of Voice*
Dominant	Strong, loud, clear, direct, confident
Influencer	High and low modulation, warm and friendly, enthusiastic, high energy level
Steady	Soft, warm, low volume, steady pace
Compliant	Direct, deep questioning, low modulation, controlled, thoughtful

Notice that some styles share some of the characteristics: Both the Dominant and Compliant are direct, for example. But the unique combination of qualities is what helps you distinguish each type. The Dominant is direct with force, speaking at a louder range and driving the words with energy and strength. The Compliant speaks directly, but with more deliberation and reserve. Both the Influencer and the Steady convey warmth and openness, but the Influencer expresses more energy and varying modulation when speaking. The Steady speaks more evenly and at a lower volume.

After you pick up on tonality, you can modify your speech accordingly. For example, when speaking with an energetic Influencer, you can add more vivaciousness and variety. If you're speaking to a Compliant, speak more controlled and more direct.

Listening for code words

The vocabulary your prospects choose is influenced by experience and perspective, but it's also shaped by their behavioral style. And by listening to the words your prospects select, you can discover a secret code that reveals that style.

For example, because Dominants have a high need to compete and win, their words, content, and analogies reflect that perspective. (If you've observed my use of sports and athletic competition throughout this book, you could easily draw the conclusion that I'm a High Dominant — and you'd be right.)

Take a look at Table 17-2 for some of the words, phrases, and expressions that can telegraph a prospect's behavioral identity. Hang this list next to your phone so you can monitor the words your prospects use in conversation. After you identify their behavioral style, then use this list as a guide to use correct words with them.

Table 17-2	Key Words to Use with Each Style
Behavioral Style	**Words and Content**
Dominant	Win, new, challenge, results, now, lead the field, compete
Influencer	Cutting edge, exciting, fun, make me look good, I feel . . .
Steady	Guarantee, promise, commitment, service, step by step, help me out
Compliant	Proven, standardized, no risk, analysis, due diligence, here are the facts

When you recognize behavioral style, this table helps you choose words that more effectively communicate to the prospect. Talking about the *fabulous, state-of-the-art* product that is *wildly popular* with the most *renowned business leaders* is bound to get the

Influencer's attention; while offering the *tested* and *proven* product that has been *backed by extensive scientific research* and includes a *no-risk* guarantee is likely to engage a Compliant.

Preparing for Questions

"Be prepared" is the motto for boy scouts and conscientious telephone salespeople alike. That's why you rehearse and practice responses to anticipated questions on a regular basis. With an understanding of the four behavioral styles, you can do an even better job of preparing for the *types* of questions each may ask. (Check out Chapter 10 for why questions can help you.)

Typically, Dominants and Influencers ask fewer questions than Steadies and Compliants. This often means that you can get to the conclusion of the process a lot faster. Although Dominants and Influencers do ask fewer questions, the questions they do ask are as critical to reaching a *positive* conclusion as the battery of queries from the others. This section looks at some types of questions the four different behavioral styles may ask you and how you can respond to them to keep your sales presentation on track.

Dominant: Getting to the point

Dominant questions are delivered directly and forcefully and are sometimes designed to intimidate you. They want to test your conviction in your product and in yourself. Prepare for questions like:

- ✔ Who else have you told this to?
- ✔ What's my bottom-line cost?
- ✔ Are you sure this is right for us?

Answer with to-the-point, brief statements that scream confidence. If you waffle, give away control, or hesitate too long, the Dominant loses respect for you.

Influencer: Seeking status

Influencers deliver their questions with warmth and even playfulness — they may lightly spar with you over price. Because establishing a connection is important to them, they may probe for your feelings. They also want answers that assure them that they're buying a product that others may envy or desire. Influencers crave the latest and greatest — as much for recognition and status as for efficiency and productivity.

Influencers may ask you questions like the following:

- Why do you feel we should buy it?
- How much newer is this latest technology?
- How many others have it?
- Can you lower your price a little?

Respond to an Influencer's questions more informally. Provide the Influencer with detail — not the facts-and-figures stuff the Compliant demands, but the emotional benefits of your product.

Steady: Avoiding "no"

A Steady's questions are typically nonconfrontational and service oriented. Steadies seek a high level of security before they're willing to make a commitment, and may request more information as a stall tactic. For example:

- Have there been times that it didn't work? Tell me about those.
- I receive good service; why should I make a change?
- How long have you been in business?
- What happens if it doesn't work?
- I need time to think it over — could I call you in a week?

Provide Steadies with answers that reassure them. Be patient and willing to spend time, but be careful of the time waster who isn't going to buy but can't tell you so. Steadies hate to say no and may drag you along for quite some time. You must get them committed to specific time frames when the decision will be made in the future. If you don't, you could still be trying to sell them a year from now.

Compliant: Working the plan

A Compliant's typical questioning process is exactly that — a process. Compliants don't do anything without a highly organized plan behind it. They want all the facts, figures, data, and studies that they can get. And they want to eliminate any possibility of risk. A 99-percent probability of success is, in many cases, too low for them. Expect questions such as:

- What is the warranty you offer?
- What qualifications do you posses?

  ✔ How long has this product been out?

  ✔ What's the return or refund rate on it?

  ✔ What other facts can you share with me?

  ✔ I don't have to decide now, do I?

Be prepared with studies, reports, resources, and references. Include facts, figures, and percentages in your responses. Compliants want reassurance, just as the Steadies do (see preceding section) — but Compliants want solid data to back up those reassurances.

Steering the Sale with Driving Forces

Everyone has some *inner motivation* — a combination of what they want and what they fear — that dictates their actions. These desires and fears are part of the behavioral profile. As you figure out how to recognize each behavioral style in your phone contacts, you're better positioned to steer your sales presentation to their driving forces. Table 17-3 identifies the motivators and fears that determine the four driving forces.

Table 17-3	**Determining the Four Driving Forces**
Behavioral Style	*Driving Forces*
Dominant	Competition, sense of urgency, change, results oriented, fear of being taken advantage of
Influencer	Communication, talking it out, trust and recognition, verbal skills, self-confidence, fear of social rejection
Steady	Sensitivity to others, adaptability, listening to others, persistence, dislike of confrontation, fear of losing status quo
Compliant	Precision and accuracy, high quality control, the details, aversion to change, fear of failure and criticism

Put this table by your phone and reference it. It can give you a peak into what actions your prospect may take and how she may react in certain situations. For example, with a Dominant you need to assure her that you'll do what you say you will do and that you're confident in the results and your delivery, because Dominants fear being taken advantage of by others.

This section explains how to shape your sales process to address these driving forces and to help you keep it on track. (See Chapter 16 for detailed descriptions of the driving forces of each style.)

Motivating your prospect to buy

After you establish a prospect's behavioral style, you're equipped to prepare a series of statements to wrap into your conversations and sales presentation — statements that are designed to motivate the prospect into taking action. By preparing such statements in advance, you're ready to say the right thing to the prospect at the right time.

You can use the following statements verbatim or adapt them to your specific sales needs. They work well verbatim when used like scripts that are delivered to the right behavioral style.

- ✔ **Statements that motivate a High D:**

  - "Our service provides you an opportunity to achieve the goals you desire right away."

  - "This product will put you on the cutting edge. We are the leader in this field."

  - "You can easily see the advantage and how, by using our service, you will beat your competition."

- ✔ **Statements that motivate a High I:**

  - "We are offering this revolutionary product to only a few initial prospects like yourself."

  - "By using our service, you will easily be recognized as a manager who is going somewhere in your company."

  - "We offer the most advanced, cutting-edge line in the industry."

- ✔ **Statements that motivate a High S:**

  - "I have a list of people who went through the same challenges as you. Our tested program really helped them. Feel free to give them a call."

  - "Others have found that this product is the perfect solution to their problems. I am sure you will evaluate the information carefully and come to the same conclusion."

  - "Here is a comprehensive packet of information that will provide you with all the information needed to make a wise decision."

  - "By moving forward with me, you will have the security of knowing that you will get the outcome that you want."

✔ **Statements that motivate a High C:**

- "After you examine all the facts, you will see that this will be the right next step for you."

- "This is a proven service. We have been in business for 25 years and have helped people like you, so you know we are someone you can rely on."

- "You can see that our warranty eliminates any risk on your part. I stand behind our service and proven results 100 percent."

- "After the presentation, you will be in the position to examine the facts, interpret them easily, and draw the conclusion that we should work together."

Turning around a wrong-way course

Even the best salespeople run into an occasional roadblock. You're in the middle of a call with a prospect and it's clear that you're losing ground: Even if this is a first conversation and you haven't had a chance to verify behavioral style yet, you can read some clues that can help you determine the style and, better yet, how to get back on track.

Re-engaging a Dominant

A Dominant prospect expresses disinterest by openly challenging or disagreeing with you. You can almost see through the phone lines that the prospect is glancing at a clock or checking e-mail for something worth attending to.

To regain the attention of the High D:

✔ **Be brief, be bright, and be gone.** The High D has more on his plate than time. He is acutely aware of that and doesn't want anyone to waste it. Hit him hard with your benefits and why he should act now.

✔ **Skip the testimonials.** The High D won't be very impressed with them. He's focused on the results. He wants to know what's in it for him.

✔ **Be direct and business-like — no small talk.** He isn't interested in building a relationship at this point, if ever. He will turn you off if you use the typical common-ground bonding type of techniques that many salespeople use.

✔ **Get to the point quickly and solve his problem.** He wants results for his problems. The more sightseeing you do on the way to delivering those results, the less likely the sale.

Warming up a High I

An Influencer makes negative or skeptical comments. It's not a good sign when the naturally optimistic I is reserved. You may also pick up on attempts to get off the phone and on to something more engaging.

These tweaks just may jazz the Influencer into listening:

- ✔ **Allow time to warm up and socialize.** The Influencer likes to interact and communicate. She wants to build a relationship, so be conversational.

- ✔ **Have focus, make it fun, and use stories.** She loves good stories that connect her to you or to the sale. The best stories are about clients that are powerful, well respected, and well known. It gives you the celebrity factor with her.

- ✔ **Hit the high points; don't be too detailed.** The Influencer isn't a detail person. She is a more big-picture, feeling person. If it feels right, she does it.

- ✔ **Present with a sizzle the new, showy services.** The Influencer likes flash, glitz, and sizzle in what she buys, so give it to her. The Influencer always has the new car when the new model comes out. Tie your product or service to the cutting edge.

Taking it slow with a Steady

Clues that the Steady isn't connecting are the most subtle of the four types. The High S hates confrontation. When you notice the points you've already covered continue to be raised, you know you've lost the prospect.

Recapture the Steady with these approaches:

- ✔ **Earn trust and friendship first — talk about family and hobbies.** The Steady is stable; family is a big part of his life.

- ✔ **Take it slow and steady.** With a Steady, speed kills the sale. If you are too fast, he can think that you're too slick, not trustworthy, and too great a risk to buy from.

- ✔ **Use plenty of proof and statistics to make your point.** He isn't swayed by a showy product or delivery. He weighs the facts. If you don't share any proof, he can assume that you don't have any. That means, to him, you're either not prepared or what you're saying is all hype.

✔ **Answer all questions and confirm agreement.** You must dig
for his views, opinions, concerns, and agreement. A Steady
will tell the waiter the meal was outstanding when it wasn't
and just go quietly and never return to the restaurant. If he
tells you everything is fine, you can be assured that it most
likely is not.

Serving up data to the Compliant

You know you're off-base with the High C when the prospect turns
evasive and unresponsive. You may get nothing more than a few
grunts and "uh-huhs." On the other hand, the Compliant may challenge you with impossible questions in order to end the call.

When you get this response, it's time to try a different tack:

✔ **Allow time for absorbing details and facts.** Your sales cycle
will be longer with a Compliant because of the need to digest
all the data. Be patient.

✔ **Use other Compliant or Steady behavioral-styled people as
sources of testimonials.** She wants as much proof as possible
because she wants to avoid being wrong at all costs.

✔ **Avoid small talk; get to the point with truckloads of support
data in hand.** She doesn't want a relationship but evidence of
a successful outcome. The more data you can provide, the
better. She believes that data lowers her level of risk.

✔ **Present only established and proven products.** If you're selling something revolutionary and new, a Compliant won't buy
it. What she hears you saying is that you're selling something
that is untested at this point.

Customizing your close

Your prospect's behavioral style dictates how you close your presentation. You wouldn't tie up the sale with a Steady the same way
you would with a Dominant. The following sections show you how
to tweak your close based on the different styles. (Check out
Chapter 14 for more general info about drafting a successful close.)

Sealing the deal with Dominants

High Dominants respond best to strong closes that offer them choices
and let them feel in control. Choices are a good way to go because
Dominants value *their* opinion more than they value yours. Having a
choice means they don't have to feel taken advantage of — which is
their primal fear.

Check out the following close you may make with a Dominant:

> *"Bob, I thought that the 4300 was the right model for you, but maybe I made a mistake. Maybe we should look at your budget range again. Maybe this isn't the model for you."*

This close, known as the *take-away,* can be very effective, but you have to be gutsy to use it. Basically, you seem to take away the prospect's opportunity to buy your product. The response from a Dominant is typically to fight for the product rather than let you win.

Wrapping it up with Influencers

With High Influencers, you find that offering choices and emphasizing status or image work well. To appeal to the Influencer's need to be admired, try this:

> *"Bob, imagine what it will feel like walking across the platform to receive the top salesperson award next year because you took the exclusive step right now of hiring a sales coach. Can't you just hear the applause?"*

The truth is that Influencers are the easiest type of behavioral style to close and sell. They naturally want to buy now and ask questions later. Remember, feelings and emotions are important to Influencers. They're quick to act when recognition, feelings, exclusivity, ego, and friendship align.

Closing with Steadies and Compliants

Both the Steady and Compliant respond well to the same type of close — their concern with making the right decision and ensuring security makes the opportunity to "test-drive" the product very appealing.

> *"Bob, I can offer you a trial period to test drive our 5600 model. This test drive periods carries a "send it back no questions asked" 30 days, so you really have no risk here — we have assumed it all. Is that something that you would be interested in?"*

Including a guarantee, warranty, trial period, no-obligation arrangement, full refund, or no-questions-asked promise takes the risk away from the decision. These slow-to-commit types find it easier to make a yes decision with this kind of protection.

Chapter 18

Staying Motivated to Succeed

*B*eing motivated and keeping that motivation is like taking a shower. Sure, the occasional workshop, a steady flow of personal-development books and CDs, and the incentive awards offered by your company certainly spark a surge of enthusiasm. But staying motivated is an every-day ablution. You need it more than once if you want it to do any good.

Telephone salespeople encounter pressures, challenges, and conflicts on a daily basis. And the more productive the individual, the more challenges are generated. A steady stream of wear and tear can drain even the best professionals.

Ah, but you have ways to stop those motivation leaks. Performing certain habits and practices daily can help you keep an "up" attitude afloat. In this chapter, I discuss some of the strategies I've passed on to hundreds of thousands of sales professionals and have used to keep *me* motivated all these years.

Getting a Grip on Motivation

To paraphrase Supreme Court Justice Potter Stewart, motivation is hard to define, but we know it when we have it. Although motivation may be hard to put into words, its results are explicit. It exposes itself via unbounded energy, intense desire to stay on task, and the ability to endure with little effort what may ordinarily be excruciatingly uninteresting or tedious. Not quite sure why motivation is important in sales or what you need to do to stay motivated? This section explains the importance of discipline and how it can improve your motivation, as well as other actions you can do to stay motivated.

Understanding why you need discipline to stay motivated

To keep the flames of motivation stoked, you need to be disciplined. Discipline isn't magical; it's merely movement. At its core, *discipline* is a self-management process that aligns with and promotes your goals, priorities, and objectives. Discipline is action oriented — an act of will, not an act of feelings. If you wait until you *feel* disciplined or until someone provides discipline for you, you may find yourself tapping your fingers for a long time to come.

Discipline is more than a building block for success; it's a keystone. Discipline can keep you upright even if other fundamentals — the economy, for example — are shaky. Discipline can see you through work upheavals and even seismic shifts in your particular industry.

Discipline means you adhere consistently and regularly to the tasks of being a top salesperson. A high-performance salesperson applies discipline to routine telephone-sales activities, such as:

- ✔ High daily volume of prospecting contacts
- ✔ Effective lead categorization and lead follow-up
- ✔ Routine practice of scripts, dialogues, and sales skills
- ✔ Regular physical workout habits
- ✔ Consistent personal development time in reading, listening, and attending personal-growth programs

In the following sections, I show you how discipline is related to motivation and how you can use discipline to make your sales plan and carry it out.

Discipline and motivation: A chicken-and-egg conundrum

When I ask salespeople which comes first, motivation or discipline, most answer with motivation. Their view is that the higher their motivation level, the more disciplined they act. That may be true — for *average* sales performers. Motivation — or a lack thereof — can certainly influence diligence to the details of prospecting, lead follow-up, honing skills, and role-playing scripts.

Money can't be your sole motivator

Too many people use money as their sole motivating factor as salespeople. This single-track focus can lead to poor results or a prolonged slump in sales growth as your sales career matures.

Don't overemphasize the importance of money as a motivator. A new salesperson may find money the supreme motivator. But it ceases to be a motivational tool when you have achieved many of your financial goals in life. After you have money and wealth, you'll need to find another motivator like service, standards, personal performance, or a personal belief system. When someone is comfortable financially, it becomes more challenging for them to motivate themselves to prospect at the same level as when they where broke if money is their most important motivation tool.

For the top salesperson, however, discipline comes *first,* and then discipline feeds motivation. The discipline expended to organize and make contacts leads to business, which increases motivation, which then generates more discipline, which results in . . . well, you get the picture.

Expecting motivation before discipline is like negotiating with a wood stove: "I will put some wood in you if you give me some heat first." I hate to throw a bucket of cold water on anyone, but life just doesn't work that way.

Relying on discipline to make your sales plan

Planning takes discipline — just as much as, if not more than, actually carrying out the work. You must set aside the necessary time to evaluate conditions, construct a strategy that takes advantage of those conditions and optimizes your skills, and identify and address weaknesses and challenges.

Then after you've developed your plan, actually implementing and staying with the sales plan also takes a great deal of discipline. Salespeople often give up on the plan before it takes full root and produces the desired results. Effort is what pays off.

Even without immediate results, discipline — when applied to a well-thought-out plan — brings about a sense of confidence and optimism. And these, my friends, are the seeds of motivation.

So how can you add some discipline into your life? First thing each morning, remind yourself that you're motivated! Keep the following tips in mind to help:

✔ **Review your goals at least once a day.** Write down your goals on small cards to keep in your wallet. Tape them to your mirror. Stick them in your sun visor. Make them your screen-saver. Looking at your goals several times a day increases your motivation to achieve them, which in turn helps you increase your discipline.

✔ **Resolve today to decide on one disciplined action you should take, and do it.** Don't wait until tomorrow; do it today. Don't wait until you feel like it, because you probably never will. Make the decision right now to do it!

Being disciplined in your calls raises your motivation level to make more calls, and when you stay disciplined and consistent in those calls, you will see results, which will further increase your motivation.

Taking care of your body

Consider your body a fuel tank that keeps your motivation running. If your energy reserves are depleted or if you fail to maintain your health, your motivation (not to mention overall performance) may stall or — worse — crash and burn.

In order to keep your body fueled and ready to go, make sure you do what it takes to stay healthy and fit. Get the rest and sleep that your body needs. (You know your body the best.) Make sure you eat regular, healthful meals and exercise, based on what your doctor recommends is right for you.

Keeping your emotions tuned up

In addition to taking care of your body, you also have another energy tank — one that holds your emotional reserves — that needs fostering. Your emotional well-being is more complex and requires greater effort to avoid depleting it. It can also be more temperamental, so operate with care.

One of the greatest dangers to your emotional balance is other people's emotions. Don't let others — whether staff, colleagues, clients, or even your boss — dump their negativity on you, which not only drains your energy, but also may do damage that could take a week or more to repair.

Overdoing it can really zap your motivation

I once coached a man who sold costly personal consulting. He was in the midst of expanding his business, but was struggling to achieve his prospecting goals each day. As I probed, I discovered he was seriously overextending himself. He wasn't getting to bed until after 11 p.m., and then was going to the gym at 5 a.m. each morning. He wasn't getting enough rest!

A little more digging and I learned that he wasn't getting to sleep until later because he didn't get home from work until after 7 p.m. most nights. By the time he had dinner (with or without the family), spent time with his children and put them to bed, caught up on world events, and talked with his wife, the clock was approaching midnight. However, after he made the commitment to be home for dinner at 6 p.m., his prospecting improved dramatically and was more consistent.

Living at a High Attitude

A positive, upward-looking attitude goes a long way toward helping you achieve your goals, whether meeting your daily prospecting numbers or attaining a lifelong dream.

So how's your attitude? Does it need an improvement? Are you positive and upbeat? If your attitude projects every obstacle as a new opportunity, success comes much easier. This section shows you how your attitude can make a huge impact on your motivational level.

Keeping your attitude in check

Having the right attitude starts with no one else but you. So what are you waiting for? Start building your attitude today. Projecting a positive attitude when faced with challenges helps you resolve them more effectively and increases your odds of making a sale. Conveying an optimistic outlook with a problem client may be the factor that transforms your encounter from "fail" to "sale." Convince yourself that you're the best salesperson anyone could hire. Until you're convinced, persuading others won't be easy.

The best way to develop and build a healthy attitude is by saying daily *affirmations*. Affirmations drive positive mental pictures into your subconscious mind — and they're so simple to use. Simply say to yourself statements affirming your positive qualities and successes — or goals you aspire to achieve.

Edison's attitude illuminated his work

You can find thousands of examples in life of how some people took lemons and, with a great attitude, made lemonade. For example, Thomas Edison was said to have developed the light bulb because darkness interfered with his ability to conduct further experiments. He wanted to be able to work long into the night. Edison could have moaned about the darkness, but that wouldn't have done any good. He used his positive attitude and solved the problem of darkness.

Make a daily habit of saying your affirmations — whether you use the ones here or create your own — out loud with confidence and conviction. I recommend doing it first thing each morning. In this way, you program your brain to be positive for the day.

Affirmations also come in handy when you have a mid-day crisis or conflict. I suggest repeating them aloud a number of times each day, such as when you're stopped in traffic or waiting to pick the kids up from soccer practice.

Some affirmations I recommend that you say include the following:

- ✔ I am a great salesperson.
- ✔ I am skilled at handling objections and getting the contract signed.
- ✔ People do business with me because I am positive, knowledgeable, and professional.
- ✔ I earn _____ (you fill the blank).

Your subconscious mind doesn't have a filter to stop thoughts, ideas, and statements from entering it as truth. That's the value of affirmations — your ability to drive deep into your subconscious mind the positive feelings of your success even before you experience the outward signs or manifestations of that success.

Controlling your environment

One of the best ways to secure a positive attitude is to guard your environment. As a salesperson, you face lots of interactions throughout your day with clients, prospects, management, and coworkers. And these interactions expose you to plenty of potential for "attitude adjustment." Of course, you can't avoid this contact — it's part of your job. But you *can* control it. Here are some suggestions:

✔ Lower your risk of attitude attack by guarding against inter-ruptions that distract you from the important work of prospecting and lead follow-up. Do everything you can to dis-courage office drop-ins and phone calls. (Chapter 8 includes some help for nipping interruptions in the bud.)

✔ For all the encounters you can't avoid, make sure your eyes are open for signs of attitude sappers: coworkers decrying management and unfair policies; the boss bemoaning the downturns in the industry; friends urging that you could do better elsewhere. When you recognize the signs, get out of the situation as quickly as you can. End the phone call, leave the room, plead a meeting or appointment, or show your guest to the door.

Putting on a little persistence

Bad things happen to good salespeople. It's a fact of life. Making mistakes, hearing the word *no,* losing sales, and falling short of goals will happen to you at some point. But these incidents aren't final or fatal — unless you choose to give up.

As discipline begets motivation (see the earlier section, "Understanding why you need discipline to stay motivated"), per-sistence fosters attitude. *Persistence* is a resolved mindset to con-tinue on even in the face of adversity or preliminary negative results. It sees you through tough times, and getting past those tough times renews your positive attitude.

"Nothing in the world can take the place of persistence." So said Calvin Coolidge, 30th president of the United States. "Talent will not; nothing is more common than unsuccessful men with talent. Geniuses will not; unrewarded genius is almost a proverb. Education will not; the world is full of educated derelicts. Persistence and determination alone are omnipotent."

So what's the best way to make persistence part of your routine? Just start. That first step is what stops most people: tying your sneakers and stepping on the treadmill or picking up the phone to make the first call. After you begin, you pick up momentum and the positive self-talk of accomplishment.

Protecting your attitude

Remember that you're the master of your attitude. You have the power to change it for the better. Unfortunately, you also have the power to hand it over to someone else who may not treat it so well. I can't emphasize enough how important it is to guard your attitude (which isn't, let me say, the same as having a guarded attitude).

Your attitude plays a major role in determining how high you'll climb in your life. Treat it as a precious valuable, and be aware that sometimes the most notorious attitude thieves are those closest to you: coworkers, friends, neighbors, family, or even your significant other!

For example, years ago, I had the pleasure of working with an outstanding coach, one of the best employees I ever had. But after some time, he let a close friend with a toxic attitude contaminate his own. He became discontented and soon left the company. Now, believe me, nothing makes me happier than when a coach or salesperson who works for me becomes so successful that he's ready to move on to greater challenges. But this man didn't leave under those circumstances. He left with a poisoned attitude that he apparently carried with him. He struggled for three years to establish a speaking and coaching career independently of my company's.

To protect your attitude, be careful of who you grant the access to affluence your life. Make the decision each morning when you wake up that you will have a positive attitude all day. Be quick to holler "Next!" when you encounter a prospect that doesn't want what you are offering.

Getting in the Zone: Taking Your Game to the Next Level

Professional athletes aspire to be in the *zone,* a place where they can't miss the basket, a putt, the target, a goal, or a home run. A few years ago, I watched David Duvall shoot a 59 in the last round to win the Bob Hope golf tournament. His longest putt that day was about 10 feet. He truly was in the zone — his mind and body were working together in a masterful performance.

Telephone salespeople can also aspire to be in the zone. In fact, I'm certain you've already been there: that day you walked away with signed contracts (at your price and terms) from every presentation, or the day every prospecting call you made ended in a lead or appointment.

Sure, every telephone-sales professional worth her salt has had such experiences. But top salespeople know how to use attitude — along with the following tools and tactics — to increase the opportunities to perform in the zone. This section highlights specifically what you can do to get yourself ready so your sales presentation is successful.

Developing a pre-activity routine

No matter what action you're taking in your sales presentation, you can establish a *pre-activity routine,* a set series of actions that you take every time to help improve your efforts and results. For example, have you ever followed a golf pro during a tournament? The golfer performs the same series of actions, in the same sequence, through each shot or putt. If something breaks the concentration during the pre-shot routine, he starts all over again.

After you establish an effective pre-activity routine, commit it to a checklist or a list of steps and make sure you follow it regularly. Here is an example of a pre-activity routine for a sales presentation:

1. **For 30 minutes before your presentation, review anticipated questions and responses.**

2. **Identify the key benefits that you want to highlight to the prospect.**

3. **Practice responses to objections you expect.**

4. **"Give" your presentation before you make it to the prospect.**

5. **Listen to music, whether in your office or in the car, that relaxes and focuses you on your task.**

6. **Take control of your emotions before you make the call.**

No matter if you're prospecting, following up on leads, giving presentations, or negotiating contracts, a pre-activity routine can put you in the right mindset and lead you to the zone on a more-frequent basis with heightened results.

Discovering how to relax

To enter the zone — to achieve peak performance — you must be relaxed. The idea that people perform best under pressure is a misconception; in fact, studies support that the opposite is true. When you're relaxed, your body works in unison with your mind. You're able to evaluate situations more clearly and make better decisions.

Think about the last time you were in a high-pressure situation — chances are you weren't on top of your game. Now, think of one of your recent sales successes. You may even recall a feeling of near serenity, as if you could step outside of yourself and see that everything was going to end positively.

You can take steps to summon that sense of relaxation. Consider the following ways to get relaxed. Some of them take a little more time than others, but they can all get you in a relaxed frame of mind:

- ✓ **Yoga.** This type of exercise may not be your sport of choice, but it does provide lessons in quieting the mind.

- ✓ **Deep breaths.** Focus on your breath for a few minutes before an important presentation.

- ✓ **Stretches:** Do some simple stretches to relax your body, which, as I discuss earlier in the chapter in the section "Taking care of your body," can also benefit your mind.

- ✓ **Physical activity:** Before an appointment, take a brisk walk to release any pent-up tension that may constrict your efforts. Find what type of activity works for you and use it.

Becoming your own coach

Everyone needs mentors, coaches, and supporters — people who believe in you and encourage you to achieve your personal best. But one individual plays a greater role than anyone else in keeping your attitude up and your motivation in high gear: *you.*

You can be your own best coach. No matter how the appointment, negotiation, or prospecting session goes, you need to be there for *you* — congratulating yourself for your successes, commending yourself for going the distance, or encouraging yourself past the occasional failures. With *you* on your side, you're destined for achievement.

To do so, have regular review or reflection periods at the following times:

- ✓ **At the end of the day:** Take 30 minutes to review your results, your contact numbers, the good calls, and what made them that way. Face what you did poorly and why.

- ✓ **At the end of the week:** Take an hour to go through the same daily evaluation, but probe the whole week. Focus on your sales ratios to determine whether they're in line with your norm. Who do you need to contact and sell next week? What are your best prospects heading into next week?

- ✓ **At the end of the month:** Take a few hours and repeat. A month is a pretty good chunk of time. Learn from your past and invest it in your future. Don't operate like most salespeople who make the same mistakes over and over again hoping for a different outcome that never comes.

Hitting the Curveballs: Staying Up during the Uncertainties

Discipline. Physical and emotional health. Nurturing a can-do attitude. Getting in the zone. Following these strategies is bound to boost your motivation level (for more info, see previous sections in this chapter), but be prepared for the curveballs! Just like a star baseball player, you can warm up faithfully and practice regularly, or you can be an all-star performer, but those curveballs — those unexpected occurrences — are guaranteed to come your way.

By accepting that you're going to be swinging at curveballs from time to time and not letting them deplete your motivation, you're more likely to increase your hits and stay positive. No matter how prepared you are and how motivated you are, you can't expect to hit everything thrown your way. You're going to get curveballs, whether uncovering a delayed order, finding out you have been selling to the wrong person in the company, or discovering their budget was just cut right as the final order and purchase order were being processed. In sales, as in life, you strike out sometimes.

Too many salespeople expect perfection. They expect to make a sale with every lead and even every call. Unfortunately, life isn't like that. You have to assume you will strike out a bunch. If it makes you feel any better, consider this: A major-league baseball player earns $10 to $15 million a year if they hit above 300. This means he can fail seven times out of ten — and still be considered a top trade.

Calm and cool: Going for the singles

Be patient with yourself when your job throws you curveballs. You may be inclined to respond to a work challenge by tensing up for the worst, while at the same time ramping up your efforts, pushing yourself hard to counter the onslaught. You may feel that the curveball has put you so far behind that you have to put forth heroic effort to compensate.

In this case, stop, take a deep breath, and recognize that there's no shame in hitting a single. You don't have to hit a home-run sale every time out. Enough singles turn into runs, which can win the game. Curveballs at work can have a devastating effect on your confidence and motivation. When faced with such a situation, be realistic and go for a small victory; rebuild your motivation one phone call at a time.

Head on: Stepping up to the plate

Sometimes when people expect that they'll face sticky situations, they find excuses to avoid them. When you anticipate you may encounter a curveball, the last thing you want to do is run away. You want to face the curveball head on. In order to keep your motivation at peak level, step up to the plate again and face your fears.

If you've been hit by a curveball, it's understandable that you'd be a little reluctant to put yourself in a position to take another hit. You find excuses to avoid anything that might bring you close to a curveball. You may push off making your daily prospecting calls or cancel appointments, or you zero in on "safe" activities that keep you away from curveballs: proofreading your sales letters, putting your files in order, updating your address list, or offering to lick stamps and stuff envelopes. But don't fall victim to the curveball; step up and try again. (Chapter 6 can give you more pointers about overcoming call aversion.)

One step ahead: Striking out the excuses

Top salespeople don't focus on excuses; they identify what needs to be done. They determine what they can and *will* do first. Don't rely on excuses if you're afraid of an outcome. Leave the excuses at the door.

I really despise the phrase "I *can't*." I don't allow people in my company, my clients, and especially my children to use it. Wesley and Annabelle know that saying "I can't" brings a swift response from Dad and Mom: "We don't use those words in our family." Asking for help is encouraged, but in our house, *can't* is a four-letter word.

"I can't" is the plainest form of an excuse. People who have more limitations in skills, abilities, and resources than you or I have accomplished much more. These champions never use the words "I can't" as a crutch.

To help you get rid of excuses you may be prone to using, I'd like to recommend this exercise: Take 15 minutes and create a list of why you can't prospect more, sell more, close more, have more money, or attain a better quality of life. Then ask yourself whether these excuses are valid. Do other people have these same excuses? Have these other people overcome these excuses? Why not me? Then take the list and burn it, so it's gone forever. This process brings to light that you can. It shows you that others have done it, so why not you. The burning of the list creates the final step to move on.

Staying In the Game through Lifelong Learning

To keep motivated, I need to have a sense of fulfillment. And to be fulfilled, I need to keep "filling up." Daily effort to increase my knowledge and skills buoys my attitude and charges me with motivation that virtually flows out of me and into others. When I can motivate others, they, in turn, motivate me.

ANECDOTE

How my "education" helped build my motivation

When I was in my mid 20s, I felt directionless. I didn't know why my career felt stalled or what to do to fuel it up. To say I lacked motivation is an understatement, that is until I went to a seminar and heard Jim Rohn, the renowned motivational speaker. He made a comment that day that hit me like a lightning bolt: "Your formal education will make you make a living; your personal education will make you a fortune." He may have been speaking to me personally.

You see, my formal education wasn't much to brag about. I graduated in the part of the high school class that bolstered up the top half. But Rohn made me see that my academic limitations were of little consequence in terms of my potential. I could still earn whatever I wanted if I attended to my personal education.

Since that day nearly 20 years ago, the education, training, and coaching I've received has transformed everything about me: my attitude, motivation, energy, passion, relationships, bank account, net worth, business, and self-image.

My progress was slow at first, but my motivation built slowly. It was so easy to come home after a hard day's work, grab the remote, and rest a beer can on my belly. Making myself read, study, journal, reflect, and replay the mental tape of my day and week was much harder. As time went on, however, the successes that I accumulated encouraged me to invest further in my continuing education. I read books, listened to personal development programs, attended seminars, and eventually, channeled into coaching and training others.

A hybrid of education, training, and coaching is, from my experience, the pathway to success. The measurements may differ, depending on your unique circumstances, but the combination of these three ingredients creates a potent cocktail for motivation. This section takes a closer look at how education, training, and coaching can help you increase your motivation level.

Taking a reality check

I spend a lot of effort encouraging salespeople to do what it takes to build optimistic energy, from attitude adjustments to self-affirming mantras. But don't think I'm suggesting that you view yourself through rose-colored lenses! In order to continue building your knowledge and sales skills, taking off the glasses and looking at yourself in the harsh light of day is absolutely essential. You must be able to recognize your weaknesses in order to gain the education you need to overcome them.

Jack Welch, the famous retired CEO of General Electric, had six rules of business: The first one was to *face reality as it is, not as you wish it to be.* Honest self-assessment is a scary thing. Who wants to be reminded of deficiencies? But doing so is critical. Review your current performance to determine what skills you need to strengthen. After you pinpoint which areas you need to improve, you can easily find classes, books, CDs, and training programs on those topics.

One of the best assessment tools? Your sales ratios. (Please read Chapters 3 and 5 for a more in-depth discussion of sales ratios.) Regular check-ins quickly reveal weak spots. In examining your sales ratios, you can clearly see the problems in your sales. For example, if you're making too many calls to produce too few leads, this usually means that your initial opening statements and probing on the phone is poor. You don't peak enough interest in the prospect to create a lead. On the other hand, if you have enough leads but aren't making sales, you have to evaluate the lead quality and the presentation you're making to the leads because your presentation isn't powerful enough to compel them to buy and buy now.

When you're feeling discouraged or unmotivated, shrinking from the reality of your weaknesses is natural. But the salespeople who rise to the top in any organization are the ones most willing to be honest with themselves. Focusing on personal honesty leads to success.

Building on information: Education

The first ingredient to a successful lifelong learning recipe is *education* — the gathering of new and valuable information to help you do your job better. Equally important is the *review* of information that you may have learned already.

You have a menu of choices when it comes to furthering your education:

- ✔ Sign up for seminars.
- ✔ Read books (congratulations; you've made a good start reading this one!).
- ✔ Listen to CDs and books on tape while driving.
- ✔ Take courses online.
- ✔ Go back to school, whether college or continuing-education classes.

Busy salespeople often complain to me that they simply don't have *time* to learn. I don't buy it. Although you may not be able to commit to a semester of evening classes, you've got prime time *every day* to get in a few new lessons while driving in your car. Even if your only drive time is a short commute to the office, you can grab a few minutes' edification by popping in a CD. Multiply those ten minutes to and from work by 240 workdays a year, and you rack up a total of 80 hours of study a year!

Putting skills to practice: Training

In order for you to stay in the game and be at the top of the pack, you need to continue taking training to expand and build your skills. *Training,* like education, involves gathering information, but at a more in-depth level and, typically, involving your participation. Education tells you how. Training *shows* you how. In a training medium, you're likely to have hands-on exercises and practice sessions — situations in which you put the lessons into action.

To help you locate some training sessions that may be appropriate for you, I suggest the following two places to start your search:

- ✔ **Sales Champions (www.saleschampions.com).** Review the training options that we have available to you. I wouldn't be much of a salesperson if I did not believe in what I was selling.
- ✔ **Business by Phone (www.businessbyphone.com).** Art Sobczak, the company president, does a terrific job in training telephone salespeople. He has numerous offerings that will help your career.

Although many salespeople commonly engage in training when they — or their bosses — spot a deficiency, I challenge you to look at training in a new light. Look at ways to attend training sessions to improve the skills you already do somewhat well. Training in your sales skills can help you boost your sales and motivation. Going to a two-day boot camp in sales to spend time learning new sales techniques, and most importantly, role-playing and practicing those techniques before you come back to the office to make your first call, can give you a huge advantage.

Creating sales champs: Coaching

Most important in ensuring your lifelong learning is enlisting the help of a coach — a *mentor* or *role-model* of sorts. Or you can also work with an individual or a consultant or sign up for a proven program, such as our Personal Performance Coaching program. In any of these situations, coaching offers you the experience of an expert, the objectivity of an outsider who can analyze you and your skills, determine skills in which you need practice, and provide you with a personalized game plan for your particular business, goals, and values.

It's no accident that, in the world of sports, those teams and individuals who've earned champion status have had coaches who are often superstars themselves. The world recognizes that it takes more than a group of healthy, talented individuals to win a Super Bowl, a World Series, or a basketball championship, and that celebrities of golf, tennis, or ice-skating don't stand alone in their glory. Behind these great successes are great coaches.

Coach Tom Landry, the famous coach of the Dallas Cowboys, said, "A coach is someone who tells you what you don't want to hear and has you see what you don't want to see, so you can be who you have always known you can be." A champion coach helps you shrink the gap between where you are and what you can be. If you believe you aren't achieving your full potential, you're a prime candidate for a coach. Whether you turn to your manager for coaching or find an outside source, a coach can help you tap into that potential.

If you're serious about increasing your knowledge base and moving up the ladder of sales, then you seriously need to consider finding yourself a coach who can share her guidance with you. This section gives you some pointers on what a coach can give you and how you can find a coach.

Knowing what a champion coach can do for you

As you seek out your own coach, you'd be wise to understand exactly what a champion coach does for you. A champion coach

✔ **Has the ability to listen and help you clarify your goals and vision in all areas of your life.** Earl Nightingale, the famous speaker, stated, "We are goal-seeking organisms." Sometimes, however, the difficulty isn't in achieving goals but in setting them in the first place.

✔ **Understands that all goals must have deadlines.** He encourages you to circle a date for when you want to make your first million. The good coach knows that timetables and deadlines help you attain those goals more readily.

✔ **Works with you to create the step-by-step game plan to achieve your goals.** Even monumental projects can be broken down into bite-sized pieces.

✔ **Helps you understand the consequences of not adhering to the plan.** Doing so forces you to face the connection between your actions and the results.

✔ **Provides ongoing motivation and inspiration during the difficult times.** Everyone needs people around them who can help them get through the rough patches.

✔ **Establishes accountability — from you to your plan — and holds you to the standard you have set for yourself.** Accountability is key. I find that many companies in sales provide too little of it, so their salespeople don't reach their full potential.

I had a client who wanted to earn more than $250,000 for the year, when the year before he had only earned $130,000. We worked diligently to identify what he needed to do in order to achieve his goal. After we listed bite-size pieces, we set up his daily routine. By simply focusing on his daily disciplines, he made progress without finding himself paralyzed by the weight of his lofty goal. As his coach, I encouraged him through some rough spots when he dropped his daily routine. In the end, he exceeded his goal: The $265,000 he brought home that year reflected an increase in business by more than 100 percent.

Finding a coach right for you

You may know you want or need a coach, but where do you start and how do you know how to find a coach who is right for you? You need to find a coach who has had success first in sales.

You can first start with your manager. Check to see if she can commit to coach you. Gain her commitment to spend a specified amount of time weekly coaching you. Have her hold you accountable to predetermined standards for prospecting, role-play practice, lead generation, and sales.

If your manager isn't available, ask your manager and coworkers for references. You want a coach who is passionate about your success. She must be able to take your short- and long-term objectives and connect them to your goals and dreams. Then she needs to teach you new behaviors and actions that help guide you and hold you accountable so your results change.

When looking for a coach, you want someone who has a system of coaching that is action- and activity-based. It can't all be theory oriented either. Ask to talk about the program's core components. Keep the following in mind to help you narrow your selection:

✔ **Get a test drive session.** Any coach worth his salt will want to spend time with you to really evaluate your situation so he knows with certainty that together you can achieve results.

✔ **Check the coaching company's experience.** More and more coaches and coaching companies enter the field daily. Make sure you get a coach who has experience in your field. For example, we have been coaching salespeople for almost ten years at Sales Champions.

✔ **Check yourself.** You play a role in the success of coaching. Are you ready to go to the next level and willing to put forth the effort? Answer the following three questions to determine whether you're ready to work with a coach:

• **Do you want to do better?** I don't mean hope, wish, or dream to do better like you wish to win the lottery. I mean do you want to do better. Do you have desire that will translate to action? Improving takes a lot of hard work.

• **Are you willing to change?** You have to change for things to change for you. If you don't want to or won't change, your sales numbers, income, and quality of life won't change.

• **Are you willing to receive, accept, and implement the advice?** In other words, are you coachable? Would you let another person that is an expert guide you to success, or are you the type of person that wants to go it alone?

If you can't affirmatively answer the questions with enthusiasm, you may want to approach the opportunity of hiring a coach with extra caution. You could hire the best in the world at coaching, but the results may fall short of your expectations because you're not truly committed.

Part VI
The Part of Tens

The 5th Wave   By Rich Tennant

"I don't take 'no' for an answer. Nor do I take 'whatever,' 'as if,' or 'duh.'"

In this part . . .

At times, everyone needs a quick fix or a fast answer. That's what you find in this part, set up in the renowned *For Dummies* Part-of-Tens format. A ready resource when time is of the essence, these four short chapters present you with easy-to-implement, easy-to-remember tactics.

In this part, you can tick off ten ways to improve the way you sound on the phone. Keep the ten do-not-use phrases at your fingertips when you've got a prospect on the line. And, finally, I include the ten commandments for phone-sales success. From one to ten, you can count on this collection of tips to ease your journey along — a journey I'm certain will be your long and lucrative telephone-sales career.

Chapter 19

Ten (Or So) Ways to Sound Like a Pro on the Phone

*J*ust because the person on the other end of the phone can't see you doesn't mean your image doesn't come across loud and clear. When you *sound* professional, you're *seen* as a professional — even if the prospect never meets you. Conveying that image takes a little more than dressing for success. This chapter can help you be the professional that you are.

Always Use a Headset

The act of putting on a headset is a psychological trigger to prepare for business — it's game time! A headset also frees your hands so you can take notes. By making a record of important information, you're better set to confirm, review, summarize, and follow up on all critical points.

And when you're not concentrating on keeping the receiver between your ear and shoulder, you're free to focus on the prospect. Using a headset also reduces neck fatigue *and* eliminates the risk of dropping the phone while talking to a prospect — blasting the prospect's eardrum with a thud on the desktop is *not* professional.

Stand Up and Be Heard

Ever notice that singers always *stand* when they perform? That's no coincidence. They know that their voice carries more resonance, range, and power when their diaphragm isn't folded over.

You can use the singers' secret for sounding more authoritative and self-assured when speaking to prospects on the phone. Stand tall and observe the energy and enthusiasm that pours forth. Slump into your desk in a question-mark curve, and feel the conviction (or lack thereof) seep out of your voice.

Spice Up Your Delivery

In order to keep your prospect's attention, don't put him to sleep. Avoid speaking in a flat monotone voice — instead, vary the delivery of your speech to grab attention. Play with the following three vocal elements to vary your speech:

- ✔ **Tune into your tone.** Your speaking voice consists of several qualities, including rhythm, intonation, and inflection, resulting in a one-of-a-kind vocal personality that distinguishes Jimmy Stewart from Pee Wee Herman. I refer to this vocal fingerprint as *tone.* Although your tone is what makes your voice *yours,* you can optimize your phone communication by paying some attention to it. Make sure your tone conveys the message you want it to.

- ✔ **Play with the volume.** I'm not talking about the volume on your headset, but the decibel of your own voice. Talk too quietly, and you generate lots of "Could you repeat that?" requests. Speak too loudly, and the prospect must hold the receiver at arm's length. Keep your volume within a reasonable range, but be sure to vary it to hold the prospect's attention and emphasize key points.

- ✔ **Mix up the pace.** Most telephone salespeople are guilty of speed talking. Chalk it up to enthusiasm, nervousness, or desire to get in the sales points before the recipient hangs up. At any rate, you want to avoid this sport. Slow talking can be just as bad — you'll have people wanting to finish your sentences for you. Moderate the pace of your speech, occasionally varying it for effect or emphasis.

Talk Less . . . Listen More

The more you listen to *others* talk, the more you find out about them. If you do all the talking, you're not going to hear anything you don't already know.

Start by asking a question or two and then let the other person talk. Tune in to discover more about the prospect, the company, its needs, and its priorities and values. You just may find that by giving the prospect a chance to talk, you discover the best way to answer those needs and meet those priorities and values. And as a bonus, the prospect hangs up marveling at how smart and knowledgeable you are! (For more on listening, check out Chapter 11.)

Limber Up Your Body

To sound better and be more effective in telephone sales, do some warm-up exercises to limber and loosen your body. Trust me, you may spend a good part of your day connected to clients by voice only, but telephone sales is a full-contact sport!

Do facial exercises before your first call. Tighten and then relax your face muscles, and clench and relax your teeth several times. Slowly yawn to limber up your cheeks, muscles, and skin. Balloon out your cheeks a few times. Loosen your neck and shoulders by shrugging and relaxing. Rotate your neck slowly to loosen the muscles. A few full-body stretches aren't a bad idea either. Stretch your quads, hamstrings, and calves as if you were preparing for a run.

Warm Up Your Voice

Your voice, like your body (see preceding section), needs warming up to perform at its best. Start out in the shower by humming a tune (no matter what others in the household may say about your operatic potential). Humming is an outstanding warm-up for your vocal chords. For that matter, croaking like a frog is another excellent vibration exercise to strengthen your chords.

Get some talk time in before your first sales call. Synchronize dinner plans with your spouse. Ask the kids what's on tap for their day. Chat with a coworker at the water cooler. And as a bonus, you may just warm up a few relationships, too.

Put In Pre-Call Practice Time

Every salesperson benefits from rehearsing base scripts and dialogues before picking up the phone. I recommend at least 15 minutes of practice before each calling session. Doing the drill out loud is preferable. Don't be put off by teasing colleagues — they won't be laughing when you lead the sales board soon. Practice it all: your opening statements, prospecting scripts and dialogues, appointment objection handling, lead follow-up scripts, and closes.

Sneaking in a follow-up practice session at the end of the day doesn't hurt. Find a supportive coworker, supervisor, or friend to work with you. If you put in the time regularly to improve your phone-sales skills, you're sure to come across in any phone conversation as the consummate professional you are.

Bundle Your Calls

For maximum effect and optimal impact, plan your call schedule to group calls by type. For example, make all prospecting calls within one block of time such as the first two hours of the morning, and then follow with a session devoted to lead follow-up calls.

Make at least ten like calls in a row. By focusing on a type, you find yourself more "in the zone," zeroed in on the skills and strengths you need to tap into for a successful call outcome. And as you tick off the calls, one by one, you find that with each call, you get better.

Tape and Replay Your Calls

Not only do you create a reliable record of the phone conversation when you tape your calls — one that you can refer back to as often as you need to — you also create a valuable tool for self-evaluation. Did you speak too fast? Talk too much? Sound too aggressive? Come across as unprepared? Hear yourself as your prospect hears you, and you're bound to discover ways that you can improve and fine-tune your sales skills on the phone.

Chapter 20

Ten Phrases to Banish from Your Vocabulary

. . . .

In This Chapter

▶ Avoiding phrases that lead to dead ends

▶ Eliminating statements that send up defenses

. . . .

*A*chieving success as a telephone salesperson is as much about what you *don't* say as it is about saying the right thing. You'll have times when you're best not to talk at all — listening to the prospect often results in key information that can help you make the sale (more on this in Chapter 11). And when you do have the floor (or the phone, as the case may be), you want to be aware of certain words and phrases that seem to halt communication rather than further it along in the direction you want. Consider the ten questions, words, or phrases in this chapter taboo for the telephone salesperson.

"Do You Have Time to Talk?"

Asking someone if they have time to talk is probably the worst way to open a sales call. Of course, you want to be respectful of an individual's time, but you can utilize more-effective ways of conveying that courtesy without giving the prospect an open invitation to say no.

A couple effective examples to determine whether the prospect has time include the following:

> *"I recognize that you have objectives for the day, so I will be brief."*

> *"I'm aware of your time constraints, so I will get to the point quickly."*

(Read Chapter 9 for plenty of ideas on how to start a successful sales call.)

"I Sent You Some Material, and I Was Wondering if You Got It."

This statement is a dead end. A common sales tactic is to mail cold leads some information with the intent of "warming up" the prospect. This tactic is rarely effective. If you're contacting a business client, chances are good that the mailing didn't make it past an assistant or secretary. So that leaves you summoning up a big, fat no response. And what can you say to that?

Even if the prospect has received the material, you run the risk that she passed it on to someone else — or tossed it. In any scenario, your chances of launching conversation in a positive direction are slim. Expect responses such as, "I don't know, maybe," or "Yeah, I think I passed it on." Not the promising start you'd like.

You're better off to begin with a more direct approach, such as "Bob, this is Fred Smith with ABC Window, the reason for my call is . . ." rather than tossing away control of the conversation's direction.

"I'll Send You Another."

I call this the "Play-it-again, Sam" approach. Salespeople typically pull out this phrase when they open with the equally ineffective "Did you receive my materials?" opening (see the preceding section). Talk about a wasted effort! Chances are, this follow-up mailing will suffer the same fate as the first one.

Before you offer to resend the information, first confirm that you're offering the prospect something that she's interested in. For example, you can say something like:

> *"I know that you're time crunched as well as I am. Would you have an interest in exploring . . ."*

> *"If I sent you our brochure, you would have it on Thursday. Would you have enough time to review it before we booked an appointment to speak for the middle or the end of next week?"*

"You Wouldn't Want a _____, Would You?"

Place anything in the blank: "a new copy machine," "to list your home," "to review your life insurance," or "to hear about our new cable packages." However, using the negative assumption results in a negative outcome. This phrase practically begs the prospect to say no.

The salesperson who uses it demonstrates a total lack of confidence or belief in the product or service — not a rousing endorsement for the prospect to listen further. Toss this question out and expect to hear a no — or the click of the receiver.

"But . . . "

But seems like such a harmless little word, thrown into your dialogue simply to connect one thought to the next. *But* . . . this innocuous three-letter word serves as a secret code to a prospect: It reveals that you're about to manipulate him. Of course, that may not be your intention at all. Consider how these common expressions can be misleading due to the *but:*

- ✔ I can appreciate your views, but . . .
- ✔ I understand your concerns, but . . .

No matter what words you choose to follow *but,* the prospect hears something like the following:

- ✔ I can appreciate your views, but you're wrong.
- ✔ I understand your concerns, but I'm going to manipulate you into buying my product anyway.

There you go, trying to be understanding and nice, and that *but* negates all your efforts.

If you use contrast and comparison in selling — and I highly recommend that you do — you want to replace *but* with a more positive link. Choose *and,* which permits the prospect to form his own conclusion. (Check out Chapter 13 for more on overcoming objections.) In addition to *but,* don't use other similar words, such as *however, yet, still, notwithstanding, nevertheless, be that as it may, all the same,* or *but's* uncultured cousin, *yeah, but.*

"You're Wrong."

Your prospects secure information about your company from many sources, including friends, business associates, competitors, and media. Frequently, their information is incorrect. Perhaps they have a partial story or the story that your competitors want to convey. Jumping in to tell them they're wrong *isn't* the way to disabuse them of their inaccurate beliefs.

A better approach is to encourage the prospect to share as much detail as possible about her concerns. Ask questions, let her talk, and try to find out the source of the misinformation. Try these phrases to uncover the source:

> *"That's interesting; I have not heard that. Can you tell me where you heard that?"*

> *"I try to keep a pulse on the industry and its developments. It sounds like you have insider information. Can you share it?"*

By allowing the prospect to talk rather than blasting her with a strong denial, you validate her perspective — and you discover the source of the misinformation. After you know where the story came from, you're likely to have an easier time turning the tide.

"We've Always Had a Challenge with that Department."

Revealing the company's dirty laundry in hopes of deflecting blame doesn't work with the customers. You may be tempted to play good cop/bad cop with other representatives or departments in your company — especially if the prospect has raised a criticism. But you're a team. If one area of your company lets the client down, you fail, as well.

You want to be an internal advocate, both for the sake of your company's reputation and for fostering confidence in your client and building a respectful relationship. Blaming another department may get you off the hook on a personal basis, but most people won't continue to do business if the service department "always" poses challenges — even if you are such an upfront person!

Rather than pointing the finger somewhere else, take responsibility for the customer's dissatisfaction and commit to resolving the situation to the best of your availability. If the situation is bad, and you know that your company can't deliver as promised, adjust the time frame or conditions so it can follow through.

"I'm Calling Because We Have a New _____."

Similar to the knee-jerk-no response (see the first statement in this chapter), this phrase triggers a reflex reaction, as well. By alerting the prospect that you're planning to pedal a new *whatever*, he is already formulating a don't-need-it or already-have-one reply.

Instead of giving the prospect a shortcut to no, lead with the *benefits* of your product. You're not selling the latest, greatest, new, and improved version of a cheese slicer; you're offering the prospect a way to make dinner parties a roaring success and reduce time spent preparing the meal.

"I'll Let You Get Back to Work"

This phrase, along with its close cousin "I won't take up any more of your time," denigrates the value of what you do by implying your sales call isn't really work or worth as much attention as the prospect's other work. You're offering an important product or service — one that may stimulate sales, decrease costs, improve customer service, retain employees, build morale, and increase productivity. That prospect is most certainly, from both of your perspectives, worth the investment of time.

Instead of closing with a statement like this, simply end the call with, "Thank you so much for your time."

"You Maintain . . .", "You Think . . .", and So On

Statements such as these send up an alarm to your call recipients — kind of like those air-raid whines in old World War II movies, warning of an enemy attack. And the prospects do the same thing those citizens did in the movies — they run for shelter.

Their defense strategy may involve shutting down, clamming up, or, in some cases, launching an attack. Keep the following types of phrases (and similar ones) out of your sales calls:

- ✔ You claim
- ✔ You omitted

- ✔ You forgot
- ✔ You overlooked
- ✔ You don't understand
- ✔ We must have
- ✔ You should

When prospects feel challenged, cornered, offended, or threatened, you can expect them to fight back and — no surprise — annihilate the possibility of a sale.

Rather, you want to use softer approaches to point out an error or point of confusion, such as

"I must not be hearing you correctly; can we explore this further."

"I am confused, so can we spend a few minutes so I am clear."

"I must not be as effective as I hoped in communicating our recommendations to you; let me try again."

Chapter 21

Ten (Or So) Actions That Promote Phone-Sales Success

In This Chapter

▶ Organizing day, time, and place for peak performance

▶ Establishing good habits for a lifetime of phone-sales success

*I*n order to achieve long-term success in any endeavor, you need to build a foundation of positive practices and productive habits. Just as saving money steadily in small increments adds up to a fortune over time, performing small actions weekly — or even daily — results in a wealth of career achievement. This chapter touches on nine things you can do to encourage success in your phone sales.

Create a Positive Workspace

Environment plays a huge role in shaping your success, so make your workspace comfortable. You want a workspace that feeds your attitude and nourishes your self-confidence. Your surroundings influence your attitude, motivation, and performance. A dank, dark, cluttered burrow of an office can translate into a confined outlook and limited vision. On the other hand, a clean, open, well-lit space can inspire optimism and clarity of purpose.

To create a positive workspace, keep the following pointers in mind:

✔ Bring in pictures and possessions that make you smile and establish a positive mood.

✔ Stock the shelves with books that give you a lift. Words of inspiration can transform doubt and discouragement into renewed exuberance.

✔ Use the walls of your space, as well. Hang up meaningful quotes and motivational passages, so you can turn to them easily for a regular reminder of your potential. Recycle the quotes every few weeks to refresh your focus. *And* leave space on your walls for your sales scripts, objection-handling scripts, and closing scripts. Having these important tools close at hand helps boost your self-assuredness.

Time Block Your Day

Time blocking — identifying and scheduling priority tasks or activities on a daily, weekly, and monthly basis — is the one skill that top salespeople hear from their clients as the most life-changing in terms of developing habits of success.

The level of your achievement — whether measured in terms of income, fame, career advancement, or emotional well-being — is directly connected to the mastery of time blocking. When you zero in on what really matters to you and *guarantee* that it gets done by putting it on your schedule, you find that those "fires" and "clusters" and inconsequential issues that steal your time no longer get in the way of the values you hold most dear.

When time blocking your schedule, consider the ebb and flow of your workday and periods of peak activity for your business. You wouldn't want to set aside time for sales calls when you're not fully alert or energized, nor do you want to contact clients during a period that they're typically tied up in other matters. (Check out Chapter 7 for more info.)

Play Early Bird and Night Owl

In order to be a top salesperson, you may need to put in extra hours and come in early and stay late. Although life balance is as critical to salespeople as it is to everyone else, sometimes you may need to devote more time and energy to your job as a salesperson.

For example, if you're new to the field or new to a company, you need to get up to speed on your job and your employer's way of working. Or perhaps your industry has been hit with a change that makes sales more challenging. You need to put in the extra time to maintain the status quo. Or maybe you want to take your success to the next level, whether you're after a promotion, a raise, or increased sales. Coming in early and staying late can help.

When I was new to sales, all I had going for me was effort. I certainly didn't have skills, so my only hope to move up was to outwork everyone else. I arrived by 7 a.m. — most of my fellow salespeople didn't come in until after 9 a.m. I stayed until 6 p.m. or later. I was willing to pay a short-term price for long-term success.

I don't propose that you put in 60-, 70-, or 80-hour weeks as a rule. But it can pay off to shoot for somewhere between 50 and 55 hours a week. Consider the extra time you put into your job an investment of 25-percent increased time — for a long-range payoff.

Become a Lifelong Learner

Make an ongoing investment in your own personal development. Just as today's dollar won't buy as much in 20 years, your current level of knowledge won't buy you as high an income level down the road. Consider the need to learn more and acquire more knowledge because of the ever-changing and competitive world we live in education inflation.

Take the classes, check out the books, play the CDs and DVDs, enroll in the seminars, and hire the coaches necessary to keep you on the learning track.

Don't rely on your company to guide you in the acquisition of skills and knowledge. You're the CEO of your own life, and if you want to be more successful, you have to be perceived as more valuable — and the best way to increase your value is to gain more knowledge.

Prepare for Each Call

Just as you plan for your time on a daily, weekly, and monthly basis, preparing for each individual sales call is equally as vital. Sure, you may make so many calls a day, and you could do them in your sleep. But taking just a minute or two to get yourself up to speed can increase your productivity tenfold. (Chapter 4 can help you plan for each call.)

Depending on the type of call, here are some questions to answer before dialing the next number:

- ✔ **Initial call:** Do you have all the background information you need?

- ✔ **Follow-up call:** What step of the sales process are you at and are you prepared for it? Where was the conversation left? Did you commit to some follow-up action? Is it done?

> ✔ **Sales presentation call:** Have you practiced your script?
> Rehearsed responses to objections? Role-played the close?

Always Ask for Commitment

No one — not even the consummate telephone salesperson —
makes a sale with every phone call. But you can't count on commitment without asking for it. Top salespeople always ask. A top
salesperson doesn't leave it up to the prospect to offer.

That said, you can still gain *some* level of commitment — even if
it's a low level of commitment. Maybe the prospect agrees to
review the information you sent. Perhaps she commits to accepting a follow-up call down the road. Use questions such as "If I send
you the literature, will you review it?" or "It seems that I have
answered all your questions, correct?" (Chapter 14 gives the complete lowdown on asking for commitment.)

Respect the Threshold Moment

Almost every sales call holds a *threshold* moment — the point in
which you become aware that the sale will or won't be made. If the
signs say the deal is near-done, then congratulations! Move into
wrap-up mode.

But when the call begins to apex in the down direction, resist the
urge to keep the prospect on in hopes of flipping him from "no" to
"go." All you're doing is reducing the number of calls, contacts, and
sales you make today. And your efforts to raise a sale from the
dead may just irk the prospect into avoiding you for the hereafter.

A negative threshold moment doesn't mean a sale won't happen,
but it does mean it won't happen on that call. After you recognize
that moment, wrap up and get off the phone — in minutes.

Review Each Call

Before you move on to the next name on your call list, wrap up the
previous call. Evaluate the call you just completed: Did you pick up
any new nuggets about what they want, such as who you're competing against, their timeframe to make a decision, or their service
expectations in their decision-making process? If you went through
all these points, make sure all the details are in your notes.

Then, review your performance. What went well with your delivery? What did you stumble over? Did you allow the prospect to do the talking while you listened? Did you struggle over any objections? What changes or tweaks do you need to make to your delivery?

Finally, make notes of those actions you want to take to your presentation. And, most important, schedule any follow-up action you committed to!

Persistence Pays Off

As a salesperson, you're going to face rejections again and again. In order to achieve success, you can't be dissuaded by this bad news. You have to remain persistent with the prospect and keep on trying. (You can find more on capitalizing on rejection in Chapter 15.)

Here's a statistic for you: 60 percent of all sales are made after the prospect has said no four times. But how many salespeople weather through *four* rejections and still pursue the business? Here's the skinny:

- Forty-four percent of salespeople give up after the first no.

- Twenty-two percent call it quits after hearing the second no.

- Fourteen percent throw in the towel with the third no.

- Twelve percent move on after the fourth no.

- And the 8 percent left who hang tough? They're the ones who garner that 60 percent of the sales business out there — and all just because they keep at it.

You can't find a substitute for persistence. Talent, skill, attitude, products, service, and marketing support — all are important in order to achieve winning results. But perseverance of spirit is what keeps a salesperson on the road to success. Working with a prospect even after hearing no four times, making your daily quota of cold calls or lead follow-ups *every day,* and staying in touch with a prospect even after he's given his business to someone else are all valuable efforts that pay off in sales success.

Index